Amalgamated Spy

Mission: Right the Wrong

A Tragicomedy / James Bond Parody

By
Anthony J. Lomas

EXPLORA BOOKS

700 – 838 West Hastings St. Vancouver, BC V6C 0A6

www.explorabooks.com

Phone: (604) 330 6795

No part of this book may be reproduced, stored in a retrieval system, or transmitted by any means without the written permission of the author.

Because of the dynamic nature of the Internet, any web addresses or links contained in this book may have changed since publication and may no longer be valid. The views expressed in this work are solely those of the author and do not necessarily reflect the views of the publisher, and the publisher hereby disclaims any responsibility for them.

ISBN: 978-1-997587-23-1 (Paperback)
978-1-997587-24-8 (eBook)

ANTHONY J. LOMAS

Table of Contents

ACKNOWLEDGMENT

I would like to thank Warren Perrin for his support in the writing of this book and also for obtaining the apology for the Cajun people. Also, the Queen of England for granting the apology, without which, there would be no book.

Paul Taranto and Jamie Wax, for their inspiring musical, Evangeline. Their lyrics captured the gist of the story and helped it along.

The MOST famous chef in all of Louisiana, whom I've always admired and even envied a little, you know who you are.

Ian Fleming, for creating the greatest spy ever. Cubby Broccoli and Harry Saltzman for bringing him to life. We all need to laugh at ourselves once in a while, I hope they're not offended.

My brother Johnny, whose personality and brand of humor was the driving force behind one of the main characters. My brother Charles, who encouraged me to dig deep when I was down. My brother Tiny, who gave me Officer Cottrell and his partner Mr. Cold Cocker. My sister Arlyne, who never stopped believing in me or this project and countless other family members whose lives I was able to blend into my characters.

My sons, Lon and Lance who were not too thrilled with my writing situation but bore with it none the less and encouraged me to continue.

My dog Solomon, who kept me sane throughout this ten-year odyssey.

Elaine, for giving me the work for expenses and all her family members for their support.

The town of Melville Louisiana, for its unique environment. Buddy and the mayor's secretary, who was so helpful in providing historical research.

Shelley, for her contributions in typing and editing the first draft in it's script format.

The universe for providing La'Nelle and her expertise in turning a script into a polished book.

My nephew Dustin, for a great cover. The folks at Edgemont Video for their technical support. And last but certainly not least, all the Cajun people everywhere. Past and present.

CHAPTER I

ew York, February 2005 — World-renowned Chef Paul Primeaux speaks to the US Culinary Team at the American Culinary Federation building in Hyatt Park, New York. He is there as a chief consultant to the US Culinary Team in preparation for the upcoming 2008 Culinary Olympics to be held in Erfurt, Germany. To break the ice and produce a relaxed atmosphere, he began telling the team about a dream he had the night before.

"I probably had this particular dream because just before I fell asleep, I was reading a book called *Scattered to the Wind*, and at the same time, a James Bond documentary was playing on my hotel TV. Somehow or other, these two events must have fused themselves in my brain and produced one hell of a dream!"

"The book *Scattered to the Wind* is about the exile of the Acadian people that began in 1755 from Nova Scotia up in Canada and continued through 1763. Because the Acadians wouldn't pledge their allegiance to the British Crown, the British had them deported by the tens of thousands. Families were ripped apart, and many were killed. The British burned the Acadians' homes and fields and loaded them onto transport ships, where many more died of starvation and disease," Paul shook his head sadly.

"It was nothing less than 'ethnic cleansing,' but the British called it the 'Grand Derangement,' and they deported shipload after shipload of the Acadians, relocating them to parts of England, France, and the United States. Many thousands were brought to the states that bordered the mid-Atlantic coast of the United States. Those that survived the horrendous conditions aboard the ships were sent into the tobacco fields to work alongside the slaves."

"Many of the Acadians ended up in Louisiana, my home state, and became known as *Cajuns*. I tell you, this dream was so real that I really felt like I was right there in 1755, right when it was all happening!"

Paul continues, "Back in 1847, a very famous poet, Henry Wadsworth Longfellow, after studying the histories of Nova Scotia families, became so disturbed about the expulsion of the Acadian people that he wrote the poem *Evangeline*, and it became the most famous work of his lifetime."

"More recently, a couple of fellows named Paul Taranto and Jamie Wax have written and produced a musical called *Evangeline*. It's one of the most heart-wrenching and heartwarming things I have ever seen."

"You know there's a Cajun lawyer named Warren Perrin down in South Louisiana that's filed a lawsuit on behalf of the Cajun people, demanding an apology from the Queen of England for deporting the Acadians from Canada all those years ago. He feels confident that an apology will come sooner or later; he just needs to keep working on it."

"But getting back to the dream, I felt like I was right there in the midst of the Acadian removal back in 1755. Then, all of a sudden, I was in London, England, at the 007 Headquarters, known as MI-6. I felt like I was suspended above everything and looking at all the activity from a distance. I saw 'N,' the chief who gives out assignments, as he opened his padded leather door to his secretary's office, and I saw Ms. Munynickle. I watched as he began giving her instructions to contact his four top agents—Sean, Roger, Timmy, and George. He told her to have them report at once for a very important mission."

"What about Pierce?" Ms. Munynickle asks.

"Not him; he's finishing up a mission."

Ms. Munynickle calls Sean, and he answers his cell phone while he's being fitted for a suit at his tailor's shop. As he's standing there in front of a full-length mirror, being told to report for a mission, the mirror becomes wavy and blurred and then clears up, and Sean sees himself the way he looked in 1962, on the Dr. Yes mission . . . a suave, sophisticated 007 agent. He agrees to report to HQ at once.

She then calls Roger, who is in bed with a woman. As he's being told to report in for a mission, he begins to reminisce about beautiful women and past missions, and he eagerly agrees to report to HQ. Munynickle's next call is to Timmy, who is in the middle of a Shakespearean play rehearsal in full costume. He's called to the phone by a stagehand.

"YES, what is it?" Timmy demands angrily.

"You need to report to HQ for a mission," Ms. Munynickle answers.

"Let me talk to the director!"

"Who?"

"The *DIRECTOR!*" Timmy shouts into the phone.

"All right! *I don't have to take this rudeness!*" Ms. Munynickle says to herself as she beeps 'N' on the intercom. "I've got Timmy on the line. He wants to talk to the director, whatever that means. I think he means you."

"Oh, I know what he means. Put him on." 'N' picks up the phone.

"Timmy, we need you to report to HQ right away."

"I can't take another part right now. I've got a contract to fulfill."

"This is not a part. It's a mission."

"I'm in the middle of a production here!" Timmy shouts.

"This mission is for the Queen. She specifically asked for you."

"Well, in that case, OK, but it's going to take me some time to get into character."

"Timmy, it's a MISSION . . . not a part!" 'N' says impatiently.

"Yeah, right. What time do you want me at the studio?"

"HQ . . . you know, *HEADQUARTERS!*" 'N' hangs up the phone and shakes his head in exasperation. He then goes into Ms. Munynickle's office and asks, "Is that it? Have you contacted everybody?"

"No, there's just George to call, but I don't see a phone number for him in the inactive file. Maybe it's in miscellaneous." Ms. Munynickle flips through the file folders.

"Oh, it's filed under Inactive-Active-Standby."

"That doesn't make sense."

"I know, but at the time it was the only way we could shut him up. After his last mission of His Majesty's Secret Service, he kept bugging us for another mission. So we gave him an active number and placed him on Inactive-Active-Standby."

Ms. Munynickle opens the bottom drawer of the filing cabinet and finds a file in the back of the drawer marked: INACTIVE-ACTIVE-STANDBY (GEORGE ONLY).

George lives in a small, simple bungalow with an attached garage in a modest neighborhood not far from HQ. His live-in girlfriend, Adena, is sitting at the kitchen table with her neighbor Susan, smoking cigarettes and drinking coffee.

"Do you think George will ever marry you?" Susan asks.

"Oh, I don't know. I don't think he has marriage on his mind. He's always sitting in his car in the garage reading spy magazines and listening to the same old song and waiting for that stupid red phone to ring. He's been waiting since 1969 or 1970. It'll never ring, but that's OK; at least I know where he's at."

Just then, the red phone rings, and both the women freak out.

"Man, that's some spooky shit!" Susan stares at the phone.

"No kiddin'!" Adena replies. "I'd better get George!"

"I'm out of here!" Susan heads for the door.

Adena hurries to the garage to tell George his red phone is ringing. Shocked, he frantically climbs out of his car and rushes inside. He trips over the threshold but manages to grab the phone before it stops ringing.

"Yes . . . speaking," he says, trying to sound official. "Yes. Yes. Absolutely! Right away!"

George hangs up the phone and suddenly looks transformed, with a certain air of importance about him.

"What is it?" Adena asks.

"I'm being called out on a mission!" he says importantly.

"WHAT?"

"I'm being called out on a mission!"

"NOW?"

"You know I've been on Standby."

"I thought it was Inactive!"

"*INACTIVE-ACTIVE* with a *STANDBY* option!" He rushes to the bedroom.

Excitedly, George begins packing. He opens the closet, grabs a suitcase, throws it on the bed, and flings it open. He pushes the hanging clothes aside in search of his 'Professor' disguise outfit, his kilt, and ruffled shirt. In one swift, stuffing motion, he has everything in the suitcase and slams it shut without noticing the ruffled shirt sleeve dangling out of the suitcase. Adena stands on the other side of the bed, feeling confused and emotional, about to cry.

"I don't understand. I never thought they would call," she says.

"I told you I was on Standby."

"For over thirty *YEARS!*" Adena wrings her hands. "INACTIVE-ACTIVE!"

Adena, with a worried look, starts to fall apart. While holding back tears, she blurts out a string of questions.

"When will you be back? Will you be all right? What if you get hurt? How will I get in touch with you? How will I know where you are?"

"Baby, that's all TOP SECRET! I can't divulge that kind of information, even to you."

"What about all those women?"

"Baby, this is no time to be jealous!" He heads toward the garage.

"I just don't understand it. Why didn't they call Sean?" she pleads.

Her remark stops him in his tracks. He turns, with a disgusted, puke-like look on his face, and shouts, "CALL WHO? *MR. PERFECT?* He always gets all the friggin' missions! They called *ME!* Now, I've got to go . . . it's my DUTY!"

George walks quickly into the garage and throws his suitcase onto the backseat of the car. He heads over to the workbench and gathers up all his important spy gadgets: his special watch, knife, pen, and gun.

He accidentally drops the gun, and it goes off! He looks sheepishly at Adena, then smiles reassuringly.

Now, she's more concerned than ever. "I don't know about all this . . . you could get hurt!"

He walks over to her, hugs her, and kisses her. "C'mon, baby, stick with me on this one."

Adena half-heartedly accepts his having to leave but cautions him to be careful and to call if he can. George jumps in his car, begins backing out, and smashes into the trash cans at the side of the driveway. He stops, gets out of the car, picks up the cans, and takes one last look at Adena. She shakes her head at George's clumsiness but smiles nonetheless, and George gives her the thumbs-up sign as he gets back in the car and drives off. While driving to HQ, he starts shoving spy magazines under the front seat and begins to psych himself up for the mission.

"Maybe I'll get my old parking space," he says to himself as he nears HQ.

As he rounds the corner of HQ, he sees Timmy's car and then spots Roger's vehicle. Slowing down, he wonders what they're doing at HQ. He pulls into the parking lot and sees Sean's car backed in at an angle, with the revolving license plate in the 007 position.

"If he's so PERFECT, why can't he learn how to park?"

Scanning the lot, he realizes he has to park across from Timmy in a spot marked VISITORS.

"That's OK," he says, trying to maintain a cheerful, positive attitude.

George gets out of his car and walks toward the office. As he passes Sean's car, he grumbles, *"That egotistical snob—he's PROFILE PARKING! That show-off. What nerve!"*

George enters the HQ office and tosses his hat at the rack in the corner where the other agents' hats are hanging. He misses the rack, and his hat falls on the floor. He begins to flirt with Ms. Munynickle as he picks up the hat.

"You better get in there. They're waiting for you!" she admonishes.

"You're late, 007! Get in here!" 'N' motions as George enters the room.

"Maybe I should say 0028 . . . get it? All of you together . . . $4 \times 7 = 28$."

Everyone laughs out loud.

"Yeah, and if Pierce was here, we'd be 0034!" George adds.

"You mean 0035?" Sean smirks.

"Oh yeah, you're right." George looks humiliated.

Sean looks at 'N' and rolls his eyes in George's direction. 'N' responds with a peacekeeping look that says, be patient.

"By the way, where is Pierce?" Roger asks.

"He's finishing up another mission right now," 'N' replies. "He'll be a few more days. Let's get to this mission at hand."

Low mumbling is heard around the room.

"But what's the deal here? Why are we all at HQ at the same time?" Sean inquires.

"Yeah, that's what I'd like to know," Timmy adds.

"As all of you know, or may not know . . ." 'N' begins to explain.

"The 2008 Culinary Olympics is coming up soon in Erfurt, Germany, and while England may be far superior in the intelligence community, we do poorly in the culinary arena. And that's got to change! For years, France and the United States have always led in these Olympics, with Canada and Germany close behind. We, on the other hand, have always been in the rear with smaller countries like Dorgo and Berzong. Well, that has to change in this upcoming Olympics! The Queen is entering her personal chefs in this competition, and she insists on a FIRST PLACE WIN!"

"You mean the Gold? As in Goldth . . . medal?" Sean blurts out.

"Precisely, and this brings us to your mission, gentlemen. In the Culinary Olympics, presentation is everything. To enhance this presentation, a clear gel, sometimes tinted, is sprayed on the food for presentation. This gel is known as Aspic. While derived from many sources, most Aspic is primarily from meat juices, which brings us to this chef, PAUL PRIMEAUX."

As 'N' speaks to the agents, he shows them film clips and slides of Paul Primeaux involved in various endeavors, shots of his restaurants and other enterprises.

"Primeaux once owned a restaurant in New York City, but now his entire operation is in Louisiana, specifically New Orleans and Melville."

"He owns a restaurant in the French Quarter in New Orleans and a ten thousand sq. ft. seasoning facility near the port of New Orleans. He ships and receives herbs and spices worldwide. His product is called *MAGIC SPICES.* More than forty countries purchase these seasonings!"

"He's trying to *MONOPOLIZE!"* Sean states angrily.

"We believe Primeaux is solely responsible for the United States faring so well in these past Olympics," 'N' continues. "For starters, he's the chief consultant to the US Culinary Olympics Team. But there's more to this guy than meets the eye. Although a US citizen, he brings to the table, no pun intended, a very unique combination of culture and technique. Culturally, he combines a French/Canadian influence handed down from his ancestry reigning from Nova Scotia, Canada, mixed with a French Creole/Spanish influence found only in New Orleans. Now this alone would be hard enough to compete with. But if you travel west from New Orleans over the Mississippi River and across the Atchafalaya Basin, you encounter the so-called 'Cajun' people, of which Primeaux identifies himself. Now, these people have an axe to grind with Britain about that expulsion from Nova Scotia that took place some 250 years ago. It's nothing, really."

"The Cajuns incorporated the German influence of smoked meats, and all of these influences combined equal a melting pot of cultural cuisine. Now this is where it gets complicated. The Germans, because of their climate, have always cold-smoked their meats. But given the climate in Louisiana . . . hot, humid, and somewhat tropical in nature, the Cajun people have taken to hothouse smoking their meats, with the exception of ONE individual."

"PAUL PRIMEAUX!" George exclaims loudly.

"Precisely!" 'N' continues.

"He's the only Cajun; in fact, he is the ONLY one we know of in the United States, according to our latest intelligence, who uses this old-world German technique of cold-smoking meats. If he is combining this German cold-smoking technique with Cajun hothouse smoking, along with his Magic Spices, in an impossible climate like Louisiana, he's had to incorporate some new-world technology!"

"This whole blend of culture, technique, and technology has left Britain at a sad disadvantage in these Culinary Olympics. The Queen's chefs don't stand a chance! Now we believe Primeaux's New Orleans seasoning facility and restaurant are just a front. Our intelligence has revealed that the REAL heart of his operation is the smoking facility in Melville where the secret to his success is hidden."

Suddenly, a huge table rises up from the middle of the floor and displays a full-scale model of the small town of Melville, Louisiana. The agents and 'N' gather around the table.

"As you can see, gentlemen, the town is completely surrounded by levees on all four sides." 'N' produces a pointer and taps at the sides of the model.

"Our intelligence tells us that a massive flood in 1928 nearly destroyed the entire town. Then, the US Army Corps of Engineers constructed those levees. Our 'friend,' Mr. Paul Primeaux, has cleverly tucked his smoking facility within these levees, thereby creating a compound out of the natural environment!"

"Man, this guy is *good* . . . hiding in plain sight!" Sean says sarcastically.

"Maybe he's just plain BRILLIANT!" George adds with enthusiasm. "Diabolical is more like it!" Sean counters.

Ignoring the outburst, 'N' continues. "Our best satellite surveillance to date indicates mostly swamp around these levees, with the exception of the East levee that borders a river. We have concluded that the river would be your best approach. There are also a few pipeline crossings above the river and a railway trestle. A ferry runs on weekdays. There's a road running parallel with the East levee, and satellite photos verify the road is impassable due to road construction."

"We know that every aspect of Primeaux's operation is computerized. Your mission, gentlemen, is to go up the river, infiltrate his compound, gain access to his computers, and bring back the data specifically related to the aspic. It is crucial that we obtain this information if the Queen's chefs are to place in the Olympics. We need to know the exact makeup of Primeaux's aspic, so we'll know what we're up against."

"That's it? Is that it? This is such a simple mission . . . so why do you need all of us?" Sean is incredulous.

"There are other aspects to this mission. There's the public relations factor. We would like to generate some PR within MI-6 to appraise the need for appropriating funds for future missions such as this one. These missions will be known as Semi-classified/Unclassified/Classified (SUC Missions). Our accounting department did some number crunching and concluded that subcontracting crews would be in our best interest. The United States is doing this with some of their smaller CIA operations. If all goes well and it proves profitable for our intelligence division, MI-6 will allocate funds for this program, codenamed AMALGA, which will become a permanent unit of MI-6, contractually, of course. Initially, the program will be experimental, and we will be on a shoestring budget, and it may involve some improvising at first until we get it off the ground."

"We have a great deal to achieve on this first mission. For centuries, the French have led the world in fine cuisine, and the world has come to expect that. Now Primeaux, with his talent and resources and unique blend of influences culminating in this bayou brand of Cajun/French cuisine, could very well turn the tide and surpass the French! The bottom line is this: we don't know if the world is ready for such a tidal wave in the culinary arts. The ripple effect could mean worldwide shortages of specific herbs and spices. We could see the development of black market trafficking in a certain spice such as cayenne, which is a main staple of Cajun cuisine!"

"You're talking about *DOMINATION!*" Roger blurts out.

"Worse than that! *MONOPOLIZING DOMINATION!*" Sean counters.

"What do the French say about this?" George asks.

"They haven't the insight to see what's going on!" 'N' assures the agents.

"Is Britain the ONLY country to recognize this attempted *DOMINATION?*" Roger frowns and looks over at Sean.

"Probably. After all, we *are* the world's leader in intelligence!" Sean leans back in his chair with an air of smugness.

"Absolutely! Our intelligence indicates this could be the beginning of the domination of the world's taste buds! We may be headed for a *ONE WORLD TASTE!*" 'N' states emphatically.

"My God!" Sean swears.

"That's exactly what the Queen said!" 'N' responds. "That's why she wants us to move as expeditiously as possible on this matter. As luck would have it, it will be Mardi Gras weekend, and everyone will be in New Orleans. Melville will be a ghost town. It's a simple job, in and out, piece of cake! There are also some fringe benefits in it for all of you. When your mission is completed, the Queen is treating you to a week of Mardi Gras festivities in New Orleans, all expenses paid!"

"That sure beats the hell out of a gold watch!" Roger smiles broadly.

All the agents agree with a big thumbs-up.

"Sean, you'll be the head of the mission." 'N' nods in Sean's direction, and Sean responds with an arrogant smirk.

"We've acquired a yacht and have anticipated everything you'll need, equipment-wise, to execute the mission. The yacht crew doesn't need to know much about your mission. Keep them in the dark. You will rendezvous with the yacht under the Hwy 190 Bridge outside the small town of Krotz Springs. From there, it will be twelve miles upstream to Melville. We have arranged plane tickets for all of you on American Airlines."

"What about transportation once we get to the United States?" Sean stands and stretches.

"You'll rent a couple of vehicles at the airport."

"Hold it right there! I'm *NOT* going anywhere without my Aston!" Sean explodes.

"Then, what do you propose?"

"Put my car on the plane!"

"Don't forget, we're on a shoestring budget; that's going to strain it."

"The gadgetry alone on that vehicle is indispensable." Sean crosses his arms across his chest defensively.

"You're right. We'll list it as a vital piece of equipment so accounting won't have a shit fit!"

'N' makes a notation on a notepad, then gets on the intercom and asks Ms. Munynickle to switch the airline tickets from American Airlines to British Airways and to have Sean's car put on board immediately.

"Your plane will be leaving soon." 'N' turns back to the agents. "Ms. Munynickle will drive you to the airport in a shuttle van. She has all the documents you'll be needing—passports, driver's licenses, and credit cards."

Everybody stands up and walks toward the door. Sean pulls 'N' aside.

"Do we *have* to take George?" he asks.

"The Queen insists. It's all part of that PR thing. Everybody knows there's bad blood between the two of you, but try to make the best of it."

Sean agrees, begrudgingly.

As the meeting is coming to an end, Ms. Munynickle sits at her desk outside the briefing room, thinking about all the years she wasted waiting on the agents when all they did was break her heart, one by one. Now, seeing them all together, it's almost too much to bear. It's a rude awakening for her.

What did I do with my life? she asks herself. *I've never married because of those carousing playboys! I have no children. What have I done to deserve this misery? They RUINED my life!*

The agents emerge from the briefing room and enter her office, everyone projecting a very high-energy, *let's-go-get-'em* attitude. They barely notice Ms. Munynickle. Sean stops at her desk.

"I understand you're taking us to the airport."

"Yes, I am," Ms. Munynickle answers icily.

"Have you sent my car ahead?"

"Yes, I have! Here are all your documents!" She flings four envelopes across the desk toward Sean.

After retrieving her purse from a bottom drawer, Ms. Munynickle leads the agents out the door to a small white van. Sean follows, while Roger, Timmy, and George collect their luggage from their cars and load it into the van. As Ms. Munynickle drives, the agents boast about past missions with beautiful women, casinos, and five-star hotels in exotic places along with fine wine and caviar. Ms. Munynickle listens to their conversation.

I can't believe the years I've wasted. I feel like an old maid librarian.

Nearing the airport, she begins to fume as the agents' laughter becomes unbearable. Arriving at the terminal, she stops in the loading zone, and they all exit the vehicle. Ms. Munynickle walks to the rear of the van and opens the doors to remove the luggage. By now, she is boiling! George, first out of the vehicle, approaches her.

"Just like old times!" he says enthusiastically.

"*ALL my time!*" Ms. Munynickle screams hysterically. "Forty friggin' years of my time! Being fooled into thinking I was *special* to a bunch of martini-sucking, high-falutin', womanizing bastards!" she yells.

Ms. Munynickle slings their luggage onto the ground in a fit of rage, all the while shouting obscenities and crying uncontrollably. She slams the cargo doors and rushes to the driver's door. Yanking it open, she quickly jumps into the seat, slams the door, and collapses into tears. Roger opens the passenger door, leans across the seat, and in his sexiest voice, he tries to comfort her.

"C'mon, baby. You know I never truly led you on. I was always getting held up. Look, when I get back from this mission, maybe we can . . ."

"You mean it?" Her expression softens and she smiles trustingly at Roger.

"Sure, baby. As soon as I get back," Roger soothes.

While Roger is comforting Ms. Munynickle, Sean steps to the back of the van.

"What the hell did you do to her, George?!" Sean accuses.

"I didn't do anything!"

"You must have done *something!*"

"I swear, I didn't do *anything!*"

"Then you must have said something." Sean turns and walks over to Roger just as he's closing the door to the van.

"As soon as I get back, baby." Roger smiles at Ms. Munynickle reassuringly.

"Now, why the hell did you say that?" Sean demands. "You know she's gonna take that bullshit to the bank!"

"I don't know." Roger looks confused. "It must have been a reflex."

The agents head into the terminal, where Sean distributes the licenses, credit cards, passports, etc. They check their bags and board the plane. The flight attendant directs them to the rear of the aircraft and to their seats. Sean is deeply offended at her suggesting they sit in coach. He's sure there must be a mistake with their ticket.

"COACH?" he chokes out.

"COACH?!" Roger echoes.

The attendant rechecks their boarding passes. "Yes, coach," she says.

"There *must* be some mistake!" Sean insists.

"You're with Universal Exports, right?" she asks.

"Yes, that's correct."

"Then there's NO mistake, sir. You're in coach. Move along, please!"

Sean and Roger walk to the rear of the plane and take their assigned seats on the left, near the toilet. Timmy and George sit up front on the right.

"I don't know why we couldn't sit in first class!" Roger says with disgust. "Those seats were half-empty! I know HQ said we were on a shoestring budget, but this is ridiculous!"

"I've *never* sat in coach! These seats are so low class!" Sean sulks.

"I wonder if this is Ms. Munynickle's idea of revenge."

"That flight attendant looks a little bit lesbian to me; perhaps I can charm our way up to first class," Roger muses aloud.

"I had a roll in the hay with a lesbian on that *Goldthumb* mission." Sean leans back in his seat and closes his eyes.

"Do you want me to try? I'm up for it!" Roger leans forward in his seat.

"Nah. Just let it ride. We'll discuss this matter with 'N' whenever we get back. He's going to have to define *shoestring!*"

Despite the seating arrangements, there's an air of excitement about the mission: Mardi Gras, casinos, women, etc. Up ahead, on the other side of the aircraft, Timmy and George discuss the possibilities.

"We're going to have a blast! I hear there are casinos everywhere down there!" Timmy rubs his hands together.

"With Sean calling all the shots, I don't know about that," George muses.

Meanwhile, Sean notices Roger hungrily eyeing the women on the plane.

"Don't be lining anything up just yet, Roger. Let's get the job done first."

"How long could it take? This mission is a piece of cake! Even 'N' said so. We could stay in New Orleans, and you could send either of those two to take care of this."

"I don't know about that." Sean rubs his chin. "Maybe we could send Timmy down there, but George . . . I don't think so."

Just then, George spills his drink, trying to be cool while flirting with a flight attendant.

Sean notices the mishap. "See what I mean? Those two never had any class!"

Timmy hurries past Sean and Roger on his way to the john to clean up. Once inside the cramped little room, as he's taking a leak, he decides the toilet looks very inviting. Distracted by his image in the mirror, Timmy lifts his chin and goes into full Shakespearean mode. "To *shit* or not to shit? To shit or *not* to shit? To shit or not to *shit?*" Timmy recites theatrically. "That is the question." He plays his self-debating game for a few minutes, then finally decides to shit.

"It's sure taking that idiot a long time. I'd better go see what he's up to. I need to piss anyway." Sean leaves his seat and makes his way to the restroom. He knocks on the door several times with no response.

"What's up? C'mon, man. You've been in there long enough! Let's go!"

Sean starts shaking the doorknob. Sensing Sean's frustration, Timmy hurriedly finishes his business and forgets to flush the toilet. He opens the door, and he and Sean squeeze past each other rather quickly.

Once inside, Sean realizes the magnitude of the stench in such a small place! He gasps and holds his breath as he quickly flushes the toilet. He starts to pee and begins to run out of air. He takes a short, shallow breath and can't believe the smell! He's running out of air again as he zips up and hesitates to take another breath. He turns, grabs the doorknob, and the door is stuck! He's running out of air! Frustration builds as he jiggles the knob and pushes, then pulls on the door in a desperate attempt to get out!

Hearing a commotion, the flight attendant approaches the door as it suddenly flies open. A cloud of stench is released, along with Sean. As he stumbles out, he has face-to-face, eye-to-eye contact with her as she politely covers her nose. Sean's face is beet-red, and he gasps for air! It appears as though Sean has generated this god-awful smell. Nearby passengers wrinkle their noses at the stench as the odor wafts over them.

Sean immediately regains his composure, looks past the attendant, and sees Timmy scrunching down into his seat, as if he's not to blame. Sean makes his way past the stewardess and to his seat.

The rest of the flight is uneventful. In New Orleans, they deplane and head to the baggage claim area, where they wait for their luggage to show up on the carousel. George's suitcase is first. As he reaches for it, Sean notices the ruffled shirt sleeve hanging out and can't resist a smart-assed remark.

"His Majesty's Secret Service, huh?"

"Yeah, and what of it?" George retorts, trying to appear unconcerned.

Just then, an airport worker informs Sean that it's going to take a while to offload his car, as they're having trouble with the plane's cargo doors.

Sean turns to Timmy and George. "Go on and rent a vehicle for the two of you. Roger will ride with me when the Aston arrives."

"Great! We'll get a Lincoln Navigator . . . all-wheel drive!" Timmy exclaims excitedly.

"Whatever. We'll have a drink and wait for you in the bar."

The agents split up; Timmy and George head to rental while Sean and Roger head to the bar. As Sean and Roger pass a gift shop, a voodoo doll in the window grabs Roger's attention and stops him in his tracks. Sean keeps on walking, stops, looks around for Roger, and signals him to come on. Breathing hard, Roger catches up with Sean.

"What is it, what did you see?"

"Oh, nothing," Roger mumbles.

At the bar, they order the usual, *martinis . . . shaken, not stirred.*

"What do you think of that, Timmy? A *Lincoln!* I told you, he's got *NO CLASS!* He's a commoner!" Sean takes a sip of his martini.

"He wants a Lincoln because the last time he was in the United States on that *License to Maim* mission, he drove a Lincoln Mark V," Roger adds.

"Huh! When I was on that '*Thunderbawl*' mission, I had to drive a Lincoln Town Car, but you don't see me craving that crap!"

"If he wanted an all-wheel drive, the least he could do is go with a Range Rover. I drove one on that *'Octofussy'* mission," Roger takes a drink.

"Do you think he even knows what a Range Rover is? If you sent George after a Range Rover, he'd come back with a four-legged animal!" Sean chuckles at the thought.

They're both laughing as Timmy and George enter the bar. Timmy nonchalantly rattles his keys, eager to drive the Lincoln.

"I take it you got a Lincoln?" Sean smirks and glances at Roger.

"Oh yeah! I just have to pick it up at the lot."

Just then, Sean is notified that his car is ready for him out front.

"Get your vehicle, Timmy; we'll meet you at the parking lot exit." Sean downs the last of his martini, and he and Roger head for the door.

Out on the lot, Timmy and George, deep in conversation, arrange their bags in the back of the Lincoln. "It won't hurt to ask," Timmy says to George as he closes the tailgate.

"Well, I doubt he'll go for it, but go ahead and ask. Here they are now."

"Hey, Sean—how about we take a quick spin down Bourbon Street, check out some casinos, and have a few drinks?" Timmy shouts over to Sean, seated behind the wheel of his Aston.

"No! We take care of the mission first! There will be plenty of time for that later. Follow us!"

"See what I mean? He wants to run the whole friggin' show! He loves to be the center of attention!" George grumbles as they climb into the Lincoln. "You know, that might not have been such a bad idea Timmy just had. We could have lined up some women for when we get back," Roger muses.

"I'm not going to New Orleans to hustle women with those two idiots! When this mission is completed, we don't even know those buffoons! They can go their way, and we'll go ours. The only reason I agreed to work with them is because of loyalty to the Crown." Sean looks over at Roger.

Roger nods in agreement.

In the Lincoln, George, irritated by Sean's cocky attitude, begins to complain to Timmy. "You know, after Sean came off that *'You Only Live Once'* mission, he said he'd had enough. That's when I took *'His Majesty's Secret Service'* mission, and it was a success except for the . . . the . . ." George, overcome with emotion, looks away, and a sad, distant stare comes over his face.

"Except for what?" Timmy asks.

"I was ready for another mission. I was ready to go back to work when that *'Diamonds Are For Never'* mission came up. And what happened? They gave it to Sean and sidelined me on an Inactive-Active—Standby! Then Sean—*MR. PERFECT*—opts for a Double O Instructor position and starts pulling strings with HQ to give Roger *all* the new missions."

George continues, "Everybody knows he's Sean's pet! Every good instructor needs a pet! And Sean taught Roger well . . . hog all the missions you can! Then when Roger starts to burn out, *MR. PERFECT* reactivates and takes the *'Never Say Ever Again'* mission! All the while, I'm stuck on Inactive-Active-Standby! You can't tell me HQ wasn't playing favorites with that *control freak!* He had to be back in the limelight! He has to have everything his way! He wants to run the whole friggin' show!"

Completely oblivious to George's upset, Timmy mutters to himself, *"Man, this all-wheel drive really handles good!"*

As Sean and Roger, in the Aston, tool smoothly down the highway, Roger asks, "How about some music?" Then he reaches back to his luggage and pulls out a CD. He slips it into the player, and the song 'A View to a Live' comes alive and wafts about. Roger leans back and lapses into a smiling daydream, reminiscing about the gorgeous women on that mission.

"That must have been a pretty good mission," Sean says.

"Oh yeah . . . except . . ." Roger's smile quickly turns to a frown.

"What? Something went wrong?"

"You know, I never told anyone this before, but I drove a *Ford Fairmont* on that mission. It was a rental." Roger shakes his head in embarrassment. "I can't believe I did that!"

Sean grimaces and looks as if he's just bitten into a lemon.

"A 4-door at that! I never felt so inadequate in my life!"

"I wouldn't tell anybody else that. Some things are better off forgotten. Remember, I told you about that *'Thunderbawl'* mission and the Lincoln I drove. I'm not doing that kind of shit anymore! That's why I told 'N' I wasn't going anywhere without my car ever again!"

Admiring himself in the rearview mirror, Sean sees himself as he looked on the *Dr. Yes* mission . . . a suave, sophisticated, young 007 agent.

"However, I did make love to *three* women on that mission!" Roger says, recovering his confidence.

"Well, that's somewhat compensating, but there's still no excuse for driving a friggin' *Fairmont!*"

Driving along behind the Aston, an aggravated Timmy begins to notice all the roadside casinos. "Man, look at all these casinos! There's a casino at every truck stop down here. There's no reason why we can't stop in at one of them for just a few minutes!"

"Fat chance!" George says with resignation. "Not with egotistical Sean running the show, no way! He won't stop . . . he's too *mission-driven!* I know him; he's too *mission-minded!*"

By now, the two vehicles have gone through Baton Rouge and are passing over the Morganza Spillway Bridge, a five-mile stretch of roadway over the Atchafalaya Basin. This Basin is a shadowy, swampy series of waterways with heavy foliage.

"I'd hate to get lost in that," Timmy comments.

"If this mission is successful, do you think it will help the Queen's Chefs win the Culinary Olympics and prevent a ONE WORLD TASTE?" Roger turns to Sean and asks.

"First of all, this mission WILL BE A SUCCESS! We're going to get the data on the Aspic . . . that's a given. And we're going to expose Paul Primeaux for the MONOPOLIZING DOMINATOR that he is!"

"What about the Magic Spices aspect?"

"Magic . . . my ass!! Monopolizers always know what they're doing!" Sean admonishes.

"It might be *voodoo!*" Roger looks sideways at Sean.

"What?"

"Voodoo! The last time I was down here on that *Live and Let Live* mission, it was a frightening factor to be reckoned with, and some of the locals believe voodoo is an underlying current running through the culture."

"That sounds like a bunch of bullshit! There's no such thing!"

Changing the subject, Roger says, "What about Primeaux's dog? We know he has one. What if there are other guard dogs?"

"I'm sure there's a tranquilizer gun somewhere in the equipment on the boat. HQ said they had anticipated everything we might need to complete the mission," Sean says smugly.

"What about the other aspects of the mission?" Roger asks.

"That apology nonsense? Man, that was 250 years ago! Some people don't know when to let go of the past! It doesn't sound like a big deal to me, but it is part of the mission, so we'll keep our eyes and ears open for anything along that line, and we'll pass it on to HQ. The main objective of our mission is to obtain the data on that Aspic."

Passing over the Spillway Bridge, they approach the rendezvous site. They exit the highway and drive below the Hwy 190 Bridge, where they see a boat docked with the gangplank extended. It's an old crew boat, once used to ferry men and equipment to and from oil rigs in the Gulf of Mexico. In its prime, this workhorse of the oil field was very dependable and somewhat fast. But this old boat of some 30-40 years has seen its better days.

"Is *that* the yacht?" Roger's jaw drops.

"What the hell?" Sean stares unbelieving.

"HQ said it would be a *yacht!*"

"Look, I'm sure it'll be OK. It's only for one night at the most. It's a simple job . . . in and out. We'll get the Aspic data and any other pertinent info, then get the hell out of Melville and head for New Orleans."

George and Timmy pull alongside the Aston. George, quietly pissed-off, eyes the so-called yacht. They all get out of their vehicles to get a better look at the shoddy boat. After grumbling amongst themselves about the rundown appearance of the boat, they all decide to accept the situation and try to stay positive. Just then, the captain steps out of the wheelhouse with a big Cajun *"HELLO"* and climbs down the ladder to the lower deck.

"Let's check this out!" George enthusiastically heads for the catwalk and trips as he steps onto it.

Sean, right behind George, leans his head toward Roger and coldly comments, "Spastic bastard!" Roger turns to look for Timmy and catches him gazing back at the Lincoln Navigator. "What is it with you and those damn Lincolns?"

"On that *License to Maim* mission, I drove a Lincoln Mark V . . . duh!" Timmy answers defensively.

The captain steps down from the ladder as the agents reach the top of the gangplank, and they meet on the deck. He smiles and shakes hands with Sean. "Welcome aboard! I am Alphonse, your captain."

"Yeah right, I take it this is all of our equipment?" Sean replies in a condescending manner.

The captain is stunned. First, by Sean's sheer rudeness and arrogance, and second, the English accent surprises and upsets him. The agents are the first Englishmen the captain has ever met, and they project an insensitive, superior attitude that the captain mentally compares to the heartless British soldiers during the Acadian exile from Nova Scotia.

"Yes, all of this is yours. Come, let me show you around," the captain says after an awkward silence.

The captain leads the agents through a door to the main living area. It's a large room containing sofas, tables, and a bar. Loud Cajun music is blasting from a TV, and a young blonde girl is singing beautifully. Jamming in the middle of the room is a longhaired, dirty-looking deckhand. The captain introduces him as Jack and begins to explain the layout of the boat.

"This is the main living area, and through those doors is the galley. These stairs go up to the wheelhouse and my quarters. The other stairs go down to the main bunkroom, which is where you'll sleep. The deckhand and engineer have their quarters down there as well, in case you need anything." He opens a door and gestures. "Here's a bathroom, and there's another one downstairs."

Sean is reminded of the restroom incident on the plane and turns and glares at Timmy.

The captain starts down the stairs. Sean and Roger follow while George and Timmy remain upstairs. Once below, they enter a small hallway with doors to the main bunkroom, the deckhand and engineer's quarters, a bathroom, and finally, a door to the engine room. The captain opens the door to the main bunkroom and says, "Here are your quarters, and like I said before, deckhand and engineer's quarters over there if you need anything. You know where my quarters are, all the way to the top, which is where I'm headed right now." He turns and starts back up the stairs.

"This is really bad! We're all in the same room with absolutely no privacy!" Roger exclaims. "There's no place in the bottom of this boat for docking an underwater craft. They don't even have sliding doors! I've never been on a job where they didn't have sliding doors!"

"You're right." Sean looks about the room with disgust. "I've *never* seen anything this trashy! HQ is going to have some explaining to do."

"In the meantime, we'll try to make the best of it. Let's give this room a once-over for bugs and cameras."

Meanwhile, up top, Timmy restlessly paces the floor, looking out the portholes and jiggling the Lincoln keys in his hand. George sits at the bar and orders a drink from the deckhand. "Martini . . . shaken, not stirred," he says smoothly.

"We got Bud and Bud Lite," the deckhand offers without missing a beat.

"Never mind."

Sean and Roger, having checked the room over, get ready to go up top, but Sean has trouble opening the bunkroom door.

"See what I mean? No sliding doors!" Roger offers.

Sean struggles with the door. "It must be jammed!"

"I've been all over the world," Roger mumbles, "on land, at sea, in mountainous caves, and underwater caverns, and we *always* had sliding doors!" After fighting with the stuck door, Sean is finally able to get it open, and they head upstairs to the main living area. Sean orders a drink from the deckhand.

"Martini . . . shaken, not stirred."

The deckhand smiles wryly. "We got Bud and Bud Lite."

"I already asked," George says with a smirk.

"Never mind!" He shakes his head and heads for the back deck.

Again, Sean has trouble with the door. He has to pull really hard to open it, and all the agents follow him outside. On the deck, Sean looks around and begins to give orders.

"Okay, let's get our vehicles unloaded."

The captain, coming out of his quarters, overhears the command. "Are you going to leave your vehicles here?"

"What do you mean? What else can we do with them?" Sean asks.

"You can drive them on top of the levee to Melville. It's only twelve miles. They'd be safer there."

"Oh yeah?"

"Yeah. You can't cross the river with them because the ferry doesn't run on the weekend, but you can drive them there."

"OK, then." Sean turns to George and Timmy. "You two take the vehicles down the levee." He hands the keys to the Aston over to George.

"And you—BE CAREFUL with my car! EXTREMELY CAREFUL!

Roger and I will go over the manifest and sort out some of the equipment here. We'll meet you in Melville." Timmy and George walk down the gangplank and over toward the vehicles.

"Wait! I need to get a few things out of my car," Sean shouts and heads down the plank.

"Yeah, I need to get some things too, especially my binoculars." Roger takes off behind him.

"We may as well go ahead and take everything with us now," Sean says.

They gather up their luggage, forgetting a pair of shoes on the floor behind the driver's seat. Sean is having second thoughts about George driving his car and yells out at him as he drives off, "YOU'D BETTER BE CAREFUL with my car!"

They take off with Timmy in the lead. As they pull up on top of the levee and round the first curve, Sean watches as the Aston spins a little in a patch of mud. A worried look crosses his face.

Returning to the boat, Sean orders the captain to proceed upriver, then he and Roger go downstairs to unpack. They make themselves at home by taking the two bottom bunks and leaving the upper bunks for George and Timmy. There are drawers under the bunks, and they decide to use them. As Sean tries to open his drawer, it stubbornly stays shut. He begins a tug-of-war with the drawer, pulling up and down and side to side on the handle. He jerks first one way, then the next; suddenly, the front of the drawer breaks off!

"To hell with this!" Sean places his luggage on the floor at the foot of his bunk.

Roger, having no trouble with his drawer, comments, "Mine works fine."

Meanwhile, due to recent rains, Timmy and George find themselves driving on top of a very muddy levee. Soon they begin to happen upon cows, and with the cows comes cow shit. The further along the levee they go, the more mud, cows, and cow shit they encounter. Before long, cows and cow shit are everywhere! The rain has caused some very slick and sloppy driving conditions that create poor traction for George, but not for Timmy. They cross through a few open-gated cattle guards, but as driving conditions worsen, they come to a cattle guard with a closed gate. They stop and get out of their vehicles to check out the situation. The gate is padlocked, but the width of the gate does not go across the entire levee.

Timmy and George get out and look the situation over. "This looks stupid. Let's just drive around the end of the gate," Timmy says.

They each fail to realize that if you drive a vehicle near the side of a muddy levee, the vehicle will very probably slide down the embankment. This may not be a problem for an all-wheel drive, but a two-wheel drive will never make it. They get back in their vehicles and drive around the cattle gate. Sure enough, Timmy's Lincoln makes it around the gate with no problem, but George and the Aston begin to slide downward and then sideways. George rolls down the window and yells to Timmy . . .

"What should I do?"

"FLOOR IT! And don't let off!" Timmy yells back.

George hits the gas, and the Aston starts sliding downward and to the side at a rapid rate. It becomes clear that this is not going to work; still, George continues to keep it floored all the way until the car hits the bottom of the levee. It comes to rest near a cattle feeder and is now settled in a veritable slush of cow shit. The car has come to rest with its rear bumper wedged against the flat ground and the front bumper angled up toward the slope of the levee. The car is literally in deep shit.

Timmy jumps out of the Lincoln and runs over to the edge of the levee. "Damn!" he shouts down to George. "Hold on, I'll look for something to help pull you out."

Finding a nylon strap in the Lincoln's road hazard kit, Timmy hollers down to George. "I've got a strap here, but it might be too short, so I'll back down the levee enough to make it reach."

At the bottom of the levee, George gets out of the car, and immediately his foot sinks in shit past his ankle, up to mid-shin! His other foot does the same. He's literally in a sink pit of shit, and the smell is atrocious! He begins to struggle toward the front of the car, and as he steps onto the incline of the levee, he slips and falls on all fours, and now is in shit up to his elbows! He grabs onto the car and pulls himself up. Holding onto the fender, he slowly makes his way around to the front of the car.

Assessing the situation, George realizes the undercarriage of the vehicle is buried up to the axles in cow shit and concludes there is nowhere to hook the strap but to the bumper. Timmy, now in position with one end of the strap hooked to his vehicle, throws the other end to George.

George shoves the strap through the cow shit muck, underneath the bumper, then up and over the middle of the revolving license plate.

After securing the strap, he begins to slop his way back to the side of the car. But again, once on the slippery incline, he falls, this time on his ass, and slides down the slope, overshooting the driver's door. He manages to grab hold of the driver's side wheel well and pull himself up.

He's now covered in cow shit from head to foot! He has to stretch himself to reach the door handle. Opening the door, he lifts his foot to get in the car, but his shoe stays stuck in the shit. He is now in a very awkward position! Standing on one foot sunk calf-deep in cow shit, with the other in a sock and his shoe somewhere below in the muck, he wobbles there, holding on to the car door for balance.

George realizes that if he wants to retrieve his shoe, he has no choice but to put his foot back down in the shit, with nothing between him and the stinking ooze but a sock. Now, he's covered from head to toe in cow shit, but somehow the idea of putting his foot down in that mess absolutely repulses him. Nonetheless, with a determined look of disgust on his face, he slowly lowers his foot into the warm, gooey shit. As his foot is slowly sinking, the feel and texture of the cow shit, along with the smell, sends waves of nausea through his body. His foot bottoms out but doesn't find the shoe.

George is sickened to the point of a gasping gag reflex. After retching a few times, he pulls himself together, bends over, and reaching his arm down into the shit, he grabs the shoe and pulls it up. "Talk about getting the shitty end of the stick!" he says, with a sickly looking grin.

After retrieving his cow shit shoe and not wanting to dirty the car's interior, George carefully places the shoe on the floorboard next to Sean's pristine pair. The contrast is like night and day. Meanwhile, Timmy is revving his engine.

"Let's GO!" he hollers down the levee.

George, covered in cow shit, hesitates to get in the car. *Oh, what the hell! There's no point trying to be careful anymore*, he says to himself.

Climbing into the car, George smears shit everywhere: on the seat, floor, steering wheel, stick shift, and even the keys. He starts the car, but before he can put it in gear and signal, Timmy begins pulling. Timmy takes off like a madman, jerking the Aston and slinging muddy cow shit all over the hood and windshield. Like a sudden pull against dead weight, as a result, the Aston's bumper is pulled out into a V-shape!

George scrambles to put the car in gear and give it gas so Timmy can tow it more smoothly. Eventually, they reach the top of the levee after a long sideways ascent. Coming to a stop up on the levee, they get out of their vehicles to unhook the strap and see the damage they've done to the Aston.

"DAMN!" Timmy exclaims.

"You shouldn't have jerked it so hard!" George says as he passes his hand over the V-shaped bumper. "Sean is gonna be furious when he sees this!"

"No, he's gonna KILL YOU!"

"There was no other way to hook it!"

"He is sure going to be pissed!" Timmy shakes his head.

"Well, when we get to New Orleans, I'll pay to have it fixed," George says with a resigned sigh.

After unhooking the strap, they get in their vehicles and continue on down the levee. The ferry ramp at Melville is within sight, and they don't have far to go.

Meanwhile, back on the boat, Sean and Roger have finished their unpacking and are upstairs as the boat gets underway. Before they start checking out the crates of equipment on the back deck, the captain informs them that he's having trouble starting one of the engines and it's going to be a while before the engineer can get it started.

"Can't you just go with one engine?" Sean is in a big hurry.

"Yes, but I'll have to stay to the right side of the river because the current is very strong. I can't get near the middle. It's too dangerous, and with only one engine, it's too hard to steer."

"Fine, let's just get this show on the road!" Sean turns to Roger. "Let's get outside and find out what kind of equipment HQ sent us."

Their exit is thwarted once again by a problem door. After a short tugging match, Sean finally gets it open. He turns to the captain behind him.

"You need to have your deckhand fix these doors! They seem to be sticking. Maybe it's the humidity down here. C'mon, Roger, let's go."

Back on deck, they take in some of the scenery as the boat begins to take off. They can hear music coming from the wheelhouse and the captain's quarters. After a short examination of the crates, Sean asks Roger to go up and ask the captain for a crowbar.

Roger goes up to the wheelhouse and passes the captain's quarters. The door is open, and Roger gives it a once-over in true agent-like fashion. The captain is lying on his bunk; the walls are covered with maps, the bookshelves are loaded with magazines, books, and films. There's a small TV and VCR and a lot of memorabilia from what appears to be the silent film era.

"What is all this stuff?" Roger gestures toward the wall.

"This is all about the exile that my people suffered in 1755," the captain rises from his bunk.

Sensing that Roger may be interested, the captain is hit with a wave of enthusiasm and begins to tell the history of the Acadian people. He then asks Roger if he has ever heard of Longfellow's poem, *Evangeline*. The captain goes on to elaborate as Roger leans in and takes a closer look at all the pictures, posters, books, films, and newspaper articles. The captain shows him memorabilia from a 1920s film of *Evangeline* and more from a 1990s musical, also called Evangeline. He inserts a tape of the musical into the VCR.

Music drifts about the room as Roger notices a newspaper article entitled, "Battle on the Bayou . . . Cajuns vs. Brits." Roger is stunned! At that moment, the music subsides, and the Lieutenant Governor of Louisiana begins to make the opening introduction. Red flags go up in Roger's mind as he realizes the political implications! Not wanting to appear too anxious for information and yet eager to report back to Sean what he's found, Roger abruptly cuts the captain off and asks for a crowbar.

Surprised by this sudden rudeness and sensing that what he has shared with Roger has fallen on deaf ears, the captain, nevertheless, accommodates Roger by going into the wheelhouse, taking the wheel from the deckhand, and sending him to get a crowbar. Unable to resist, the captain tells Roger that the town of Melville just so happens to be one of the first places where the Acadians crossed the Atchafalaya River into what is now known as Acadiana. And the settlers became known as Cajuns. A song from the Evangeline musical grows louder, and drifting into the wheelhouse, it catches Roger's attention.

"That's a catchy little tune," Roger remarks.

"That song is *The Village of Grand Pré*. It's about how my people carried the village within themselves and how they could not be destroyed. That film I mentioned about Evangeline really tells the story well." Just as the captain begins to tell the story of Evangeline, the deckhand returns with the crowbar and gives it to Roger, who thanks him and heads for the door.

"Later, if you have time, you're welcome to watch the film," the captain calls out after him.

"Sure." Roger is out the door and climbing down the ladder. He says to himself, *That* guy is clearly living in the past!

"What took you so long?" Sean asks when Roger rejoins him at the crates. "Did you get the crowbar?"

"Yeah, and that's not all I got! You're not going to believe this! You know the other half of the mission we're supposed to keep our eyes and ears open for?"

"That 250-year-old thing?"

"Exactly! The captain is up to his eyeballs in that nonsense!"

Sean looks around suspiciously and immediately goes into agent mode. "Yeah, go on. What did he say?"

"It's not so much what he said as what I saw. His whole cabin is full of maps, books, films, documents, and newspaper articles. One article in particular, entitled *"Battle on the Bayou . . . Cajuns vs. Brits,"* is about the exile from Nova Scotia and the demand for an apology."

"A *demand!* No wonder the Queen is reluctant to offer an apology. It's not exactly front-page news, but it could get out of hand! What else?"

"Well, the captain keeps referring to this poem Evangeline."

"What?"

"The poem, *Evangeline*, written by Longfellow. The captain says it's a love story about a woman named Evangeline who lost her love, Gabriel, during the exile in 1755."

"*Again*, with the 250 years ago!" Sean is adamant.

"Evidently, this love story has a lot to do with the Cajun people's heritage and somehow it tells the story of the exile," Roger says.

"A lot to do with their *sensitivity!* You know how sensitive the French can be!" Sean counters.

"This *Evangeline* poem must have been popular in its day. The captain even has a 1920s film and a more recent musical about Evangeline."

"Evidently, this poem from the past is fueling the demand for an apology. Some people just don't know when to let the past go!" Sean shakes his head wearily.

"These people are *definitely* living in the past!""They try to steal the Culinary Olympics and, at the same time, wage a war on the political front using the media. Friggin' MONOPOLIZERS! If they want a battle, we'll give them a battle!" Sean sets his jaw.

"The captain invited me to watch that old film."

"Good. You can befriend him and find out whatever you can. When Timmy and George return, I'll send them to get the data on the Aspic."

"I thought you didn't want to trust them with this."

"True, but with this apology thing falling in our laps, we'll have to divide our manpower. When I report to HQ, I'll inform them we've hit the *Mother Lode!*" Sean grabs the crowbar and starts opening crates.

Arriving at the East ferry ramp across the river from Melville, Timmy and George turn off the levee and drive down the ramp to the water's edge. George makes a U-turn and parks Sean's car a short way up on the ramp, facing the levee, so the damaged front end can't be seen from the river. Timmy parks the Lincoln close to the water. It's a quiet, desolate place with heavy foliage. A railroad trestle is in the upright position, and half hidden behind thick bushes, there's a railroad maintenance vehicle abandoned on the tracks at the foot of the trestle. George puts his shoe back on and gets out of the car. He sloshes down to meet Timmy at the bottom of the river ramp.

"There's sure not much here," Timmy says.

"This must be the place because there's the railroad trestle that 'N' spoke about in the briefing." George slings his leg out to the side and shakes it. "I can't take any more; I've got to wash this shit off me!" He strides into the river, shoes and all, and begins stripping off his clothes.

"Sean is gonna freak when he sees that car!" Timmy says from the bank. "He won't understand. It's a good thing you parked it like that. He might not notice it right away, but eventually he'll find out!"

"It was unavoidable!" George replies. "I plan on paying for all the damage!"

"That won't be good enough. He's probably gonna want to kick your ass!"

"Just let him try! I'll kick *his ass!* I've had enough of him calling all the shots!"

As George finishes washing up, he realizes the only things salvageable are his shoes, now minus most of the cow shit. He tosses them up onto the bank, then he pushes his clothes down into the river's muddy bottom with his feet.

"Hey Timmy, grab my suitcase, will you?" Stark naked, he walks out of the water and up the ramp.

George takes the suitcase from Timmy and lays it across the hood of the Lincoln and quickly opens it, grabbing the professor disguise. As he dresses, he thinks about his shoes.

"I sure need another pair of shoes. Sean has an extra pair behind the drive."

"Are you *crazy?* He has those shoes handmade in Italy! He'd kill you if you wore them!"

"Well, my shoes sure stink! That smell won't come out!"

"That's cow piss ammonia! It's not going to come out for a while; it has to wear off! You better make the best of it." Timmy walks to the water's edge and looks downriver. "That boat should be here soon."

Hugging the right bank, the old crew boat slowly makes its way up the river. Sean and Roger are trying to make sense out of all the crates when the captain steps out of the wheelhouse on the upper deck.

"The engineer tells me we must have taken on some bad fuel and that's why the engine wouldn't start. Now we're beginning to have trouble with the generator. Even the engine we're running on seems to be a little sluggish."

"What can you do about it?" Sean looks up from the crates

"We can transfer the bad fuel and then pump good fuel into the main tank if the pump holds up."

"Well, just do it then!" Sean snaps.

"We're nearing Melville. Do you want to come up to the wheelhouse and have a look at where you might want to dock?"

Sean goes up to the wheelhouse, and Roger follows. As Sean walks by the captain's quarters, he glances in the door, then looks back at Roger with a thumbs-up. The captain is at the wheel, looking upriver and scanning the banks.

"OK. What have we got here?" Sean says to the captain.

"Well, coming up on our left is the ferry I told you about. It'll be docked at that ramp all weekend. Up that ramp and over the levee is the town of Melville. To your right is the East ramp for the ferry crossing."

"Can you dock between the railroad trestle and that pipeline north of the trestle?"

"Yes, normally, I could get through right now because the bridge is open, but it's too dangerous to venture out into the middle of the river with only one engine. We can't chance it. Those currents are really strong. I wonder why the bridge is open like that. They normally don't open it unless a vessel requests passage. It must be stuck. They're always having trouble with those things. It's because they don't use them enough."

Just then, the generator goes out, and the one sluggish engine also dies. There's an eerie silence.

"We've got to pull over NOW!" The captain leans into the wheel and begins to maneuver the old boat toward the bank.

Sean spots Timmy's Lincoln parked on the ramp near the water, with Timmy and George standing nearby.

"How about on the north side of that ramp where that vehicle and my guys are?"

"We're going against the current, but I think we may have just enough momentum to drift over there." The captain picks up the PA and radios down to the engineer in the engine room.

(SCRRRRR) . . . "Start up the auxiliary generator!"

(SCRRRRR) . . . "I can't start it until I get some of this good fuel pumped around into the main tanks. I'm more worried about that bilge filling up."

(SCRRRRR) . . . "Do the best you can, then."

"What's with the bilge?" Sean asks.

"Well, the bilge pump won't run without the generator, and the bilge pump is what keeps the rudder room from filling up with water. If that happens, the boat will start to sink, but we won't let that happen, even if we have to pump it out by hand."

"This boat sure has its problems!" Sean looks around the wheelhouse.

"Yeah, I know she's seen her better days, but in the thirty years we've been together, she's always come through. This may be her last voyage. The office is talking about sending her over to the bone yard."

They have just enough momentum to drift to the bank a little north of the ramp. The captain orders the deckhand to drop anchor off the bow and extend the catwalk on the rear starboard side of the boat. As the boat drifts to a stop, Roger is scanning the Melville side of the river with his binoculars.

"There's got to be some women around here somewhere," he mumbles.

There's not much to look at except a levee, a few fishing camps, and some large-leafed banana trees fluttering in the wind. The leaves part now and then in the breeze, just long enough to reveal the head of a garden scarecrow. Roger gets a fleeting glimpse of the scarecrow and perceives it as a voodoo figure! It stops him cold! Stunned and shaking, he quickly pulls the binoculars away from his face.

"What is it? What do you see?" Sean asks.

"Uhhhh . . . uh . . ." A blank stare comes over Roger's face, and he's unable to reply.

"What's the matter with you? C'mon, let's go! Let's get something done!"

Sean leaves the wheelhouse and goes down the stairs to the deck. Roger, in a daze, follows quietly behind. They meet Timmy and George as they cross the catwalk onto the boat.

"God! What's *that* smell?" Sean wrinkles his nose.

With wide-eyed, shoulder-shrugging, open-palmed gestures, Timmy and George both say, "I don't know."

"You guys smell like shit!" Sean exclaims. "Now, let's get to work. We've only got a couple hours of daylight left, so we have to get *something* done! Give me that crowbar, Roger!"

Roger stands woodenly and doesn't respond.

"ROGER, give me that damn crowbar!" Sean yells.

Roger, still dazed, slowly hands the crowbar to Sean.

"What the hell's the matter with you?!" Sean looks quizzically at Roger as he takes the crowbar. With no answer forthcoming, Sean's thoughts return to the job at hand.

"The first thing we need to find is that tranquilizer gun." Sean looks over the crates, trying to decide which one to open first.

"What do we need a tranquilizer gun for?" Timmy asks.

"Where were you during the briefing? We know Primeaux has at least one dog; he might have guard dogs all over the damn place! We're going to need a tranquilizer gun! None of the codes on the manifest match any of the codes on the crates! We'll just have to start busting them open. At this point, it's potluck! Let's try this one."

Sean rips the lid off a smaller crate. It's full of standard issue "00" specialty spy watches, and in his excitement, George grabs at the pile, and two of them go off! One shoots a dart that narrowly misses Roger as it whizzes, then thunks into a nearby crate! The other watch shoots a bullet that grazes Sean's upper coat sleeve, tearing a slit across the shoulder! Pissed off to the max, Sean is ready to cuss George out.

"Don't look at me!" George shouts defensively before Sean can say anything. "I'm not the one who packed this mission! It was probably the new Quartermaster!"

In the interest of moving things along and for the sake of the mission, Sean manages to control his anger and urges everyone to be more careful. As he turns back to the crate, he glances over at Roger, who is still somewhat dazed.

"You don't look so good. Maybe it's the heat. Why don't you go inside and cool off, work the deckhand and engineer, see what you can get out of them?" Roger stumbles off in a zombie-like trance.

"You two, open that big crate over there," Sean directs Timmy and George. Sean tries to hand the crowbar to Timmy, who's daydreaming and looking up the ramp at the Lincoln. "Hey, pay attention." He puts the crowbar in Timmy's hand.

"So, what are YOU gonna do?" George asks sarcastically.

"I'm gonna have a look at some of these other crates. Maybe I can match up a code. It'll save some time." Sean walks around toward the back of the crates.

"Who does he think he is?" George nudges Timmy. "Saying . . . *pay attention!* I'll bet you he wouldn't speak to me like that!"

Timmy doesn't seem to hear George at all or be bothered by Sean's treatment of him. He's in his own little world. Meanwhile, Roger is up in the main living area where he finds the deckhand standing in the middle of the room, toolbox in hand, jamming to a Cajun rock and roll band on TV. The music is blaring, and he's lost in the rhythm.

"Man, that's one bad little babe!" The deckhand nods at the Britney Spears look-alike on the TV.

"Yeah, she looks real good!" Roger seems to regain his bearings.

"Do a lot of the women around here look that hot?"

"Yeah, pretty much, but they're all at the Mardi Gras right now."

"Hmm . . . Mardi Gras sounds like FUN!"

"I'd like to stay and chat, but the captain wants me to check out some of these doors." The deckhand turns and walks away.

"Guess I'll go downstairs for a while," Roger says.

Back on deck, Timmy and George have lifted the lid on that large crate and find a two-man vehicle designed to ride inside pipelines.

"It's the pipeline pig!" Timmy exclaims.

"A what?" George examines the odd-looking vehicle.

"It's the pipeline pig I used on that Living Daylites mission." The *Living Daylites* theme song goes off in Timmy's head, and he asks George, "Do you hear that?"

"Hear what?"

Confused, Timmy looks at George, then after a moment of puzzled silence, he says, "This is one wild ride here!" He runs his hand along the pig.

"Hey Sean, come and take a look at this!" he hollers.

Sean saunters over and, seeing the pig, exclaims, "Hey, that's great! We can really use that, and I think I found the crate with the tranquilizer gun." He points at a long crate atop several others. "Timmy, back your vehicle up to the catwalk, and you all load the pig and take it down to the base of the pipeline. There's got to be a valve station there with a pig trap that you can use to load it into the line. I'll get the gun."

Down in the engine room, Roger was hoping to extract some useful information from the engineer. Instead, he finds the engineer poring over the boat's blueprints, and he gets a lecture on Boatology 101. The engineer explains how they took on bad fuel and what all he has to do to correct the problem, how he's running low on filters for the generators and the engines, and how it's going to be a real juggling act to move the bad fuel into a spare tank while, at the same time, pumping water around the boat in order to keep it level.

"We may list back and forth and side to side, but it's nothin' to worry about. We're not gonna sink or tip over or anything like that," he assures Roger.

Up top, Timmy and George have the pig loaded, and Sean is giving them last-minute instructions. He hands the tranquilizer gun to George and orders him to be careful with it. George places it next to the pig in the rear of the Lincoln.

"And here's your walkie-talkie." Sean hands a two-way radio with an isolated frequency to Timmy.

"When you get on the other side of the river, head for the back levee. As you get close, you may be able to smell your way to the main smoking facility if there aren't any other obstructing odors." Sean looks at George's shoes.

Timmy and George get in the Lincoln and drive up the ramp. Sean, noticing the back of the boat is sitting somewhat lower in the water, heads to the wheelhouse to talk to the captain.

Impressed with the Lincoln's ability, Timmy says, "Boy, this all-wheel drive really pulls good on the uphill!"

"If this ramp was a little steeper, I could ski down and across the river," George says as they crest the top of the levee.

"No way! The current's too strong!"

"I skied down a whole damn mountain on ONE ski!" George exclaims.

Proceeding down the other side of the levee, the two agents turn onto a gravel road and head north along the bottom of the levee toward the base of the pipeline. The road crosses under the railroad, and they spot a railroad maintenance vehicle sitting on the tracks above. It's a rather new, high-tech looking piece of equipment resembling a milk truck with various antennas and satellite dishes. On the door is a Union Pacific Railways logo.

"Hey, look at that!" Timmy points to the vehicle. "It looks abandoned."

"They were probably doing some work on the bridge. They must have gone to the Mardi Gras," George muses.

They drive on. Meanwhile, Sean goes into the wheelhouse and finds the captain sitting at the wheel, watching a small TV/VCR next to a radar screen. The musical *Evangeline* is playing, and a Cajun with a really heavy accent is singing one of the songs, *"Matt From Ville Platte."*

"Who is that IDIOT?" Sean motions toward the music.

The captain says nothing. Sean walks out the side door of the wheelhouse to the bow of the boat. He hopes to see what Timmy and George are up to, but he can't see the base of the pipeline because of the levee. He begins pacing back and forth across the bow of the boat. Meanwhile, Roger has had an earful of the engineer and comes up to the wheelhouse.

"What's going on?" Roger asks the captain.

"Your boss man is out on the bow. I guess he's looking for your other two guys. He seems kind of nervous, keeps pacing back and forth."

"He's under a lot of pressure. Do you mind if I look at some of your books?" Roger asks, standing in the doorway of the captain's quarters. "Oh no. Sure. Go ahead, help yourself."

Arriving at the valve station, Timmy and George unload the pig at a small gate, and after a struggle of pushing, pulling, and dragging the pig some twenty-five yards, they reach the pig trap hatch. Timmy begins to open it.

"We're having to do all of the HARD work while Sean and Roger are taking it easy on the boat! Sean is playing favorites with Roger!" George huffs as he positions the pig. "I've heard of brown-nosing before, but Roger is so far up Sean's ass, it looks like he has four legs! If anything, I should be the leadoff hand on this mission. After all, I do have seniority over Roger!"

Timmy opens the hatch and finds things a little rusty inside the pipeline, indicating a lack of use. He looks at a row of gauges, and they all read zero. He taps a few of them to see if they're working. "There's no pressure on this line! This line is dead!"

"So, what does that mean?" George asks.

"Without any natural gas pressure, we have nothing to propel the pig down the line and over to the other side of the river."

"Maybe it's because of Mardi Gras and everybody's gone. That's where we should be!" George grumbles. "We need to get this shit done!"

Back on the boat, Sean realizes he's not going to be able to see any sign of Timmy and George and decides to lie down on a bench next to the wheelhouse on the bow of the boat. Roger rummages through the captain's quarters as the captain watches his *Evangeline* musical.

At the pipeline, Timmy reaches out and runs his hand along the pipe. "This thing sure is sweating. If it wasn't so slippery, we could damn near walk on top of it to the other side."

Just then, an excited look comes over George's face and he cocks his head. He's recalling how he hand-walked across cables on his last mission.

"You hear something?" Timmy asks.

"No, uh . . . look, why don't I just use my cable watch to pull myself up to the line, grab hold of those cables, and hand-walk them over to the other side?"

"Are you crazy? Those cables are HOT!" Timmy replies.

"On my last mission, I encountered cables that were cold and full of grease. All I had to do was tear out my pant pockets and use them as gloves. It's nothing. Quick! Give me your pockets!"

"I don't know. Maybe we ought to check with Sean. Tell him the pig won't work and see what he wants to do."

"There you go again!" George sighs. "What HE wants to do! Does everything have to be what HE wants? Aren't we allowed to show some initiative of our own? Aren't we allowed to improvise if need be? Why does everything have to be HIS way?"

"I don't know. He's the Direct . . . uh, I mean, he's the head of the mission."

"Oh hell! Let's just get this over with so we can get to New Orleans! We're missing all the festivities! Give me your pockets!"

"What?"

"Give me your pants pockets! Tear out your pockets and give them to me! I told you I already used mine on my last mission."

Not quite understanding, Timmy tears out his pockets and gives them to George. George puts them on his hands, as though they were gloves, and begins walking toward the levee. Timmy follows, and as they pass the Lincoln, he grabs the tranquilizer gun and continues up the levee. At the top of the levee, George aims and fires his watch, which shoots a wire cable that attaches itself to a thirty-foot-high brace holding up the pipeline. Feeling very proud of hitting his aim, George turns to Timmy and boasts.

"Wasn't that a beautiful shot?" Suddenly, without warning, the watch malfunctions and begins pulling him upwards.

"Wait! You forgot the gun!"

George manages to stop the cable watch and is just hlanging in mid-air.

"C'mon down a little ways, and I'll throw you the gun!"

"Right!" George tries putting the cable watch in reverse to lower himself, but it only moves a few inches. "It must be jammed!"

Timmy, standing below, looks up at George and shouts, "Try going up a little and then back down!"

"OK!" He moves another inch or two, then stops. "It's still jammed!"

"Well, try coming down again!"

"Damn!" He tries, but the cable won't move. It won't go up or down. "Keep trying! Jerk around on it!" Timmy encourages.

Back on the boat, from his seat in the wheelhouse, the captain has been watching this whole fiasco with Timmy and George. He hollers for Roger, who's still looking at books in the captain's quarters.

"Hey, come here a minute! Take a look at this! Isn't that one of your guys there hanging off that pipeline? He looks like a big catfish dangling on a trotline! And isn't that the other one on the levee there?"

"Yeah, that's them. Looks like a slight hang-up." Roger heads out to the bow of the boat and rouses Sean from his past mission daydreams.

"Sean, Sean, get up! Take a look at this!"

"What?" Sean grumbles.

"Take a look over at that pipeline, near the brace. Here, use my binoculars."

Sean lifts the binoculars and sees George hanging there. "What the—? I *knew* it! I *knew* it! He just had to play with the friggin' watch! I knew he was gonna try to use that friggin' watch!"

"It was working fine until I stopped! This thing is supposed to coil and recoil on demand!" George says.

"Sean is gonna be pissed!" Timmy yells up.

"He better not blame this on me! Pierce is probably the one who broke this watch on his last mission!"

"I'll go back to the boat and see if I can find something to get you down." Timmy heads for the Lincoln.

"Don't tell Sean, if you don't have to! He'll raise hell!" George yells.

Timmy puts the gun in the back of the Lincoln and closes the tailgate.

Driving down the ramp, he sees Sean coming off the ladder from the wheelhouse deck. Just as he stops and opens his door, Sean tears into him.

"What the hell is going on? Why is that idiot hanging there like that? And why aren't the two of you riding the pig to the other side?" Sean yells.

"The line is dead. There's no pressure to propel the pig," Timmy tries to explain.

"Doesn't that pig have magnetic propulsion capability?"

"No."

"Damn, they give Pierce all the good equipment!"

"Well, uh . . . what about George?" Timmy asks cautiously.

"Whose idea was it to try that watch cable?"

"We had to improvise. That's what the scene called for. George wanted to get up near the line and hand-walk the cables to the other side. He said he'd done that on his last mission."

"*Last* mission! *Last* mission! His only friggin' mission! Take a watch with a laser over to the pipeline and cut him down. Then, the two of you get back here, PRONTO! I found a hot air balloon in one of the crates. We'll get it aired up and ready to go first thing in the morning. Tonight, I may send you over in the Lincoln if I can locate the GPS system that's listed on the manifest. It's got to be in one of these crates."

"Where's Roger?" Timmy asks.

"I've got him working on something else. Go ahead and get going. I've got to report in to HQ about some of these delays."

In the captain's quarters, Roger stumbles across a voodoo book, and it brings to mind the voodoo doll he saw at the airport and the voodoo figure he may have seen behind the banana trees. Shocked a little, paranoia begins to set in. Timmy locates the laser watch in the crate full of watches and heads back to help George. When he arrives back at the pipeline, George is still dangling.

"What took you so long? My arm is getting numb!" George complains.

"Sean saw the whole thing from the boat! He was pretty pissed and started giving me instructions a mile a minute!"

"That bossy big shot! Have you brought something to get me down?"

"I've got a laser watch; I'm gonna cut you down."

"Cut me down?! I'll fall right in that cow shit!" Looking down at bayou sludge laced with cow shit and cow piss. "Didn't they have a block and tackle on that boat? Or SOMETHING!"

"This is all Sean sent me over with, and he said to hurry!"

"But I'll fall right in that shit, man! This is my professor's disguise outfit! I'm running out of clean clothes!"

"Are you ready? We've got to get going!" He starts cutting.

"Wait a minute!" George yells.

"It'll be a soft landing!"

"NO! WAIT!" He drops with a SPLAT!

The combination of water, mud, cow shit, green slime, and cow piss is only a few feet deep, but George falls so fast and hard that he plunges beneath the vile sludge! He comes up slowly and pauses for a moment in disbelief.

"I can't believe this is happening to me!" He slowly wades out of the slimy filth, up the levee and toward Timmy.

"Oh man! That STINKS!" Timmy shakes his head in disgust. "I'm going to need a bath!"

"There's no running water on the boat. The generator is still busted."

"Oh man, I'll have to wash off in the river near the ramp!"

"You're NOT getting in my truck like that!"

"YOUR truck? It's a rental!"

"Why don't you ride back here?" Timmy opens the tailgate.

George sits on the tailgate with his legs dangling about six inches from the ground. Timmy turns the vehicle around on top of the levee and takes off toward the boat. They hit a small trench in the levee, which causes the Lincoln's rear end to slightly bottom out, and George's feet are dragged through a big pile of soft cow shit that cakes up the back of his heels.

"Oh man!" He quickly lifts his legs to avoid more shit.

Arriving at the boat ramp, they notice the boat listing toward the bank. George jumps off the tailgate and runs down the ramp and into the water. Timmy takes the tranquilizer gun up onto the boat and places the gun on a crate near the catwalk. He returns to the Lincoln and begins to clean off the tailgate.

"Hey, Timmy! Could you get my bag again? I'm going to need my kilt and ruffled shirt."

"What are you going to do with your professor disguise?"

"Shove it underwater in the mud like I did with the suit I took off earlier."

"You know they're not going to stay in the mud very long with that current. They're going to work loose and surface eventually," Timmy warns.

Meanwhile, Sean is down in the bunkroom trying to contact HQ on his cell phone/walkie-talkie, which has an isolated international long-range frequency. It's early morning, British time, and after a few rings, Ms. Munynickle answers the phone.

"MI-6," she says tiredly.

"Top of the morning to you, Munynickle!" Sean says heartily.

"What do YOU want?" she asks, sounding irritated.

"Got up on the wrong side of the bed, did we?"

"I'm not in the mood for your crap! What do you want?"

"Is 'N' there?"

"HOLD ON!" She presses the office intercom button.

"Yes, Ms. Munynickle?" 'N' answers.

"The great Sean is on the phone!" she says sarcastically.

"Thank you, Ms. Munynickle." He picks up the phone. "Sean, how's it going?"

"It's not! It's a JOKE!"

"What do you mean?"

"Well, let's start with JOKE number one, this so-called yacht! It's more like an old oil-field crew boat that's falling apart and sinking at the same time! The only thing holding this tub together is the rust! I heard the captain say it was ready for the bone yard!"

"I sure am sorry about that, Double O. It's the fault of those guys down in Accounting. I swear, they're so tight, they squeak when they walk! I'll have a talk with them. What about the equipment?"

"You mean JOKE number two?"

"What do you mean?"

"This garbage looks like it's been around the world twenty times! The crates are so marked up that it's impossible to compare them to the cargo manifest. All we can do is open one at a time and hope for the best. It's like potluck!"

"Again, that's the fault of Accounting! They hopscotched that stuff over there on a number of cut-rate freighters to try and save money instead of just paying for a straight run."

"We did find a 'Model T' pipeline pig in one of the crates, but we couldn't use it because the line was dead. It's doubtful that it would have worked anyway!"

"They must have turned it off because of Mardi Gras. We hadn't anticipated that. We knew it would be a ghost town, but we didn't think they would shut it down to that degree."

"Who in the hell loaded this job, anyway?"

"It's that new Quartermaster. The one who took 'Q's place."

"He should have loaded the magnetic propulsion pig that Pierce used on *The World Is Enough* mission."

"The pig got blown up on that mission."

"Knowing Pierce, that's no surprise! We found the jet pack I used on that *Thunderbawl* mission. It looks like it blew up in the crate!"

"Pardon?"

"It's in a million pieces!"

"Well, from port to port, longshoremen can be pretty rough, and no doubt, that equipment went by way of the North Sea. That's pretty rough, too."

"I would think the new Quartermaster would have refurbished the equipment to some degree and packed it better."

"Well, yes. But he claims his department is also experiencing budget cuts and he's allotted only so much time and money to spend on this mission."

"We *never* had this kind of Problem when 'Q' was running things!"

"Well, remember what we talked about in the briefing? About our shoestring budget and having to improvise?"

"Yeah, I tell you though, that word 'improvise' brings to mind a little mishap we had with one of our watches and George and Timmy. When I questioned Timmy about the incident, he insisted the *scene called for some improvisation!*"

"What do you mean? The *scene* called for?" 'N' asks curiously.

"Yeah, what kind of lingo is that?" Sean continues, "And earlier, when I gave him a short-range radio, he said to me, *when that comes on, that'll be my cue,* I tell you, it's like he's using actor 'speak' to communicate!"

"Yes. He doesn't talk much, but when he does, he uses a lot of that terminology. You know, he studied Shakespeare quite extensively. In fact, he was on stage when we called him for this mission."

"If you ask me, he still thinks he's on stage!"

"Well, you know, Shakespeare once said, *All the world's a stage and we're actors upon it.*"

"Yes, I know, and Timmy seems to be taking that literally. I don't see how you can justify sending someone like him on a mission. Wasn't that the reason he was sidelined?"

"Remember, this is for the Queen. Just give him some time. I'm sure he'll come around."

"I hope you're right. I plan on him running some reconnaissance around the Western levee with a homing device and a radio."

"That sounds good."

"As long as I can monitor his coordinates through the GPS and communicate via the radio, I might be able to keep him out of Shakespeareville!"

"What about George? How's he doing?" 'N' asks.

"Besides having two left feet, a bad sense of timing, and a screwed-up wardrobe, you could say he's doing all right. He's always trying to complicate things by throwing in his two cents' worth!" Sean says.

"What do you mean?"

"He constantly gives everybody the benefit of the doubt. He's too naive, too trusting... not good qualities for a Double O."

"He may be a little out of touch, especially after what happened on his last mission."

"Look, I'm not interested in what happened on his only mission! I'm interested in *this* mission!"

"You know, that may be part of George's problem. No one wants to talk about what happened back then. Roger is the only one who ever touched on it. Timmy... well, you can't expect much. Pierce sure as hell never dealt with it. I don't even think it's a part of his consciousness."

"I don't want to go there either. It's too damn mind-boggling! Look, the bottom line is, and I hate to say it, but George is just not Double O material! Never has been... never will be!"

"Everybody has their place, and there's a place for everybody. George just has to find his niche in all of this. Give him time. He may prove to be vital to the mission."

"I'm going to send him into the compound on that balloon that Roger used in the *Octofussy* mission. We don't anticipate any problems. The wind is in our favor, and there's not much that can go wrong with a balloon. We'll launch at first light. Get in, get the Aspic data, and get out. Then head for New Orleans!"

"I'll bet Roger can't wait to get to New Orleans."

"Yeah, all these substandard conditions are not exactly his cup of tea, with the 'yacht' the way it is and all. I think it has him a little disoriented. You know, he doesn't function well in a situation like this without women around."

"I can't imagine Roger being disoriented. He's been down in New Orleans before on that *Live and Let Live* mission. Unless... uh..."

"Unless what?" Sean asks.

"Well, when he returned, he did show some signs of a somewhat distant demeanor... a little off-kilter. The boys in the Psych Department attributed it to a sociological aftermath stemming from that mission and involving..."

"Don't tell me—that hocus-pocus voodoo bullshit!"

"I know it sounds like bullshit, but there may be some validity to it. He was *stealthily* examined; unbeknownst to Roger, he was treated and desensitized to certain aspects from that particular environment."

"Stealth examination, huh? Go ahead, I'm listening."

"The long and short of it is, there may be some things in the environment sensitizing him and triggering a relapse. A relapse in which he perceives a slow, subtle, spiritual kidnapping."

"And these sensitizing triggers are...?" Sean leans forward.

"It could be a number of things... a spear, a deck of cards, a snake, a doll, or even music."

"We're talking about one of the best Double O's that MI-6 has ever produced! I helped train Roger myself! He's been in life-and-death situations that created enough fear and danger to kill or paralyze a normal man. And now, you want me to believe he thinks a spear-wielding doll with a deck of cards and a pet snake is kidnapping him? GET REAL!"

"This voodoo is a bona fide religion," 'N' continues. "Besides, all religions share the principal foundation of voodoo, which is the giving up of oneself to a higher power."

"Look, there's nothing those guys in the Psych Department love more than overcomplicating things by blowing shit completely *out* of proportion to try and build a mountain out of a molehill, just to fund their own department! *Stealth examination!* In the real world, we call that screwing with your head! If they want to screw with somebody's head, let them screw with Timmy's! They could have a field day with him!"

"Again, I must emphasize, this is a bona fide, ancient, African religion with some fifty million or so believers. Voodoo is practiced in countries like Brazil, Trinidad, Cuba, Haiti, and Jamaica, with a strong following in New Orleans. According to our latest intelligence, voodoo has filtered down into the Cajun community, *your very location!*" 'N' is adamant.

"Yeah. Roger mentioned this voodoo on the way down here and how it was an underlying current running through the culture. He's well aware of that. He also realizes that religion, of any kind, is the opiate of the masses and that you also have to believe in *something* to establish a moral compass. Before Roger could be swept away by such a current, he would have to get near the edge and choose to lend himself to that mindset. The ultimate decision to jump in would be his, unless he slipped or was pushed by an intoxicating stimulant!"

"You mean drunk or drugged?"

"Any kind of stimulant! Drug, alcohol, chemical, money, a woman, even a belief itself could be alluring enough and prove to be a slippery slope!"

"You sound like an addictionologist," 'N' speculates.

"I've studied addiction quite extensively. When I was instructing, I taught my Double Os to maintain an *unscented* lifestyle and to be aware of anything that could be construed as a central nervous system stimulant, such as perfume, cologne, fabric softener, pesticides, air fresheners, etc. The list goes on and on. Although the effects are not as obvious as drugs and alcohol, over time, these other stimulants can be even more destructive! In the short term, they can disrupt one's sense of smell, causing *olfactory blindness,* thereby jeopardizing a Double O's mission!" Sean states emphatically.

"I realize everything is a stimulant and those targeting the central nervous system are especially harmful, and even more so when combined with belief systems. But with respect to voodoo, I just thought that since it was ancient and all..." 'N' raises his brows questioningly.

"We have no qualms with the ancient. My God, if we didn't know where we had been, we wouldn't know where we're going! But Double Os have to stay in the present, the here and now. I can't believe I'm having this conversation!" Sean shakes his head. "Do you think Roger is simply alive from the neck up, living in some analytical atmosphere, subject to being blown about by the slightest gust or fad? HELL, NO! I've known Roger for over thirty years. He may be a little spoiled, but I can assure you, he has both feet on the ground!"

"The boys in the Psych Department say there could be some pretty powerful forces at play here."

"To hell with the boys in the Psych Department! I'm telling you, Roger's whole problem is a combination of the ratty accommodations on this alleged *yacht* and the lack of women on this mission thus far! Unlike most Double Os, Roger doesn't function at full capacity in the absence of women, but he more than makes up for it in their presence! He's unique in that way. Average it out on a mission-to-mission basis, and it's more of an asset than a deficit. Believe me, when we get to New Orleans, he'll snap right out of it!"

"Well, I hope you're right." 'N' seems reluctant.

"I KNOW I'm right!" Sean counters adamantly.

"OK. Enough said. To change the subject, what happened to Ms. Munynickle on the way to the airport? She came back to HQ mad as hell. Cursing, crying, and slamming things around!"

"I don't know what happened. George said something to her, and she came unglued. Roger was able to calm her down. See what I mean about Roger?"

"Well, his *calming down* didn't hold. Like I said, she was madder than hell when she got back. And later in the day, I was in her office when Pierce showed up. By the way, he completed that mission he was on. So anyway, he barely got a 'hello' out of his mouth when she tore into him screaming, *'Don't you dare try and flirt with me, you high-falutin' bastard!'* We were both shocked! I was surprised she was even capable of such vulgarity. I've never seen her like this. She must be having some kind of a breakdown."

"Aw, she'll be all right," Sean says tersely.

"Speaking of Pierce, he offered to go over to Melville and give you a hand."

"Nah. I don't think so."

"You'd still be head of the mission. That's a given."

"Well, naturally! But I don't think so."

"Pierce has a lot of respect for you and would consider it an honor to work with you."

"That's nice, THANKS, BUT NO THANKS!" Sean snaps.

"You know, he really idolizes you," 'N' says, still trying to persuade.

"NO! The truth is we don't need him. I could probably go there myself with nothing more than a slingshot and get the Aspic data. Besides, he breaks everything he touches, and everything we have here is either already broken or barely working as it is. The last thing we need down here is Pierce!"

"I just wanted you to know he has a tremendous amount of admiration for you and that he was making himself available."

"Look, with all the trouble we're having, I just don't think I could handle adding Pierce to the mix! Every time I turn around, this friggin' tub of a yacht is leaning in a different direction! It's like a roller coaster ride sitting still."

"Why is that?" 'N' asks.

"Well, they keep moving water and fuel around into different tanks, and it's causing the boat to list, sometimes back and forth, then from side to side."

"They're working on solving the problem, aren't they? After all, we're paying them…"

"Yes, but in the meantime, it's damn hard trying to walk on this tub!"

"I'm sure they'll get it ironed out. All of you should have a few martinis and get some rest."

"You just don't get it, do you?" Sean asks in exasperation.

"Get what?"

"This is NO FRIGGIN' YACHT! There are NO MARTINIS! There's NO ELECTRICITY! NO RUNNING WATER! We're sweating buckshot here! We'll be lucky if we ever get a friggin' bath!"

"Well… uh…" 'N' hedges.

"Look, I've got to go check on the guys and see how they're coming along with that balloon. If all goes well, by this time tomorrow night, we'll be in New Orleans. Oh, I almost forgot—we stumbled upon quite a bit of info concerning that apology thing; it will all be in my report."

"Be specific, but watch the wording in that report. You know how those Americans tend to misinterpret reports. And do try to keep me updated throughout the mission, even though it will be a quick in and out."

"OK. I've got to go."

"Good luck, 0028!"

Yeah, right! 0028, how corny! Sean mumbles to himself. I just don't know where some people get their sense of humor!

Sean steps out of the bunkroom to head upstairs and sees the captain and engineer at the end of the hallway. They're looking over blueprints of the boat and engaged in a discussion about the tanks. Sean makes his way up to the wheelhouse, where he finds Roger in the captain's quarters, standing near a bookshelf. A glazed look on his face, he's staring at a voodoo book with a bright red cover.

"You really don't believe in that nonsense, do you?" Sean asks.

"Well, I... uh..." Startled at Sean's voice, Roger searches for words.

"That stuff can't affect you unless you believe in it! And the only way to believe in it is to know a lot about it and to practice it. If you don't know a lot about voodoo, it can't affect you. And you certainly don't practice it! If these people want to believe in that religion and it's a part of their culture, so be it. You're NOT part of these people! You're NOT part of this culture! We've got to keep our mind on the mission!" Sean nudges Roger and cracks a smile. "I can't wait 'til we get to New Orleans! It'll be like old times: WOMEN, casinos, and fine food and wine! C'mon, let's go! We have to get busy!"

The men head out to the back deck and find George and Timmy sitting on a crate. George, cleaned up and dressed in his ruffled shirt and kilt, is still wearing the same wet, shitty shoes and stinking more than ever.

Sean can't resist... "His Majesty's Secret...?"

"Don't say it! OK? So, I'm running out of clean clothes!"

"OK. Did you two see anything interesting by the pipeline?" Sean asks.

"Nothing but a railroad maintenance vehicle. It seems to be operative, as if the workers just left it and went to the Mardi Gras. Look, you can see it from here if you step over by this crate."

"*Maintenance vehicle*... my ass! That's a compound surveillance vehicle if I ever saw one!" Sean exclaims.

"But the logo..." George begins.

"That logo doesn't mean a damn thing!" Sean interrupts. "They're in New Orleans, all right. And they left that vehicle to block the tracks, and they left the bridge up to prevent entry to the compound."

"Maybe the bridge is broken," George offers.

"Yeah, right. That's what the captain said. Give me a break! They probably have the tracks blocked on the other side of the compound as well!"

"But..."

"But nothing! You can't put anything past these friggin' monopolizers! Maintenance vehicle, huh! And that bridge is in perfect working order! This is all diversion and defense tactics! Your problem, George, is that you always think it's anything other than what it is! You've got to stay focused and fine-tuned to the obvious! Now listen up..."

Sean's treatment of George regarding the maintenance vehicle is causing George to feel furious! He wants to lash out at Sean but restrains himself and curbs his anger. After all, discipline of emotions is a top priority for a Double O!

"All right, here's the game plan," Sean explains. "We've got a little daylight left. Roger, you and George can start unpacking and airing up that balloon for the morning. Timmy, you and I will go through some of these smaller crates. According to the manifest, there should be a homing device in one of them. We'll find it, try it out, and if it works, I'm sending you around to the Western levee in the Lincoln. The homing device will allow for greater freedom of movement and continual contact. It's also a backup communication if the walkie-talkie stops working. We've got to cover all the bases and stay one step ahead of Primeaux and his gang! A monopolizer of his stature never sleeps! Let's get to work!"

Roger and George drag out the balloon and begin to air it up.

"Man, this balloon sure brings back memories," Roger says. Suddenly, the song 'All Time High' goes off in his head. "This is the same balloon I used on that Octofussy mission—to fly over to an island with a woman farm on it! A farm with NOTHING but women!" Roger smiles at the memory.

"When I was on that His Majesty's Secret Service mission, I went to a clinic up on a mountaintop where there was nothing but women! Well, almost nothing but women; there was one male doctor," George reminisces.

"Hey, Timmy!" Sean shouts. "I found the homing device! It's a lapel pen with a note attached, instructing us to substitute this laptop computer for the tracking unit. It says here that the companion watch that goes with the pen is broken. That figures! Probably that friggin' Pierce broke it! Well, let's give it a try. Here, put it in your shirt pocket. Or, better yet, pin it under your shirt collar for concealment and to make sure you don't lose it! And while you're at it, clip the radio to your belt."

Sean opens the laptop, turns it on, and instructs Timmy to walk across the catwalk and stand over on the ramp.

"Good! It seems to be working. Now, go left... no, LEFT! Your right, my left... the other way... back up... now, come forward! OK! Right... now, LEFT! We're probably too close to one another. Maybe it'll work better from a distance."

"Now listen carefully—both of you." Sean looks at Timmy, then over at George working on the balloon. "Timmy, get on the levee, go back to Hwy. 190, take a right, and cross over the bridge, then head west through Krotz Springs. Just outside the city limits is a levee running north and south. Turn right on top of the levee. You'll be headed north. At the end of the levee is a forest. You'll then head east through the forest. Our maps indicate some logging roads and hunting trails through there. However, they may be difficult to follow due to the heavy underbrush. There may be some swampy areas also, so be careful! These topographical maps are helpful, but they don't show everything. We'll be in constant radio contact, and I'll be tracking you via the homing device. Once you've made your way through the forest, you will have reached the rear levee on the west side of Primeaux's compound."

"Once there, Timmy, I want you to stand by and wait for George. He'll be making an aeronautical approach and will have a clear shot at tranquilizing the dog or dogs, whichever the case may be."

"Did he say *standby*?" George whispered. "Yeah," Roger replied.

"Once you hear gunfire and the dogs are silenced, proceed over the levee and meet George as he lands the balloon. From there, the two of you will bust into Primeaux's main control facility, retrieve the data on the Aspic, drive over the rear levee, and backtrack through the woods onto the north/south levee to Hwy. 190. You'll cross over the bridge to our original rendezvous site and drive beneath the bridge where we boarded the yacht. Roger and I will be waiting there. Did you get all that? George—*George?!*"

"Yeah, I heard," George replies, seeming a little overwhelmed.

"Good! Then I won't have to repeat myself. OK, Timmy, get going!"

George and Roger have the balloon positioned and begin to air up the envelope. Everyone is jubilant that the equipment is working as expected, and this small success brings about a renewed sense of accomplishment and enthusiasm that infuses them all. It also gets the attention of the captain, who is now in his quarters, lying on his bunk and listening to the musical Evangeline. He gets up and goes into the wheelhouse to look out at the back deck to see what all the commotion is.

The song *"Father Forgive Them"* echoes from his quarters. Having watched so many historical films about the Acadian exile, the captain again envisions the agents as British soldiers in 1755.

Roger notices the captain staring at them and calls it to Sean's attention. Sean looks up at the captain, now in a trance-like state with a pained expression on his face.

"That's one weird dude," Roger speculates.

"Maybe something's bothering him," George adds.

"Yeah, right! I'll tell you what's *bothering* him," Sean says. "He's probably having trouble formulating his part in this monopolizing diabolical scheme. For all we know, he could be working for Primeaux. Why, they could have used this very boat to haul supplies in and out of Primeaux's compound!"

"He certainly knows the river well enough," Sean continues. "He's not to be trusted! Remember in the briefing how adamant 'N' was about keeping the so-called yacht crew in the dark?"

"Well, he looks harmless," George adds.

"Harmless?! Huh!" Sean snorts. "Think about it. Take this *yacht*, for instance."

"What are you getting at?" Roger asks.

"Just see if you can follow me on this. This *yacht* was obtained through a CIA pencil-pushing operative, rubbing erasers with our pencil-pushers back at MI-6. Together, they do a minimal amount of background checking when they acquire a boat and crew. They reason that no amount of intelligence is 100 percent foolproof, so they do their 'best' and leave the rest up to the agent in the field, who is expected to adjust, compensate, and adapt to the situation. In other words, work it out... make do! These guys don't know what goes on in the real world!

They're sitting behind a desk! I'll bet the bulk of their focus on this whole mission was how they could squeeze a quarter out of a dime! Now, if they can be duped into believing this friggin' tub was a yacht, they can be just as wrong about its crew!"

"BRILLIANT, Sean!" Roger nods in approval.

"Well, maybe we shouldn't suspect *everybody*. I mean, on almost every mission there are people who become our allies," George interjects.

"Yes," Sean says. "But judging from the captain's quarters and the amount of material he has stockpiled on this apology thing, I'd say he's obsessed and probably hell-bent on seeing it through! Or else, this is a hell of a front for Primeaux!"

"Or maybe he's just passionate about it."

"Look, George, everyone knows it's not a big leap from passion to obsession," Sean says. "I'll tell you what... when you're finished airing up the balloon, the plan is to spread out around the boat. We'll go up to the captain's quarters, and you can have a look for yourself. Talk to him; he's friendly enough. Roger said hello to him, and he damned near talked his ear off! He even invited Roger to come and watch a movie. So you can judge for yourself what kind of cloth our Captain Passion is cut out of... friend or foe."

"All right!" George responds eagerly.

"OK, but now I've got to go down to the bunkroom and try to raise Timmy on the GPS and see how he's coming along. You two continue on here. Make sure the balloon is securely tied before it gets too full. We don't want it taking off!"

"Yeah, this balloon sure brings back fond memories of that *Octofussy* mission. I forget how many women I made love to on that mission. There was a whole island full of women!" Roger reminisces dreamily.

"On my last mission, that clinic on the mountaintop had a ton of beautiful women! I made love with THREE!" George counters.

Sean, below deck on his way to the bunkroom, notices the captain and engineer at the end of the hallway. He says to himself, *Now the captain's back down here. It's like he's following me! He sure sneaks around a lot!*

The captain and engineer are unaware of Sean's presence. Standing outside the engine room, they're once again busy studying the boat's blueprints, and Sean startles them.

"This damn boat sure is leaning!" he complains. "I know. We're working on it," the captain replies. "Good. Get it fixed!" Sean stalks off.

Sean enters the bunkroom and closes the door behind him. With the generator broken and no electricity, it's very dark. There's one small emergency light on the wall and some moonlight coming through the portholes. It's a full moon, but very little moonlight is able to shine through the dirty portholes. For some reason, these portholes happen to be square. Sean sits down and opens the GPS laptop. Luckily, the laptop is battery-operated and has a very bright screen, so he can see well enough to monitor Timmy's movements.

Timmy is just getting off the levee and onto Hwy. 190. Sean picks up his signal as Timmy crosses over the bridge. Timmy is listening to the song *"License to Maim"* from his *License to Maim* mission. The song has taken Timmy back to that mission... literally! As he's coming off the bridge, he spots a small nightclub on the left called Bargehead Bar, and there's a Lincoln Mark V parked near the front door.

There's my Lincoln near the door! I hope they're ready for me on the set. Timmy pulls into the parking lot and parks next to the Lincoln.

What the hell is he stopping for? Sean watches the screen. *Probably a friggin' casino! I should have insisted that he not stop anywhere!*

Sean grabs his radio/walkie-talkie and tries to contact Timmy. When the radio comes on, it produces a scratchy noise as the frequency transmits. Timmy hears the SCRRRRR sound.

"That's my cue!" Timmy says and jerks open the vehicle door. The radio, clipped to his belt, rubs against the armrest and accidentally keys the mike. The mike button stays stuck in the 'ON' position due to its age and poor design. Now Sean can't talk to Timmy but can hear everything. As Timmy enters the bar, lively Cajun music can be heard along with loud conversation, laughter, and the ring of slot machines.

DAMN casino! He had to stop! I should have known! Sean is irate. Timmy... Timmy... come in, Timmy! Do you copy? Damn, I sound like Pierce! Come in, Timmy! It's no use! Damn, he's liable to be there for hours!

Timmy saunters through the bar. It's a small, crowded, smoke-filled room with a row of slot machines along the back wall. The dim lighting and the excitement of a woman dancing on a table add to the exotic flavor of the place.

Timmy makes his way over to the bar and asks the bartender, "Hey, man, do you know Pauline Beauvier?"

"I know Pauline Boudreaux. She's the blonde right over there at that table." He points to a nearby table.

"OK. Thanks." Timmy turns and walks toward Pauline's table. *That bartender must be having a hard time with the pronunciation of these French names.* Arriving at the table, he sits down and says to Pauline, *"This is an unexpected surprise!"*

A bit startled because she doesn't know him, has never seen him before, and yet he's acting as if he knows her, Pauline is intrigued by Timmy's accent and good looks and decides to play along.

"Where do you come from?" she asks in a sexy voice.

"The hospital... intensive care! Exactly where you'll be if you don't get out of here, fast! Sanchez has letters and files with your name all over them!"

Sensing something amiss, Pauline says, "You know, I'm not here alone. I'm with those two big guys at the bar, and they're waiting for Dureaux, my..."

"What'll y'all have to drink?" a waitress interrupts.

"I'll have a beer," Pauline answers.

She's supposed to say 'wine.' She doesn't know her lines! The director's not cutting the scene. I'll just go with it, then. "I'll have the same," he says.

Just then, Dureaux and a friend enter the bar. Pauline, still alarmed by Timmy's remark about intensive care, warns him, "My boyfriend Dureaux and his friend used to be pro wrestlers; they don't take shit from anybody!"

Did she even read the script? Timmy says to himself. *None of this is in the script! She's improvising, and they're not cutting it! I guess I'll just have to go along with it!* He responds to Pauline's warning, "Just the kind of guys that Sanchez would send!"

Dureaux and his friend walk toward the table. Timmy is waiting for Pauline to say her line. *{Are you carrying?}* That's Timmy's cue to open his jacket and show his gun. The line does not materialize.

Where in the hell do they get these second-rate actors? Timmy wonders.

Dureaux and his friend walk toward the table as Timmy becomes more and more agitated with the situation. He grumbles. *The director's still not yelling CUT! It looks like I'll have to ad-lib the whole damn scene!* He opens his jacket slightly, showing Pauline his gun.

Pauline, seeing the gun, begins to panic as Dureaux and his friend sit down at the table. "Hi," she says, fearing the worst.

"Hey, baby!" Dureaux slips his arm around her shoulders.

"Get your hands off her! She's with me!" Timmy orders.

"What?!" Dureaux starts to get up and kick Timmy's ass.

Pauline steps on Dureaux's foot and grabs him by the arm. She tries to get him to sit back down so she can warn him about the gun.

Dureaux leans over the table and stares into Timmy's eyes. "Don't I know you? Didn't you fly charter planes for Pro-South Wrestling?"

Totally pissed off now, Timmy asks himself, *"Why is this guy looking at me and asking me that? He's supposed to be looking at her and asking her a question, and that's not even the right line! Am I the only one who read the script? Where in the hell is the director? Is he going to stop this or what?"*

The waitress steps between the two men and sets her tray on the table. "Two beers, that'll be $3.50," she says.

"Run a tab!" Timmy snaps angrily.

"OK. Would your friends like something to drink?"

"Yeah, but first, I gotta take a leak." Dureaux's friend stands up to go to the john. Suddenly, Timmy stands, elbows him in the gut, and slams his head on the table!

"He's had enough to drink!" Timmy says harshly.

Dureaux comes unglued! He jumps up and slugs Timmy from across the table, knocking him to the floor! Dureaux shoves the table out of the way and starts to jump on Timmy.

"He's got a GUN!" Pauline hollers.

"CUT!" Timmy yells.

A *really* big bouncer runs over and gets between Timmy, who's on the floor, and Dureaux, who's ready to pounce again.

"What the hell is going on?" the bouncer demands.

"CUT!" Timmy shouts again.

"Are you cut?" the bouncer asks, leaning over Timmy. "Did somebody pull a knife?"

"That son-of-a-bitch *really* hit me!" Timmy struggles to his feet.

"It's only supposed to *look* like he hit me!"

"What are you talking about?! What's all this *cut* shit? Are you cut?"

"He's got a gun!" Pauline screeches.

"Are you carrying?" the bouncer asks.

"NOW THERE'S THE LINE!" Timmy says triumphantly. "Do you have a gun?" The bouncer pulls open Timmy's jacket.

"I've got the prop." Timmy rubs his throbbing eye as the bouncer removes the gun. "Are you the director?"

"What?" the bouncer asks.

"Are we still rolling?" Timmy looks around.

"Yeah! You're rolling right the hell out of here!" The bouncer grabs Timmy like a rag doll, and dragging him with one arm through the bar, he throws him, wild west style, right out the door.

Timmy hits the ground, tumbling over a few times and landing next to the old Mark V. He is dazed, confused, and disoriented! A young couple in a nearby car are listening to an oldies radio station, and lo and behold, the song "License to Maim" from his *License to Maim* mission is playing! Upon hearing the music, Timmy climbs into the old Lincoln and cranks it up. The patrons in the bar hear the loud, busted muffler as Timmy takes off in a tire-screeching, haul-ass mode!

"That's MY car!" yells an old Cajun named Jagneaux, sitting inside the bar. He and the bouncer run outside, closely followed by Dureaux, Pauline, and several others. "He stole my car! He stole MY car!"

"That bastard's crazy!" says Dureaux's friend.

"You should have let me at that sombitch!" Dureaux says to the bouncer.

"No! He's SICK! I could tell by the way he was talking out of his head!"

"No shit!" Pauline agrees. "Why, he could be in an alcoholic blackout."

"We'd better call the cops." The bouncer turns to go inside. "He could be an escaped mental patient! He might hurt himself or somebody else!"

In the Mark V, Timmy rubs his bruised and swollen eye and tries to check it out in the rear-view mirror. *Oh, shit! It's sure to be a shiner! If they want to act rough like that, they're gonna have to get me a double! I ought to file a complaint with the Actors Guild against that director! He can't just throw me off the set and into the next scene like that! Queen or no Queen, I don't have to take this shit! My agent's going to hear about this!*

Just then, Timmy spots the levee that he's supposed to turn onto. He turns right and crosses a cattle guard. He's now on his way! It's going to be a fifteen-mile ride on top of the levee.

Meanwhile, back on the boat, Sean is still engaged in conversation with the engineer and captain about the water and electricity. They've been giving him the whole nine yards on the workings of the boat's tank system.

"All right! I've heard enough!" Sean says angrily. "What's the *bottom* line? When will we be able to take a shower?"

"Maybe by tomorrow morning."

"All right! All right!"

Sean climbs the steps to the top deck. As he goes through the living area, he's forced to walk uphill because the boat has shifted once again with the bow nearly on the river's bottom, and it's really hard to walk.

He passes the deckhand who's watching TV and munching on fried pork rinds.

"Hey, if the generator is out, how the hell is that TV working?" Sean demands.

"Auxiliary batteries. We got them hooked up to..."

"OK, OK! I've heard enough!" Sean rudely cuts him off.

"Hey man, want a Bud and pork rinds?" the deckhand offers.

With a disgusted look, Sean walks to the back door. He has trouble opening it. He pushes, pulls, turns the knob, pushes some more, pulls, and is ready to cuss out the deckhand for not fixing the door when suddenly, it opens!

Sean glares at the deckhand. *Damn lucky,* he mutters.

Outside, Sean sees that George and Roger have finished with the balloon. "It looks like you got everything done. Good," he says.

"Yeah, she's ready to go," Roger responds.

"What's the story on Timmy?" George asks. "Were you able to track him with the GPS?"

"Yeah, I tracked him... right to *a damn* casino!"

"What?!" Roger asks, obviously jealous.

"A casino! I should have ORDERED him NOT TO STOP anywhere! *I should have known!* He's been crying casino ever since the plane landed in New Orleans!"

"He was talking about casinos *on* the plane," says George.

"He's probably got a gambling problem! He's liable to be there for hours!"

"Longer than that, if he meets a woman!" Roger adds. "He better have his ass on that back levee by daybreak!"

"I'm sure he'll make it," George responds.

"He better!"

"What's next? What's the game plan?" Roger asks, trying to change the subject.

"Well, the captain and engineer are downstairs working on the tanks and generator, and the deckhand is watching TV. Now would be a good time for us to look through the captain's quarters concerning that apology crap. With all three of us on it, we're sure to turn up something. If there's anything worth turning up, it shouldn't take long," Sean speculates.

"We'll go up the outside ladder and through the wheelhouse," he continues. "That way we won't alert the deckhand. Are you sure the balloon is secured?"

"Absolutely!" Roger nods affirmatively.

"Do you think it'll stay inflated all night?" George asks.

"We'll give it another blast of hot air before we turn in tonight and leave it on a low flame all night. Let's go!" Sean heads for the ladder.

"What about a shower?" Roger inquires.

"It won't be fixed until sometime in the morning."

"That sucks!"

George doesn't say anything. The thought of a shower just reminds him that he doesn't have any clean clothes. They climb the ladder up to the wheelhouse and go into the captain's quarters. Sean and Roger enter first, followed by George, who stands in the doorway because the room is too small. It's about 8' × 10' with one porthole over a small bunk. A desk and bookcases are filled with posters, books, films, and maps. Newspapers and magazines are stacked in every corner, nook, and cranny, giving the illusion of a round room. There is also a small TV/VCR that was left on, and the movie that's playing is an old black-and-white silent film.

"See what I mean, George?" Sean waves his arm about. "If you tried to put one more nugget of info in here, you'd have to hang it from the ceiling!"

"Yeah, I see." He surveys the room with both surprise and curiosity.

"The captain left his TV on." Roger reaches over and turns up the volume knob. "Hey, there's no sound! I know this TV had sound when I was up here before."

"It's a silent film... before the talkies! Man, talk about living in the past!" Sean shakes his head.

"I wonder if this is the movie he invited me to watch? I don't want to see this old crap!"

Sean and Roger begin to search through the captain's belongings, while George is intrigued watching the silent film.

"Here are those newspaper articles that I told you about." Roger hands the newspapers to Sean.

Sean thumbs through the articles. "These were all written by the same guy, named Perrin. Warren Perrin. No doubt, a front man or diversionary expert for Primeaux! These guys are unbelievably clever! Better look under the bunk."

"Maybe the captain has a blow-up rubber doll under here!" Roger begins earnestly searching under the bunk.

"The captain sure seems to be passionate about all this stuff," George observes.

"More like *OBSESSED!*" Sean contends. "What we're looking at here is a typical pack rat, a political pack rat at that, with a historical axe to grind!"

Just then, Roger, down on his hands and knees, finds a small wooden box hidden among the papers, books, and videos. He opens it. Inside the box, there's a chicken's claw, a dried-out beak and tongue, and a colorful feather arrangement. All objects, he knows, are commonly used in the spiritual practice of voodoo. Roger freezes on all fours!

"Maybe this will tell us something. It's titled *The Truth About the Cajuns.*" George pulls a book from the shelf.

"The truth about harboring a worn-out, old grudge and a diabolical plan!" Sean jeers.

"With respect to the grudge factor, maybe the captain just cares about his people. Maybe they're a misunderstood people. Maybe all this stuff is justifiable," George offers.

"MAYBE! Maybe! Maybe! Damn it, George! Take a good look at this friggin' rat hole! There's nothing here but 'spilt milk' and a shitload of tears!"

"I was being *objective!*"

"NO! You're being OBTUSE! Look, this is one of two things. It's either a hell of a front for Primeaux to throw us off the trail of the Aspic or it's one hell of a wasted life! Holding onto this 250-year-old grudge would drive any man into a hole like this... justifiable or not!"

"Well, we should try and give him the benefit of the doubt."

"We're not here to give anyone the *benefit of a doubt!* We're here to get the Aspic data and put that dominating, monopolizer, Primeaux, in his place! Try to stay focused on the MISSION! Damn it, George!"

Sean turns his attention to Roger, still frozen on all fours, halfway underneath the bunk. Sean nudges Roger's foot with his own.

"Have you found something?" Sean asks.

Roger, somewhat dazed, backs out from beneath the bunk. He stands up slowly with an open-mouthed, blank expression and tightly clutching the box. Sean loosens Roger's grip on the box and opens it.

"What's this?" Sean pokes at the contents. When Roger doesn't answer, Sean closes the lid, turns the box over, and sees a voodoo symbol.

Just then they hear someone coming up the stairs. "Damn! It's the captain! Quick! Split up!" Sean shoves the box back under the bunk.

Roger is stunned. Finding the voodoo paraphernalia almost took him over the edge. Sean realizes he has to get Roger away fast. Sean pulls him by the arm.

"C'mon, let's go!" he says in a commanding tone.

George steps into the wheelhouse. "I think I'll stay here for a while," he says.

"Well, try not to be so naïve; keep your guard up!" Sean pleads in exasperation. He pulls Roger along behind him as he walks past George.

Reaching the upper deck, Sean turns to Roger and shakes him. "Are you all right? Hey—Roger, you all right?" Sean asks anxiously.

"Uh... yes, uh... yeah, I'm OK," Roger responds weakly.

"C'mon, man! You can't let that kind of nit shit get to you! That's nothing but a box of cheap trinkets! I thought we discussed that voodoo shit! Don't pull a 'George' on me! C'mon, man! You've got to stay with me on this! That box and everything in it is nothing but symbolism. It can't affect you unless you believe in it!"

"Yeah, yeah. I guess you're right."

"I KNOW I'M RIGHT! Look, there's nothing wrong with being a little superstitious, but when you take it too far, it becomes supposition, and then you're flirtin' with left field! Left field is littered with fear and doubt and a thousand slippery slopes! It's a false/positive bonanza."

"Look at the trouble I'm having with George. You heard what went on in the captain's quarters—*maybe, maybe, maybe!* George voiced the same doubt when he argued with me over that surveillance vehicle. He just doesn't grasp the gravity of the situation! To tell you the truth, he's starting to get on my nerves! He's driving me crazy with this benefit of a doubt shit! He exhausts me! He's too *damned feeling!* Thank God, by this time tomorrow, we'll be in New Orleans and well rid of him and that other wanna-be, Timmy!"

Sean guides Roger over to the ladder and down to the rear deck. "I've got to check on Timmy. You check on the balloon and give it another blast of hot air. While you're there, take your binoculars and check out the nightlife on the other side of the river. There may be a shapely silhouette over there! After I get a fix on Timmy, I'll be up to meet you."

"Yeah, that lucky little shit! He's probably with a woman!"

"Either that or glued to a crap table!" Sean scowls.

Sean and Roger split up.

CHAPTER II

The captain returns from downstairs and walks into the wheelhouse where he and George encounter each other. George forgets he's still holding the book *The Truth About the Cajuns*.

The captain notices the book in George's hand. "Have you been in my quarters?" he asks.

"Oh, I just came up and stood in the doorway to watch the movie, and I saw this book on the edge of the bookshelf. Sorry, I..."

"Nothing to be sorry about. Through the years, I've always shared my books and information with anyone onboard who's interested."

"You have quite a film collection here. Even silent films—you don't see many of them anymore."

"This film is only partially silent. There's sound toward the end. But it's not just any old silent film. Everything in this room is either directly or indirectly related to that film, my people, and their exile from Nova Scotia in 1755."

"What's the film about?"

"You may have heard about Longfellow's epic poem *Evangeline*?"

"No, I haven't."

"Evangeline was a very real person who spent her entire life waiting for her lost love to return. To the Cajun people, she's the symbol of true dedication and virtue—a sad example of stagnant emotions and a wasted life. Her story is our most famous legend."

"*Real,* huh?" George asks, his curiosity getting the best of him.

The captain continues. As he begins to tell the story, he is almost transformed into a poet laureate.

"Early one morning in the little village of Grand Pré in Nova Scotia, not one, but two babies were born in an old Acadian farmhouse. The two children, a girl and a boy, came into the world just moments apart. The story of these two soul mates would go on to touch the lives of all who had ever loved and lost."

"Growing up together, the children developed a very special bond. As the years passed, they remained good friends. When they were both seventeen years old, Gabriel proposed to Evangeline, and she accepted. Shortly afterwards, the exile began. Evangeline's father was killed, and she and the local priest, Father Felician, stayed behind to bury him. Thus, she was separated from Gabriel. Father Felician and Evangeline left on the last ship, but when they landed in New England, Gabriel was nowhere to be found. Ships carrying my people arrived at different destinations, scattering the Cajuns among the American colonies."

"Evangeline and Father Felician wandered like a band of Gypsies, without a home. Everywhere they went, they saw the Cajun people struggling to sustain a little joy and a sense of community, all while trying to start over and mend their shattered lives. Everywhere she went, Evangeline would ask about Gabriel."

"The years passed by, and Evangeline and the priest found themselves wandering along the Mississippi River.

They'd heard about a large number of Acadians that had settled in the Louisiana territory. Evangeline was sleeping one night when two oarsmen rowed their pirogue past them in the dark. One of the young men was Gabriel."

"Evangeline and the priest traveled the next day to an encampment mostly comprised of people from their village back home. There, they were reunited with many of their friends. One was Madame Hébert, a dear, hospitable soul who invited them to stay a while with her. Again, Evangeline asked for news of Gabriel, but no one knew of his whereabouts. Evangeline's friends worried that she was living in the past; it had now been more than four years since the expulsion. They told her that surely it was time for her to move on! In tears, Evangeline ran to the water's edge. Her friend, Madame Hébert, followed to comfort her."

"Evangeline, don't let them cause you to doubt yourself. Faith is a rare and precious gift," Madame Hébert says kindly.

The captain continues his story, "Several days later, a trapper stopped by, and Evangeline was thrilled to learn that he knew Gabriel. She and the priest decided to accompany the trapper to his village of St. Martin, where they would find Gabriel. Once there, they met another old friend, Basile, who told them that Gabriel was away for several days on a hunting excursion. Evangeline sat beneath the branches of an oak tree beside the water and waited for him each day."

"Although Evangeline waited patiently, Gabriel never returned. Five years passed, and Evangeline and the priest established a church in St. Martin. Evangeline worked with Father Felician as well as the village physician. But still, every spare moment she had, she spent beneath the oak tree, waiting and watching for Gabriel. Before long, the entire region had heard of the beautiful young maiden who watched and waited so patiently each day."

"After some time, Evangeline and Father Felician once again began to travel, visiting one settlement or another, ministering to the sick and despairing. One day, not far from their old village of Grand Pré, a dying trapper was brought into their makeshift hospital. His beard was bristled and gray, and he was delirious with fever. As Evangeline bent over to minister to him, she saw immediately that it was Gabriel."

"Gabriel," Evangeline whispered.

"Evangeline," he says. "I stayed true. I always knew we'd meet again someday, and I'd be with you."

"I knew you would, and I always felt the same," she said.

Evangeline held Gabriel's body close as he took his last breath. Father Felician knelt beside her in comfort."

"Was it worth it, Evangeline? Was it worth your entire life?" he asked.

"Yes, all that and more." She smiled as she spoke through her tears.

The captain wipes away a tear of his own and finishes the telling of Evangeline's heartrending story. "Still stands the forest primeval. But far away from its shadow, side by side, in their nameless graves, the lovers are sleeping. Under the humble walls of the little Catholic church yard, in the heart of the city, they lie unknown and unnoticed. Still stands the forest primeval, and in the fisherman's cottage, maidens still wear their Norman caps and their girdles of homespun, and by their evening fire, repeat Evangeline's story. While from the rocky caverns answers the wail of the forest."

"Whew!" George exclaims to the captain. "It sounds like you've damned near recited the whole thing."

"Well, that was just the gist of it, although I do know it in its entirety." The captain adjusts his cap and wipes his hand across his forehead as if to clear away the remains of Evangeline's sad story.

Glancing over at the silent film on the TV, George says, "You know, you sort of look like that character, Gabriel. You don't think you're *reincarnated*, do you?" he asks jokingly.

"No. But I've been told about the resemblance before. It's not *reincarnation*; it's more like *saturation*. For the last thirty years, I've been researching the exile of my people and the aftermath from 1755 until now. Anytime you submerge yourself that deeply in a subject for that long, it alters you, and you take on that persona. It's much like an actor who studies for a part."

"I know somebody like that!" George exclaims.

"You've heard the old saying: *you become whoever you hang around with.* I'll bet if you look deep enough inside, you'll find traits in yourself that are much like those of your friend."

More than you know, George says to himself. "But that story sure was something!" he says out loud.

"That was just one version, and a romanticized one at that."

"Once they were settled in this part of the country, the Cajuns began to form their own identity. They became farmers, fur traders, ranchers, and fishermen and had little contact with Europe."

"This is all very interesting," George encourages.

"They built an ingenious levee system and turned marshland into fertile fields," the captain continues. "They traded surplus grain to the garrisons or to the New England colonists for fabric, tools, and metal.

They became so prosperous that they attracted the attention of Britain, who..."

"Britain, huh?" George interrupts.

"Yes. In fact, Britain fought with France for control of Acadie. The colony changed hands a total of ten times before Britain took control for good in 1713. By then, the Acadians had been here for more than a hundred years. Yet during this whole time, even though they were able to remain neutral, the Acadians held on to their French language and their Catholic religion."

"Not much different from the French of today," George muses.

"That's right. In this new land, far from Europe, they forged a separate frontier identity that was neither French nor British but Acadian. The first new identity forged on the North American continent. In 1755, British mistrust of the Acadians mounted as a new conflict with France approached."

"British mistrust, huh?" he interrupts again.

"Yes. At the beginning of the French and Indian Seven Years War, the Colonial government demanded an oath of allegiance from the Acadians. But the Acadians refused to take the oath. As a result, Lieutenant Charles Lawrence gave orders to his officers. Here's a copy of the actual document." The captain unrolls a piece of parchment.

"*Actual* document, huh?" George shows his amazement.

"Yes. It reads: *'It will be necessary to keep this measure as secret as possible to prevent the Acadians from attempting to escape and to carry off their cattle. You will endeavor to fall upon some strategy to get the men, both young and old, especially the heads of the families, into your custody and to detain them till the transports shall arrive.'* His commanders combined *FORCE* with *DECEPTION in order* to deport over ten thousand Acadians. That was in 1755." The captain shakes his head sadly.

"That has a familiar ring to it, *force with deception,*" George rubs his chin.

"Yes, force with deception." The captain repeats, then draws George's attention to a map entitled ACADIE, THE ODYSSEY OF A PEOPLE. The map traces the deportation of the Acadian people along with their immigrations. The captain begins to explain the Odyssey to George.

Meanwhile, Sean is down below decks trying to track and talk to Timmy. Sean doesn't have any problem getting a fixed position on him via the GPS and laptop.

Thank God! He left that damn casino! Sean says to himself. *"He appears to be right on course, heading north on the levee."* He tries to reach him on the radio. "Timmy, Timmy, come in, Timmy!"

But it's no use. The mic on Timmy's radio is still keyed. Sean can't talk to him, but he can hear what's going on. There's a loud background noise like a missing muffler. Sean immediately concludes that Timmy bottomed out the Navigator and tore off the muffler. He can also hear Timmy talking. It's not clear if he's talking to himself or someone else.

The studio's going to hear about this shit! Timmy says adamantly. That director's days are numbered! I don't have to take this kind of treatment! My agent's going to have his ass!

Sean tries again, "Timmy! Timmy, come in, Timmy! Do you copy?" *Damn! I sound like Pierce again!* he says to himself. *There's no reaching him, I guess. Well, at least he's heading in the right direction. I'll just try again later.*

Sean heads back up to meet Roger out on the deck. Back in the captain's quarters, the captain is literally taking George on an odyssey as he explains in gut-wrenching detail what the Acadians were forced to endure.

"The war between the British and French was imminent. British authorities in Nova Scotia decided to expel the Acadians to prevent any Acadian alliance with the French. Fearing reprisals from both sides, the Acadians refused to swear an unqualified oath of allegiance, and the deportation began," the captain says.

"Just minding their own business. They were no threat," George reflects.

"Exactly, they were a peaceful people. The deportation was carried out by two thousand New England troops assisted by 250 British soldiers. Lieutenant Colonel John Winslow directed the deportation from the area of Les Mines. They were allowed to take only what they could carry."

"That's terrible! That's criminal!" George protested.

"Yes, it was!" the captain agrees. "Absolutely HEARTLESS! Approximately 2,200 Acadians were deported from Les Mines between mid-October and the end of December." He bows his head at the shame.

This guy's a walking history book, George says to himself. He continues to listen intently.

The captain continues. "And then, approximately 1,600 Acadians were taken from the Port Royal area in December 1755, thus ending 120 years of Acadian settlement! Transport vessels carried approximately six thousand men, women, and children, their families often separated, to the American colonies on the Atlantic seaboard."

"The exiles were only allowed what personal effects they could carry. All other property was forfeited to the British Crown. The nine American colonies to which the Acadians were sent were unprepared to receive them. In some states, the Acadians were allowed entry but had to seek refuge elsewhere. Many times, they were scattered in small groups and forced to work alongside slaves in the tobacco fields. Their makeshift accommodations were often squalid."

"That's *HORRIBLE!* Relegated to slave labor!" George says in disbelief.

"Many Acadians died before reaching the colonies because of overcrowding and disease on the transports. By 1758, some 3,500 Acadians in St. Jean alone were deported to France, and seven hundred perished when two of the transport vessels sank. On December 13, 1758, another transport vessel sank with three hundred Acadians."

Each time the captain spoke of a sunken ship, his whole demeanor seemed to sink also. He seemed to be falling down inside himself as he fought to hold back his tears. George had an urge to give him a hug for comfort but restrained himself. The captain continued on with great passion.

"The approximately 1,100 Acadians who were refused entry into Virginia after the 1755 deportation were taken to England, where many died because of sickness. In 1763, when the war ended, approximately

750 survivors were repatriated to France. A final deportation to Massachusetts in 1762 failed. The exiles were refused entry and returned to Nova Scotia. Deportation continued until 1764 when another ten thousand were deported, most of them to the American colonies south of Nova Scotia."

Just then, the silent movie is no longer silent, and their attention is turned toward the TV as they watch and listen.

Meanwhile, Sean has made his way out to the back deck, where he sees Roger, who is gazing up at the full moon. Sensing Roger is deep in thought, Sean approaches slowly and stands beside him. "*Moonmaker,* huh?"

"Yeah," Roger replies somberly.

"That was a pretty far-out mission, if you know what I mean!" Sean says with a sarcastic smirk.

"At least we had some women on that mission!" Roger replies, almost whining.

"We'll have women! By noontime tomorrow, we'll be in New Orleans. There'll be *plenty* of women! Hell, if that pipeline had been pressurized, we'd be on our way to New Orleans right now! Who would have thought they would turn off the pipeline for Mardi Gras? Another glitch in the background intelligence!"

"HQ should have anticipated that. Everybody knows how these people are... the French, in general. When it's time to work, it's time to work. When it's time to play, it's time to play! You've got to admire that!" Roger turns and smiles at Sean.

"Yeah, you're right. All work and no play makes for a dull agent!"

"Hell, we'd already be in New Orleans with the right equipment. If we had that Lotus I used on *The Spy Who Liked Me* mission, the one with the submarine-like transformation option, I could drive right down that ramp into the water, undetected, to the other side of the river," Roger reminisces.

"In *that* current? I don't think so!" Sean laughs. "The Lotus was good for running around lagoons and calm water, but its shape would make it too vulnerable in this current, and it wouldn't have sufficient underwater propulsion capabilities. It had plenty of horsepower at the wheel but suffered at the prop. You'd end up in the Gulf of Mexico! No, you would need something like the underwater jet I used on that *Thunderbawl* mission. Still, I wouldn't try it. The captain says this river is over a hundred feet deep in places with a violent undertow. No, an underwater approach is out of the question," Sean says adamantly.

"Yeah, I guess you're right," Roger concedes reluctantly. "But in that large crate over there, I did see the manned alligator flotation device I used on that *Octofussy* mission. I guess that's out of the question, too, huh?"

"Totally! I don't understand why HQ would even send a piece of equipment like that on a mission like this. That thing relies on manpower alone. It's nothing more than a paddleboat disguised as an alligator."

"Yeah, I guess you're right."

"Not to mention, it was designed as a female to avoid territorial disputes with males, and this is the mating season. With all the male alligators out there, you'd be screwed... literally... before you got to the other side of the river!"

"No shit!" Roger suddenly realizes the implications of his suggestion.

"Another glitch in the background intelligence! I know that no amount of intelligence is 100 percent accurate, but shit like this is *inexcusable!* This will all be in my report!" Sean turns to go. "I'd better go check on Timmy again. You keep on scheming. It won't hurt to have a Plan 'B' in the event..."

"I thought we were on Plan 'B'!" Roger interrupts.

"OK... Plan 'C' then. You can never have too many backup plans. Like we were always taught, *always leave yourself an out.*"

"OK." Roger returns to his moon gazing. *Alligators screwing! At least something is screwing! There's got to be a woman around here somewhere.* He picks up his binoculars and begins to scan the opposite shoreline for a female silhouette. Pausing at the banana trees, he recalls what he saw earlier. *Was it or was it not a voodoo image?* he asks himself.

Back in the captain's quarters, the captain and George have finished watching the Evangeline film.

"That was a *really* sad ending," George laments.

"Yeah, and you missed the beginning. The film is similar to the poem, only sadder. The musical is both sad and heartwarming. Here, I have a CD; let me put it on. We can listen while we talk."

George is mesmerized as the captain continues to regale him with the epic tragedy of the Acadian people.

"After the migration, the Acadians set off in all directions. Following the peace of 1763, many of them relocated to Louisiana and the American colonies. Others arrived from Quebec, Saint-Pierre-Miquelon, and France to join their compatriots in remote areas of Nova Scotia and what is now New Brunswick and Prince Edward Island. Louisiana became a focal point of the Acadian exile migration. It was the one true place of welcome."

"Here, they were given land, tools, and clothing, first by the French and then by the Spanish Colonial government. Spain sought to populate its newly acquired territory with these hardworking farmers who could grow food for New Orleans and discourage British forces from crossing the Mississippi."

"Discourage the British, huh? The Acadians were just being used," George thinks out loud.

"Oh no! Louisiana was like *'coming home'* after all they had been through, and they were grateful for everything. They adapted quickly to every aspect of living, including coming from a wintry-type climate, where temperatures were sometimes 20 degrees below zero, to a subtropical climate, where temperatures reached 90-100 degrees."

As enthusiastic as George is to hear all this, he still has his *"agent"* antenna up, and the word *"climate"* takes him back to the briefing at HQ when he first learned about the Primeaux technique of cold-smoking meats in a tropical climate.

"It was amazing how quickly the Acadians learned to build houses that expelled heat as opposed to ones that retained heat. They also learned to adapt to different foods and clothing. By the nineteenth century, the migrations were over."

"Although scattered, the Acadians maintained their sense of identity. They were bruised but not broken. Unlike many people today who seem to be blown about by every whim, fad, or belief that comes down the pike, we could all learn something from the experience of the Acadians," the captain speculates. "When I think about the pathetic war in Iraq, it will be interesting to see if the Iraqi people will be able to retain their identity. The Acadians should serve as an example to follow, but many times they've been ridiculed in the media and movies. Don't forget, theirs was the *first new identity* formed on the North American continent. They were neither French nor English, but Acadian neutrals. They embodied the real values and truth of what America is supposed to represent."

"*REAL,* huh?" George nods in agreement.

"Yes. Their focus was on land and family, not wealth, unlike the greed that governs today! They formed an egalitarian society where the poorest Acadian was no less worthy than his wealthiest neighbor. This was a view carried from Nova Scotia. *Slavery did not exist in old Acadia!"*

"Culturally, the Acadians maintained their religion, speech, food, music, and dance. Before the Civil War, they worked for comfort, not luxury. In the 1840s, English was becoming the language of business, and many Acadians crossed over to French Creole, then English, and sought to distance themselves from their poorer cousins. The Acadians, or Cajuns, as they came to be known, were viewed as backwards or ignorant. Because they held fast to their Catholic religion, Protestants viewed them as intolerant of other religions. Because of their strong family ties, they were thought to be inbred."

"Not wanting to go far from home, a lack of education, and refusal to assimilate, the Cajuns were thought to be un-American. They were seen as low class and lazy, but that view was a distortion of the truth. The Cajuns just didn't want very much; unlike the French of New Orleans, where a man's measure was gauged by his wealth and holdings, the opposite of an egalitarian society. The poor Acadians retained more of their culture. The only revered Acadian was Evangeline. She was an Acadian everyone loved.

"Ah, yes—Evangeline," George smiles, remembering.

"In the 1920s, the forces of assimilation came down upon the Cajuns once again when their children were forbidden to speak French on the school grounds. This form of oppression created fear, shame, and doubt in addition to overall feelings of being *'less than.'* The twentieth century brought high-paying oil field jobs, and the Cajuns could afford luxuries they could not as farmers. World War II came, and some Cajuns who were stationed in France discovered that their French language, which they had once been forbidden to speak on the school grounds, came in quite handy, and they were needed as translators."

"Having a newfound sense of self, when they returned home from the war, they embraced their Cajun traditions and were eager for dance, music, gumbo, etc. This began a restoration of the Cajun heritage. Yet it would not be until the *1960s* that French was reintroduced into the school system. However, some Cajun middle class rushed to embrace postwar 1950s mainstream America and rejected any Cajun tradition as too *Cajun.* Cajun music was considered *chankee chank.* Cold War fears led some Cajun people to downplay any semblance of Cajun culture, and many Cajuns tried to live like the well-to-do upper class of St. Martinville and Lafayette, which was considered the hub of Acadiana."

"Then they were not being *honest* with themselves!" George surmised.

"Yeah, you're right! They forgot that denying one's own heritage to try and fit in, in the name of progress, style, or whatever, produces a false sense of self. This fragmented the Cajun community as a whole, resulting in many of its ills, such as the abuse of alcohol. When you lose sight of who and what you are, *you lose sight,*" the captain said knowingly.

"Yes, go on," George urges.

"Well, these so-called upper class Cajuns began to celebrate the Bicentennial of the Deportation as the *Grand Derangement*, a romanticized reenactment based largely on Evangeline lore. Afraid the observance would frighten tourists or offend non-Acadians, they referred to the expulsion as simply a *migration!*"

"All that death, destruction, misery, and murder... a *MIGRATION?!*" George practically yells.

"By this time, Cajuns no longer knew their own history. They didn't understand their own past. As I said before, in the late 1800s and early 1900s, Longfellow's poem, *Evangeline*, attained worldwide popularity and came to be regarded as an accurate history of the Acadian exile.

Telling and retelling the story led people to believe it was an actual account."

"So it wasn't REAL?" George queried.

"Oh, it was *real,* in that it illuminated the darkest hour of the Cajun people. Literature and legend could only tell of one couple among the thousands whose stories have been forgotten and will never be told. *The light of truth is often packaged in a tale.* It's the blur between romance and reality that's confusing."

"Then how did they ever come to know and understand their past?" George asks. "I'm getting confused."

"Well, in the 1960s, an awareness of ethnic and social issues arose around the world. Some Cajuns set out on a fact-finding mission to find the truth."

"Yeah... FACTS... MISSION... that's it!"

"In 1967, the University of Southern Louisiana (USL) obtained Louisiana French Colonial records on microfilm from the France National Archive. This inspired the Center for Louisiana Studies creation. Then, in 1975, Spanish Colonial records from Havana and Madrid were obtained. After much study by scholars and historians, an accurate picture began to take shape regarding the arrival and establishment of Acadians in Louisiana."

"Now this is the *REAL story?*" George questions.

"Yes, completely real! In 1978, the first book was written about the Acadians entitled 'The Cajun History and Culture.' It was edited by Glen Conrad, a professor at the University of Southern Louisiana. The book tells the story of the exile in 1755 until present day and the role Cajuns played in shaping Louisiana. It's a fascinating and informative book that encourages long-forgotten pride and appreciation for the Acadian people."

"A *REAL* professor, huh!"

"Yes, a real professor. Then, in 1987, the USL historian, Dr. Carl Braseaux, also wrote a book. In Dr. Braseaux's book, *The Founding of New Acadiana,* 1765-1803, he told of the *largest forced* migration of whites (the Acadians) in colonial North America and how the Cajuns got to Louisiana and adapted to life here. This book certainly unearthed more than romance," the captain says confidently.

He continues, "It told how Acadians resisted the British with guerrilla tactics and women who hid in the woods with them. It told of the hope of reunions with families. It told of Louisiana settlers who fed New Orleans and pioneered the cattle industry in Louisiana. The book names *real* people and *real* heroes."

"Wow, that should have given the Cajun people something solid to hold on to," George nods approvingly.

"The first 200 Acadians who arrived in New Orleans in 1765 were given tools, land, and a contract to raise cattle on land that is now called St. Martinville. That tiny village and the population began to swell with Acadians. The exiles called their newly adopted land 'home.' Having discovered all of this through the research, the local residents decided that a tribute was in order. They already had the live oak honoring the city's ties to Acadian literature and legend."

"Ah, the tree that Evangeline sat under?" George asks.

"Yes. And the only other monument to the Acadians was far away in Nova Scotia, a lonely iron cross overlooking the Minus Basin," the captain shakes his head sadly.

"Go on, man. What happened next?"

"Well, in 1990, the city of St. Martinville decided to designate the area around the oak tree as a park. Then, in 1991, the Louisiana Legislature designated St. Martinville as home of the world memorial to all Acadians who ended their exile in Louisiana. That same year, the city council, led by Mayor Bobby Aucion, who has since passed away from cancer... much too young, I might add... well, anyway, they dedicated and began renovating the old city hall on the Bayou Teche next to the oak tree."

"Why, the city of St. Martinville even commissioned a well-known international artist, Robert Dafford, to paint a wall mural depicting the arrival of Acadians in Louisiana. It's quite beautiful. It's about 10′ × 30′, and the Old World style depiction covers the years 1764-1788. It's sort of a timeline painting, with actual Cajuns posing as their ancestors."

"Man, I'd really like to see that! A *REAL* artist and REAL Cajuns?!"

"Why all these questions about *'real?'* Don't you know what's real and what's not?" The captain cocks his head and looks at George.

"Oh yeah... yeah, sure! I'm just trying to keep the story straight. Go on, I want to hear the rest."

"Well, on a wall opposite the mural, a symbolic reunion of all the Acadians who came to Louisiana was unveiled in 1987. There's a wall display of twelve bronze plaques with the names of three thousand Acadian refugees who were documented in early church and civil records, where they came from and the dates of their arrival in Louisiana."

"*REAL* records?!" George seems to be trying to convince himself.

"Yes, real records," the captain answers patiently. "Near the bronze plaques, there's a phrase which reads three thousand *Unique Individuals... Read My Name and Remember.* The fact that these dispersed Acadians regrouped and found the will to rekindle their fragmented culture is indeed a true testament to the human spirit. This fact is commemorated at the Eternal Flame in the Memorial Garden that's located on the Bayou Teche in St. Martinville."

"The flame also honors what Colonial Governor Aubrey called *their sacred attachment to their homeland.* Especially remembered are the several thousand Acadians who died as a result of their exile, *never to find refuge.*"

These last words tear at the captain's heart. He lowers his head.

"C'mon, man, hold it together," George admonishes.

"The flame also burns as a reminder that all who are oppressed can rekindle the spirit to reclaim their humanity. The flame is centered on a polished granite oval with an inscription that reads, *A People Without A Past, Are A People Without A Future*. This is a quote by the Cajun poet, Antoine Berque. The renovation, the mural, the wall plaques, and the Eternal Flame all came together, and the museum opened in 2001. Exhibits tell the story of old Acadia, the Deportation, and the establishment of Acadians in Louisiana. St. Martinville's ties to Evangeline are also explored. The museum shares the historical location with the African American Museum, which traces the arrival of Africans and the establishment of free people in this area in the 1700s and 1800s. Together, the two interpretive areas make up the St. Martinville Heritage Center."

"The whole Center is *REAL?* It really exists?"

"Right down there on the banks of the Bayou Teche!"

George continues to listen rapturously as the captain relates the unfortunate events and experiences of the Cajun people and how they came to have a museum dedicated in their honor in Louisiana.

Meanwhile, having no luck reaching Timmy, Sean decides to rejoin Roger on the back deck. Leaving his room, he notices the engineer is still studying the blueprints in the engine room. Sean dodges a conversation with him.

"I don't dare speak to the idiot or he'll tear my ear off with all that 'tank' talk," Sean mutters to himself. He walks on up to the next level and through the galley, where he passes the deckhand who's enjoying TV.

Lazy little shit! Sean thinks as he puts his hand on the doorknob. It better open. He turns the knob, then pulls, pushes, and jiggles it. He's just about to curse when the door opens. He glares at the deckhand as if to say, *Once again, you're damn lucky it opened!*

Out on the back deck, Sean can see Roger standing near an open crate and studying the contents.

"What have you got there?" he asks.

"It's the hang-glider I used on that *Live and Let Live* mission. I could take it up to the highest point on the railroad bridge and come off there with a pretty good tailwind. I could make it to the other side with no sweat."

"Nah, that's no good! You could catch a wind shear that would plunge you right into the river. It's too risky! The combination of the dangerous whirlpools and that treacherous churning could quickly suck you under! No, I wouldn't try that," Sean speculates.

"Yeah, you're probably right," Roger says.

"If that jet pack I used on the *Thunderbawl* mission wasn't in a thousand pieces, we could fly right over the water to the other side and be low enough to avoid radar detection. As it is with the balloon, we may not be able to avoid detection. We'll have to get in and out *quickly* before they have a chance to respond with reconnaissance aircraft! This is a no-fly zone, and they're sure to respond."

"Hell, it's a *simple* job! We'll be in and out before that. What's the story on Timmy?"

"He's still got his mike keyed. I can't talk to him. Hell, come to think of it, I can hardly talk to him *in person*, let alone on the radio!" Both the agents chuckle at the thought. "Speaking of radios, have you noticed how much into music these people are? The engineer has a radio playing down below, the deckhand stays in front of the TV with music on, and listen... you can even hear music coming from the captain's quarters. They have music on every level of this tub."

"George sure must be getting an earful! He's been gone for quite a while," Roger looks at his watch.

"Or getting sucked in!" Sean infers. "Seems like these people can't live without music. According to the deckhand, they have it hardwired into the 12-volt electrical system. That's why, when the generator went out, they *never* skipped a beat."

"Oh, they skipped. There was a *slight* moment of silence. It was eerie, too."

"It only seemed eerie because we went from the noise of the generator running to a sudden silence and then the music playing."

"Well, I think it was more like a *long* pause," Roger says.

"Maybe it was some kind of a purposeful delay, maybe a fire safety feature like a circuitry protection device. Listen to me with the *maybe*. I'm starting to sound like George!"

"That was a pretty good-sized lapse for something that's supposed to be hardwired."

Sean senses that Roger is edging toward the voodoo thing. "Do you see where you're going with this? You've over-analyzed this 'delay' into a fish story. You started out with a *slight moment* that grew into a *long pause,* and now you're caught up in *a pretty good-sized lapse*! Add a teaspoon of fear and a conspiratorial twist to the mix, and you could probably stretch it into an hour and a half of left field time!"

"I don't know...," Roger hesitates.

"Or you can look at it logically. It's a big step down from 110 to 12 volts! This friggin' tub is over thirty years old, and everything on it is either broken already or in the process of breaking! We're lucky it didn't catch fire and sink when the voltage switched over!" Sean exclaims.

"Yeah, I guess you're right." Roger seems to come to his senses.

"I *KNOW* I'm right! Even the captain said this boat was on its way to the bone yard!"

Meanwhile, in the captain's quarters, George and the captain are listening to the *Evangeline* musical, and the song *"Trust Your Heart"* begins playing. The lyrics hold George's attention in a thought-provoking way.

"Can you back that up and play it again?" George asks.

"Sure," the captain complies.

George listens intently as the lyrics embrace his heart and mind...

Sometimes you just cannot trust what you see with your eyes.

Sometimes your ears only hear mere conjecture and lies.

All your senses may betray what's true.

Sometimes you need more than reason when faced with a choice.

Sometimes to see your way clear and to hear the voice of God,

you must turn from your senses and learn to trust your heart.

George is mesmerized and in awe as the words resonate within the core of his being.

Meanwhile, back on deck, Roger wonders about George. "It sure is taking George a long time! What could he be up to?"

"He's probably getting pulled in... hook, line, and sinker! When he gets out of there, he'll be stumbling over *'what-ifs,'* puking up *'maybes,'* and passing out *'benefits of a doubt'*! He'll be *impossible* to reason with!"

"You think so?"

"Absolutely! It'll be written on his tombstone... *Try To Give Them The Benefit Of A Doubt.*" Sean shakes his head and laughs. "I'm going to try Timmy again via the GPS and hope I can reach him on the radio this time. You go ahead and give the balloon another boost and keep your eye open for any compound activity."

"I've been looking for hours. There's *nothing*. They're all in New Orleans," Roger states wearily.

"There could be a straggler or two. You never know; they could have left a skeleton crew."

"You mean a party pooper who stayed behind? I guess there's one in every crowd."

In the captain's quarters, George and the captain have been enjoying a number of songs from the Evangeline musical, and now the song *"A Sort of Friend"* is almost finished. This song causes George to reminisce about another time and place. He lingers with his thoughts for a moment.

"That song, *'We Have All The Time and The World'* reminds me of another one," he wistfully comments. "When I was..." He stops abruptly.

"Was what?" the captain asks.

"Oh, nothing."

The music continues to play and wafts its way about the old boat. Down in the bunkroom, Sean is on the GPS and can see Timmy still heading in the right direction.

Well, at least he's going the right way, thank God! Now, if I could just get him on the damn radio! Sean turns up the volume and hears what still sounds like a broken muffler. He hollers, "Timmy, Timmy! Come in!"

Timmy is speeding down the levee, looking like a madman. His clothes are crumpled and torn, and he's sporting a swollen, black eye from the bar fight. With the song *"Living Daylites"* playing in his head, Timmy sees the levee come to an end up ahead.

"BRACE YOURSELF!" he shouts.

"The vehicle flies off the levee and plunges into the swamp!"

Sean hears Timmy shout, *"Brace yourself,"* followed by the sound of the crash. "Timmy... Timmy... Come in! Are you all right?! Come in!" *He must be with someone,* Sean thinks as he checks the GPS. *The muffler is silent, and that movement indicates that Timmy's in motion. He must be walking, so he must be OK,* Sean surmises, and tries to reach him one more time. "Timmy, Timmy, come in, Timmy. Come in, Timmy." Damn.

Deciding it's no use trying to reach Timmy on the radio, Sean closes up the laptop and heads out of the bunkroom. Quickly walking by the engine room, he can see the engineer bent over the blueprints, and as he looks up from the prints, he begins to say something. Sean almost runs from him to avoid a conversation! The engineer doesn't get a single word out before Sean is gone. Walking through the living area, Sean does the same thing to avoid the deckhand. When he reaches the door, he struggles for a moment with the knob, but then it opens, and Sean strides out onto the deck.

"Did you finally reach Timmy?" Roger asks as the binoculars dangle from his neck.

"Nah," Sean replies. "He still has his damn mike keyed! But I could hear him. It sounded like he crashed the Lincoln!"

"What?"

"It sounded like he crashed! He must be OK, though. The GPS detected a walking motion. But he must be with someone because just before the crash, he shouted— *'Brace yourself!'*"

"That lucky son-of-a-bitch! He's probably with a *woman!*"

"No doubt he's with a woman. I just hope she isn't working for Primeaux!" Sean worries.

Up in the captain's quarters, a few more songs have played, and the song *"Blessed Lady,"* sung by Gabriel, is just ending. This song is a prayer for Evangeline's protection. After it ends, there is a short narration by the priest.

"Just imagine how much Gabriel must have loved Evangeline," the captain speaks. "How awful it was to lose her and the uncertainty of not knowing if she was even alive."

"I once knew a love like that," George says with a dazed stare. He's beginning to sense the love Gabriel must have felt for Evangeline.

"The next song is called *'Worth The Wait,'* " the captain informs. "It describes how Evangeline sat under that oak tree for years, waiting for Gabriel's return, how all of her friends thought she was wasting her life, and what that wait had cost her. *Was it worth it?*"

As George and the captain listen to the song, an awakening truth falls over both of them, and they realize how their lives have paralleled Evangeline's. George—he sat in his garage for thirty years waiting for his next mission and believing that any day the call would come. The captain—he sat on his boat for thirty years relating the story of the Cajuns to countless passengers and anyone who would listen and hoping, against all odds, the apology would come. The song ends, and the captain pauses the tape and looks up at George, and at the same time, they both say...

"You know, I'm like... my life..."

"I'm sorry. Go ahead," the captain says.

"No, that's OK. You go ahead." George gestures toward the captain.

"Well, what were you going to say?"

"You first," George insists.

"You know, some might say, I'm like Evangeline," the captain begins. "I've never married. I've spent my whole adult life on this boat... thirty years trying to rally the Cajun community behind the apology and to right *the wrong* my people have suffered. Most people couldn't have cared less, but some did. I have to ask myself what Evangeline's friends asked her: *is it worth it?* Am I a fool for sitting on the sidelines of life, living in the past as life goes by?"

"I wouldn't say you're a fool. I've done the same thing sitting in my garage waiting for a call. My sideline was *getting sidelined.*"

"We need to ask ourselves... do we learn anything sitting on the sidelines of life, or is it all in vain? Surely, people on the sidelines have a better view of the game as opposed to a player who only sees what's in front of him," the captain surmises.

"Yeah, we see the big picture, all right. But then, we want some action, too. We want to jump in," George adds.

"The only action I want is an apology for my people, to help heal this cavitation in our society as a result of the deportation of the 1750s and the assimilation of the 1920s when we were made to feel less than worthy. I feel that with this apology, my people will begin to realize their strong sense of identity and feel validated. I mean, isn't that what every human being wants at their deepest level? To know and to be known... *validation.*"

George thinks about what the captain has just said. He draws a parallel for himself by realizing that he's maintained his *'agent-ness'* through all his years on the sidelines with little or no validation.

"I know what you mean. I feel the same way about my situation," George remarks, realizing the truth.

"History has a way of repeating itself. Getting the apology and taking another look at what happened to the Cajun people could be beneficial to all segments of society that have been wronged throughout the world... both past and present."

"Maybe so," George admits.

"How about listening to the rest of the musical?" The CD has ended. The captain removes the disk and inserts another.

"Sure, but I'm gonna have to get going soon."

Back on the deck, Sean and Roger have been talking, discussing old missions and speculating about new ones.

"Damn! There goes that music again!" Sean says angrily. "He's going to be in there all the damn night!"

"Oh, I'm sure that whatever the captain's dishing out, George is eating it up!" Roger adds. "He must be on his third helping by now! He's too *damn* trusting! That's why he'll never make a good Double O! It's not really his fault. It's that *Australian* side of him."

"He does have a little of that 'down under' mentality."

"Down under, my ass!" Sean retorts. "Down-and-out-of-it is more like it! He refuses to take anything at face value and call it what it is. He's always looking for a *deeper* meaning in everything! You saw the way he argued with me over that compound surveillance vehicle, and now he's up there getting sucked in by *Captain Passion*. He'll be more obstinate than ever! For all we know, these Cajun people couldn't give a damn about that apology! It could just be another front used to distract us while they double their efforts toward a one-world taste. That's how these damn monopolizers operate! But do you think George will ever see that? Hell, no!"

"Like you said, it's probably that Australian side of him."

"Without a doubt, it's his breeding. Australians are by-products of English prisons, so what do you expect? George is a genetic twist of fate."

"Does Australia even have an intelligence community?" Roger asks.

"I don't know. I thought I heard something about a James McGillacutty once."

"McGillacutty?" Roger questions.

"Yeah. Man, is that a mouthful! What's your name? *McGillacutty, James McGillacutty.*"

Both men laugh at the thought of an agent McGillacutty. Meanwhile, back in the captain's quarters, the captain and George are listening to the last song on the CD, *"Trust Your Heart."*

"There's that song again," George says, once again falling under the spell of the simple but insightful words. Somehow he senses that the unpretentious truth revealed in the words of the song is speaking directly to his soul.

Sometimes you just cannot trust what you see with your eyes.

George closes his eyes and allows the words of the song to enter his heart. The philosophy of the lyrics has a profound effect upon him. The last words of the song float away.

You must turn from your senses and learn to trust your heart.

The lyric's truth has taken hold of George's heart. "I could listen to that song a thousand times and never get tired of it."

"It really does hold a great deal of meaning," the captain says solemnly. "I must have listened to that song a hundred times, but each time I hear it, the words seem even more powerful. And this time, more than ever before, it seems even more real."

"Yeah... yeah! Tha... that's IT! *REAL!* That song makes you think about what's really *REAL!*" George exclaims excitedly.

"Not only real but *relevant*," the captain says, nodding in agreement. "Everyone in life has a mission. Evangeline's was to find her lost love. Mine is to right the wrongs done to my people. And what do you think *your* mission might be?" The captain turns to face George and looks him in the eye.

"Well, I... I... my... er... *my*... mission? I'm really not sure. I have to leave now. Thanks for everything." George is unsettled by the captain's sudden question about missions and turns to leave.

"Remember, be true to thyself!" The captain leans out the door and shouts at George's retreating back.

"Sure thing. Thanks again, captain," George hurries off. Feeling a bit stunned yet excited by what he's learned, he quickly descends the small spiral staircase.

"Be true to thyself," he mumbles to himself, the "Trust Your Heart" lyrics continuing to play in his head. He reaches the galley and passes by the deckhand without seeing him; he is so preoccupied. With so many thoughts and feelings racing through his mind and heart, George says to himself, "*Everybody* has a mission!"

The back door is open. George walks out onto the deck and heads for the rear of the boat. Sean and Roger are standing next to the cabin. They're hidden by the shadows, and George walks past them without noticing. They hear him mumbling to himself, and Roger starts to step out of the shadows when Sean pulls him back.

"Let's see what he does," Sean whispers. "He's walking pretty fast; he probably needs to piss."

"What a sight! The only thing on this mission in a skirt, and it's George!" Roger shakes his head sadly.

"If you think that's a sad sight, wait till he hikes it up to piss!" Sean chuckles.

George is bee-lining it for the back starboard side of the boat, and oddly enough, the boat is level at the time. At the railing, he pulls up his kilt and starts peeing in the moonlit river, still talking to himself.

This captain is for REAL! Sean's just wrong! George tries to make sense of all he's just learned. The captain is not living in his head. His mission is REAL! Everything he just told me is based on historical facts; it's even documented on microfilm! It's the historical aspect of it all that has MR. PERFECT believing that the captain is living in the past. But our mission is based on intelligence, and that intelligence is faulty or inactionable; it could very well lead to a failed mission! George wrestles with this newly acquired knowledge. If his facts are true, then the Cajun people are definitely owed an apology!

On the other hand, if he's fronting for Primeaux... well, he's one hell of a good actor! Because when he talks about his mission, he has an affidavit face. But what if he is working for Primeaux? What if I'm wrong about the captain? If I tell Sean that I think that maybe the captain's on the level, he'll never believe me. Sean's too damn mission-minded! He'll think I'm trying to sabotage our mission! George looks over his shoulder and sees Sean and Roger walking toward him. I'd better keep this to myself for now and see how things unfold.

Sean is giving Roger instructions concerning the balloon. "Better go check the flame and adjust it just high enough so the wind won't blow it out, yet low enough to conserve fuel." He then turns his attention to George.

"You and *Captain Passion* enjoy your little visit?" he says with a sneer.

"It was OK." George looks first at the water, then up to the stars.

"He's living in the past, right?"

"Sort of."

"I thought so. Look, we're going to leave that balloon on a low flame to be sure it stays inflated through the night. We'll be lifting off at daybreak. We better turn in."

"I'll be down in a minute."

"OK. Don't be long! I want you to be fresh in the morning!" Sean walks away, leaving George to continue to wrestle with his thoughts.

George gazes out at the moonlit river with the song *"Trust Your Heart"* replaying in his mind along with the captain's parting words, *"Be true to thyself."* George struggles to put everything into perspective.

So if the words in the song are right, the heart can hear the heart, but the head can't hear the head. The heart can hear the head, but the head can't hear the heart. Or is it that the head can hear the heart, but the heart can't hear the head? This is basic communication, with heart to heart being the best. The bottom line is don't let your head outrun your heart... so, trust your heart.

The captain's like me, I'm like him, and we're both like Evangeline. He needs an apology to fulfill his mission. She needed to find her lost love to fulfill her mission. I need a successful mission to fulfill my mission. He sat on a boat. She sat under a tree. I sat in my garage. The similarities are striking, with the common denominator being hopeful stagnation.

Well, guess I'd better turn in. George turns away from the railing and heads toward the bunk room, his thoughts spinning about in a confusion of newfound possibilities.

Below deck, Sean and Roger are trying to get things situated so they don't stumble over anything in the dark. The only illumination is a dim emergency light over the door and the moonlight casting a long speckled shadow through the dirty porthole.

"This sure as hell isn't a five-star hotel!" Sean grumbles.

"It's not even a ONE-star! It's friggin' space debris!" Roger adds.

"There he goes with that 'Moonmaker' shit," Sean thinks.

"No water, no electricity, no sliding doors, and HOT AS HELL!" Roger continues. "Thank God we'll be in New Orleans soon!"

George enters the bunkroom, and Sean announces, "Roger and I took the bottom bunks; we left the uppers for you and Timmy. He won't be here, so take your pick. That reminds me, I'd better check on him." Sean reaches for his radio and gets a whiff of George's shoes.

"What the hell is that smell?" Sean wrinkles his nose in disgust.

"It's the whole damn boat! The whole thing stinks!" Roger complains.

Meanwhile, Timmy has come across and stolen an oil and gas exploration vehicle. It's a giant 4-wheel drive with 6' tractor tires and swivel capability. When he climbed on the vehicle, his radio scraped against a lever, de-keying the mike and clearing the radio for transmission.

Sean switches the radio on.

(SCRRRRR)... "Timmy... Timmy... Come in, Timmy! Do you copy?"

(SCRRRRR)... "Is that you, Pierce?" Timmy asks.

(SCRRRRR)... "NO! It's Sean!"

(SCRRRRR)... "For a minute there, you sounded like Pierce."

(SCRRRRR)... "Pierce is nowhere around; he's *across the ocean!* Never mind that! Where are you? It sounds like you've yanked the muffler off the Navigator!"

(SCRRRRR)... "I ditched it. I commandeered another vehicle."

(SCRRRRR)... "YOU WHAT?!" Sean shrieks.

(SCRRRRR)... "I ran the Lincoln off the levee and into a swamp."

(SCRRRRR)... "Are you all right?"

(SCRRRRR)... "Yeah, but it scared the *Living Daylights* out of me!"

Sean leans over to Roger. "*Living Daylights,* wasn't that...?"

"Yeah, *Living Daylights* was one of his missions."

"You don't think he...?"

"I don't know. HQ was having some problems with him when he was classified 'Inactive.' I heard he had a tendency to take things a little too... uh, seriously."

Listen to this voodoo-warped guy! Talk about the pot calling the kettle black! Sean thinks.

George, up on his bunk, is half-listening to the conversation below and thinking about the lyrics from *"Trust Your Heart"*... *Sometimes your ears only hear mere conjecture and lies...*

(SCRRRRR)... "Timmy, are you there? Are you there? Come in, Timmy!" Sean is back on the radio.

(SCRRRRR)... "Yeah."

(SCRRRRR)... "What's all that noise? Is that the vehicle you're on?"

(SCRRRRR)... "Yeah, it's loud! I think it's some sort of logging vehicle. It's clearly designed for this type of terrain! It almost has snake-like capabilities; it seems *unstoppable!*" Timmy shouts above the noise.

(SCRRRRR)... "Have you found the roads we talked about?"

(SCRRRRR)... "No need! This thing makes its own roads!"

(SCRRRRR)... "See anything else? Can you see the rear levee?"

(SCRRRRR)... "No. But every now and then, I run across a bunch of ground wires strung out over the terrain."

Sean looks over at Roger. "Sounds like seismic surveillance sensors. No doubt, they're part of Primeaux's compound security system!"

"Yeah, they're probably sensors," Roger replies.

"It's lucky that all of Primeaux's people are in New Orleans, or they'd have Timmy spotted by now!" Sean speculates.

"Yeah, those systems are super sensitive. I've heard they can tell what size shoe you're wearing!"

George ponders another lyric. *Sometimes you just cannot trust what you see with your eyes...*

(SCRRRRR)... "Timmy! Can you see the levee at all?" Sean asks.

(SCRRRRR)... "Not yet. There's moonlight out here, but not enough to see very far."

(SCRRRRR)... "I'll raise you on the GPS and point you in the right direction." Sean opens the laptop.

(SCRRRRR)... "Go ahead. Good idea!"

(SCRRRRR)... "OK, Timmy. I've got you. Turn east. NO! You're headed the wrong way! Not *north... east!* NO, not *west!* OK, now go *right...* NO, not *left! My right... your left!* OK, now *south.* NO! The other way! OK, now go *right.*"

(SCRRRRR)... "You're breaking up!" Timmy yells.

Roger offers a guess... "It could be something interfering with the homing device. Maybe there's *something* in the air."

"There's nothing in the air but mosquitoes and humidity," Sean says, while thinking, *don't give me any of that voodoo shit!*

(SCRRRRR)... "Timmy! Keep looking for the levee! If you haven't found it by daybreak, just head toward the sun. That's east, and you're sure to run into it."

(SCRRRRR)... "You're breakin'..."

"Damn, that boy's got no sense of direction! He'll be driving around in circles till morning!" Sean shakes his head.

"It shouldn't be that hard for him to find his way. Cypress logging was once a big industry down here, and there should be plenty of old logging roads for him to follow," Roger suggests.

"Should be... yeah, but I'll bet my left nut on a choppin' block, Timmy will be lost until morning!"

George contemplates another lyric. *All your senses may betray what's true...*

"Do you think Timmy's out in left field?" Roger asks.

"Nope."

"Do you think he's in right field?"

"No. He's in another friggin' world!" Sean says adamantly.

"You're probably right."

"George, are you asleep up there? You're awfully quiet," Sean queries.

"No, just thinking," George replies.

"Well, how was your stroll down memory lane with Captain Passion? Did you learn anything that might help us?" Sean looks over at Roger and smirks.

"Yes. He feels very strongly about..."

"Whoa, whoa!" Sean interrupts. "*He feels*, huh? Maybe we should call him Captain *Compassion!*" Sean laughs out loud, and Roger joins in.

"Sorry, George, go on."

"Like I was saying, he feels very strongly about what his people went through, and it's his life's mission to obtain an apology. He could be on the level, you know."

"You mean his life's *OBSESSION!*" Sean says gruffly.

"I don't understand what the big deal is about this apology," Roger says. "With the political climate the way it is today, politicians are apologizing right and left."

"Sure, for a slip of the tongue here and there." George sits up on his bunk. "But one country apologizing to another, that's not so common."

"I know one thing... you give *these* people an inch, they'll take a mile! I can see why the Queen is reluctant to administer an apology. It may not even be warranted. The next thing you know, they'll be calling for an International Apology Day... everybody can be sorry for *everything!*"

"Well, the captain did suggest an International Inventory Day when people would take stock of their lives and countries would take stock of their policies," George offers.

"You see, the mere fact that he would *suggest* such a thing *proves* he's OBSESSED!" Sean rants. "Inventory, apology... it's all hogwash! It would never work! Human nature being what it is, most people can only see the wrongs that others have caused them, unaware of *their* own wrongs. That 'Inventory Day' would be the biggest blame *game* the world has ever seen! It could result in TOTAL ANARCHY!"

"Well, inventory and apology aren't *hogwash* if they're rooted in real truth and forgiveness! The result of an International Inventory Day could be the greatest PEACE the world has ever known!" George says earnestly.

"That's *wishful* thinking! The world's not made that way. I'm telling you, it would lead to TOTAL ANARCHY! A monopolizer's dream!

Then Primeaux and his people would succeed, and what kind of a message does that send to other monopolizers in the world?" Sean continues his tirade. "As I've said before, there's a fine line between passion and obsession. Crossing that line will blind a man and distract him from his mission."

"Maybe the *real* distraction and danger to any mission is when an element of force goes against the natural flow of things."

"Look, George, I know you like to give everyone the benefit of the doubt, but it's just that... DOUBT! How do you know the captain's not working for Primeaux? You don't!"

"True. But on the other hand, the moment of absolute certainty never really arrives, does it?"

"Enough of this shit! We're here to get the data on the Aspic, the Queen needs a win, and we've got to get to New Orleans. PERIOD!" Sean rails.

"That's what I say!" Roger agrees heartily. "I think I'll start with a brunette... or maybe a blonde!"

"If it hadn't been for all the glitches in the background intelligence, we wouldn't even be having this conversation! We'd be in New Orleans right now!" Sean tries to fluff the pillow on his bunk.

"If only we had the boat that Pierce used on *The World Is Enough* mission, we would have been in New Orleans a long time ago! I'd probably be on my *fourth* woman by now!" Roger laments.

"That thing was busted up while still in its developmental stages." Sean smooths the wrinkles from his blanket and carefully folds a corner back.

"I can't believe the trouble we're having getting across one damn river!" Roger shakes his head.

"We can play these 'what-ifs' until hell freezes over! That still won't get us to the other side! So let's quit with the bullshit and focus on a *successful* mission. For right now, all we can do is get some shut-eye and hope the wind is in our favor in the morning."

"Yeah, you're probably right. Goodnight, Sean. Goodnight, George." Roger yawns and sinks back onto his bunk.

"Goodnight, Roger. Goodnight, George," Sean says.

"Goodnight, Roger. Goodnight, Sean," George answers from above.

The three agents drift off to sleep, with Roger fantasizing about all the women in New Orleans, George lost in his musical reverie, and Sean, with a vision of his younger self, cruising down a winding mountain road.

And then there's Timmy... he's somewhere, out in the night, making his own roads!

Down the hallway, the engineer and deckhand are in their bunks, having their own conversation.

"Man, it's been a *long* day!" the engineer exclaims. "I haven't worked this hard in years! Thank God, it's only for a couple more days! This damn boat's a mess! I can't see how that other engineer kept it going! He must have known what was what because I can't figure that mess out. All that piping is like a big pile of spaghetti. He must have had a magic touch or something."

"I doubt that. He was always down there beating and banging on something and yelling and cussing, so he must have had his bad days too," the deckhand replies.

"There's enough by-pass valves and lines down there to plumb *two* boats! I can't make head or tail of it. There's been so many changes over the years that nothing matches up with the blueprints. So the blueprints are useless, and the captain's not much help, either. I left that one transfer pump running. I'm *not* staying up all night to watch it. If she burns up, she burns up! If the pump don't kick off, we'll be listening to starboard when we wake up in the morning," the engineer yawns. "Speaking of the captain, is he all right? He seems kind of distant."

"No, that's just the way he is. He's been a little depressed ever since he got word from the office that they were sending his boat to the bone yard. He's been with this old girl a lot of years. Hell, we were on our way to the bone yard when they called us to go on this job! But he'll be all right."

"We'll be lucky if this thing ever makes it to the bone yard on its own! Between the bad fuel and the bilge pump, it might never start. Why, it could sink right here!" The engineer shakes his head and continues. "Yeah, losing his boat must have taken a toll on that old captain. He really looks tired, weird even."

"If you want *weird*, what about that gang we got on board? You've been down here working all day and haven't seen the half of it!"

"What do you mean?" the engineer asks.

"For starters, we picked them up *under* a bridge instead of at the docks! And look at the way they're dressed... they're not exactly roughnecks! And that *cargo*... that's not oilfield equipment! Whatever that stuff is, it's been all over the world! And now, they got a hot air balloon inflated out on the back deck. No telling what those guys are up to!"

"A hot air balloon? Yeah, that is strange for out here."

"And that boss-man, he gives a whole new meaning to the term, *hard-ass!*"

"Which one is he?" the engineer asks.

"He's the one beating the hell out of all the doors!" the deckhand exclaims.

"Yeah, I met him. He really is rude! He asked me when they'd be able to take a shower, and when I started explaining to him how I was transferring water and fuel around and how much time it'd take, he cuts me off and says, 'OK, *I've heard enough!*' and turns right around and walks off."

"Well, he told the captain to have me go 'round and check *all* the doors 'cause they seemed to be sticking. There's nothing wrong with the doors! It's him! I saw him when they first got here! Almost like he didn't even know how to open a door—pushing and pulling on the doorknob and turning it back and forth and back and forth with no coordination at all but plenty of frustration!"

"Guys like that need sliding doors," the engineer says.

"You got that right. I was in the galley area watching TV when he first came through. He never said HELLO, GOODBYE, GO-TO-HELL, SCREW YOU, nothing! At the very least, he could have had the courtesy to say something!" The deckhand smirks. "I must have rubbed him the wrong way when he asked for a martini and I offered him a Bud or Bud Light. He looked at me like he was fixing to kill me!"

"A *martini?* On this frigging tub? Talk about reaching for the sky! That guy is definitely out of his element," the engineer laughs.

"He's outta something! Patience, for one. That old bastard's heading for a stroke, sure as shit! But he don't scare me like that other sombitch!"

"Which one's that?"

"The one driving the Navigator."

"I didn't see him. I never went up top."

"Oh man! You really missed it then!" The deckhand continues. "He had *MANIAC* written all over him! A violent, crazy-looking sombitch. I tell you what. I've been in jail with sombitches like that! You sleep standing up, with your back against the wall and one eye open. I'm sure glad he's not here tonight, and I hope he don't come back!"

"What about that old boy running around with them binoculars hanging off his neck? What do you think he's looking for?"

"*Women!* That's one horny old fart! He was asking me about the women round here and in New Orleans and if I thought there'd be a lot more during Mardi Gras," the deckhand chuckles.

"Come to think of it, he asked me about women, too."

"If he's looking for women with them binoculars, you've got to give the old guy credit! He's still got it!"

"Yeah, or else he's all pumped up on that Viagra!" the engineer adds.

"The one I can't figure out is the guy in the skirt!" the deckhand laughs.

"You mean the one in the kilt? I just caught a glimpse of him going in their cabin. He must be Scottish or something like that."

"I don't know, his accent is kind of different from the rest of them, but I don't think it's Scottish. Maybe more of a Crocodile Dundee Australian accent."

"Then, I wonder, what's the deal with the kilt?"

"I don't know. When they first came aboard in Krotz Springs, he had on a fancy suit like the rest of them. Then when we got here in Melville, he had on what looked like a professor's outfit. And now he's got on a skirt. Tomorrow... who knows? He may be a weird dresser, but he sure hit it off with the captain. Tonight, they were up in the captain's quarters talking and listening to music for hours."

"Well, speaking of night... I've got to get some sleep."

"Yeah, me too. Goodnight."

Up in his quarters, the captain is laying in his bunk, staring out of his moonlit porthole, thinking about his encounter with George.

He's like me, I'm like him, and we're both like her. All these years, I've been shoving the Cajuns' exile experience and Evangeline's story down anyone's throat that would lend an ear, and I never realized that I was just like Evangeline. I know it wasn't all in vain. Some of what I shared must have resonated with someone. But that old boy, George, I think he was really interested. Anyway, I hope he finds whatever it is he's looking for and that God blesses him.

During the night, Sean wakes up tossing and turning. He decides to check his laptop GPS to see how Timmy is doing. The laptop screen lights up, and Sean can see that Timmy is going in circles; at times, he's almost off the screen.

Like a friggin' goose in a rainstorm! he mutters, then closes the laptop, rolls over, and goes back to sleep.

CHAPTER III

The next morning, as predicted by the engineer, the boat is listing sharply to the starboard side. Sean is the first one awake. When he rolls over to get out of bed, he rolls right out of his bunk, onto the floor, makes another full roll, and ends up with his face in George's filthy, cowshit/cowpiss, stinking shoes.

DAMN! I KNEW it! That's where all the stink is coming from! I ought to shoot that moron! No, I'm not going to let him get to me! I've just got to get George on that balloon, get the data on the Aspic, and then get the hell out of here!

Sean quickly dresses, then shaves with his electric razor. He grumbles as he rouses George and Roger. "Get up, let's get going! I'm going up to check on the balloon. Hopefully, the wind is still in our favor. I'm taking the radio and GPS with me so I can contact Timmy and make sure he's in position."

Roger and George begin to get dressed. George feels like crap because he's out of clean clothes. He hesitantly hops down from his bunk and sits on the one folding metal chair that's over the manhole cover. After a moment, he grabs his stinking shoes and filthy socks, then sits back down in the chair.

"Is that what you're wearing?" Roger asks.

"Uhhhhh... yeah?"

"The last time I flew that balloon, I wore this." Roger takes a neatly pressed safari outfit from his bag and begins to put it on. "Too bad we're not the same size," he says.

"Well, this is all I have." George screws up his nose as he begins to pull on the still damp socks. "I'll buy new things when we get to New Orleans. I hope I can find a good tailor."

"Hey, I have an extra pair of clean socks, here you go." Roger pitches a pair of white socks over to George, then turns back to the mirror to finish his shave.

"Thanks. My razor's in the Lincoln. I'll shave later."

Up top, Sean goes through the living area, where he finds the deckhand and the engineer sitting at a table watching an early morning French language program on TV. Sean is having trouble walking up the slanted floor.

"Damn! Why can't you guys get this damn boat level?" he grouches.

"I left the pump runnin' all night," the engineer explains. "It was supposed to kick off when the boat leveled out, but the float mechanism malfunctioned and the bilge pump never..."

"Aw, I don't want to hear that shit!" Waving his hand through the air in disgust, Sean heads for the door. He grabs the knob and begins his rattling routine.

The door finally opens and flies outward because the boat is leaning so much. Once outside, Sean stumbles against the door, takes a step or two to right himself, then slams the door behind him.

"Did you see that? See what I mean?" the deckhand asks. "I'm telling you, he's a stroke waiting to happen!"

"Man... that's one rude sombitch, all right! I'd hate to be a door at his house!" The engineer turns to leave. "Well, I've got to get working on that generator."

"Yeah, what's the story on that?"

"Now that I finally got the bad fuel pumped out and some good fuel in, it ought to start right up. Sure took a hell of a long time, though! I didn't think the tank had that kind of capacity!"

Roger and George enter the galley area. Roger is clean-shaven in a safari outfit, and George, badly in need of a shave, is in his filthy kilt and ruffled shirt. They pass the two other men with a 'good morning' nod. A song is just finishing up on a French TV program, and the announcer says, *"That was a great performance by the Big Daddy Voodoo Band."* Roger immediately stiffens. He stops and quickly glances from side to side, a look of panic on his face.

"I'm fixing to get that generator going, and we'll have some coffee here pretty soon," the engineer says.

"That sounds good, thanks," George replies as he gives Roger a shove, and they pass on by and out the door.

"Did you see the eyes on that one with them binoculars? He looked like a deer caught in the headlights," the deckhand comments.

"Maybe he needs those damned things just to see! I get what you mean about their clothes! Not exactly roughnecks!"

"That one in the skirt is a long way from a roughneck!"

"That's the damnedest-looking crew I ever saw! I wonder what kind of business they're in," the engineer shakes his head.

"Don't know. The captain asked them when they first came aboard about the job and how long they'd be, and the boss-man told him, *'Look, you just run the boat!'*"

"Well, whatever they're doing, I'll be glad when it's over so I can get back to my regular boat." The engineer heads for the engine room.

Out on the deck, Roger immediately goes to the side of the boat and starts scanning the Melville side of the river with his binoculars. George approaches Sean, who has his laptop open and is talking to Timmy on the radio.

(SCRRRRR)... "Timmy, you're right where you need to be." Sean turns to George and Roger. "George, go ahead and get the balloon ready. Roger, what's it looking like?"

(SCRRRRR)... "You're break..."—Timmy's voice cracks.

(SCRRRRR)... "OK, Timmy. All you have to do is head east!" Sean yells.

(SCRRRRR)... "You're breaking up!" Timmy screeches back.

George climbs into the balloon gondola as Sean watches from several feet away. The gondola is dangerously leaning to one side, and the rope holding it is stretched tightly from the all-night heat.

(SCRRRRR)... "Just head for the sun, Timmy! Head for the sun!" Sean admonishes as he turns to George and the balloon. "George, don't forget the tranquilizer gun!" he yells.

George jumps out of the gondola to get the gun, takes a couple of steps, and catches his kilt on a nail sticking out of a crate. He's yanked backward by the nail, loses his balance, and falls on the rope that's holding the balloon. The rope snaps, and the balloon, suddenly free, is buoyed aloft! Sean, watching the whole mishap, dashes for the rope dangling from the basket. He trips over George, who is tugging on his kilt, still unaware that the balloon is lifting off.

In a mad dash, Sean chases the dangling rope to the end of the deck. Desperately grasping, he makes one last-ditch effort; he dives for the rope and almost falls off the boat as the balloon lifts and flies away! Lying there in disbelief, he sits up and lowers his face to his hands for a moment. He raises his head and watches in disbelief as the balloon ascends. He turns and glares at George, sitting on the deck, speechless and wide-eyed with his mouth open.

"I ah... I uh... ah..." George struggles to speak.

"THE BRIDGE!" Roger yells excitedly.

"Look! It's coming DOWN!"

Sean jumps up from the deck. Watching the bridge, his senses begin to heighten, and he quickly assesses the situation. He spots the railroad maintenance vehicle on the tracks near the foot of the bridge. With the balloon gone and the mission in jeopardy, he realizes it's time for *raw* courage. With no time to think, he takes off for the vehicle! Running past George and across the boat, he leaps off the gangplank onto the bank. He sprints full blast toward the foot of the bridge.

Sean reaches the vehicle and jumps in, only to realize there are no keys in the ignition. Frantically, he searches the dashboard, under the seat, on the floor, and finds the keys in the ashtray. He starts the truck and floors it!

The tires spin on the slick rail, and Sean gets no traction. He lets up on the gas a little, then gradually gives it more gas, and the rail truck picks up speed quickly.

The captain and the deckhand are in the wheelhouse and have gotten a bird's-eye view of what's going on.

"He's stealing that railroad truck!" the captain is shocked.

"That sombitch is *CRAZY!* Holy shit! The bridge is going back *UP!*" the deckhand yells.

Sean sees the bridge going up and hits the brakes, but the truck continues to slide on the slick rails. Watching from the boat, the captain is on the radio trying to alert the watchman to lower the bridge, but it's too late; Sean is going too fast! Everyone on the boat watches in shock as the vehicle flies off the bridge!

The truck sails into the air as if in slow motion and falls to the water in a belly-bust splash. When it hits, it begins to sink, then suddenly resurfaces and radically bobs up and down in the whirling current. Uninjured, Sean struggles out of the vehicle and desperately swims toward the boat. The deckhand grabs a life ring and throws it out to Sean, but the water is so turbulent that the life ring zips right past him. With all his might, Sean thrashes against the current and swims toward the stern of the boat. Everyone on board has gathered at the back of the boat to urge him on. He's tiring quickly against the strong and treacherous river while whirlpools threaten to pull him under! Just as he reaches the boat, he slips under for a few seconds, but then suddenly bobs up with George's discarded underwear wetly draped over his head and face; the classic skid mark cuts across the bridge of his nose. A filthy pair of pants is wrapped around his neck, and a muddy scarf hangs from one arm.

Roger and the deckhand are the closest to Sean, and they quickly reach out and pull him onto the boat, which is listing low in the water. Once on deck, Sean angrily resists their help in peeling off the excess clothing. In a fury, he yanks the filthy garments off his body and flings them aside.

"Are you all right?" George reaches out in concern.

"*That bridge sure is acting strange, going up and down like that for no reason,*" Roger muses, looking worried.

Sean pushes everyone out of his way and quickly walks the uphill grade of the deck to the back door of the cabin. Assuming the door will be stuck, he grabs the knob and pulls with all his remaining strength.

The door comes completely off its hinges! Sean falls to his back and slides downhill a ways. After a bit of stumbling, he manages to stand up, still holding the door by the knob. He slams it down on the deck, then heads through the galley area and down the stairs where he spots the engineer.

"Can I get a shower, NOW?!" he yells, his face beet red and his nostrils flaring.

"Yeah, sure. I just got it fixed."

In the bathroom, Sean starts to strip. He hears the pumps running and feels the boat begin to level out as he steps into the shower and turns the faucets. The warm water is both refreshing and comforting; he closes his eyes and begins to relax when suddenly the boat lists sharply and slams him against the shower wall!

"Friggin' roller coaster!" Sean yells. He's barely regained his balance when he screams, "DAMN!" Rubbing his eyes furiously, he backs out of the shower. "Damn, it's pouring diesel!"

The engineer comes running from the engine room and the captain from the galley; they race to the bathroom. Sean is standing in the shower, drenched in diesel.

"What the hell? Look at this shit!" Sean screeches in disgust.

"So that's where that fuel went!" The engineer throws his hands up. "Man, I sure am sorry!" The captain approaches to help.

"Out of my way!" Sean pushes his way between the two men. They turn and follow as he furiously stomps his way to the bunkroom. He steps over the threshold and slaps his bare foot into an oily pool of diesel! "Now, what's this shit?!" he hollers.

Sean turns on the light to find his shoes floating on a sea of diesel, with more bubbling up from the open manhole. His bag, on the floor next to his bed, is sodden with the oily mixture

"Oh man!" the captain says, turning to the engineer. "You couldn't figure out what tank that bad fuel was being pumped into? There it is, right there!"

"I'll be damned! So that was where all that fuel went! I kept thinking it was going in one of the rear tanks, and all this time it was being pumped up here." The engineer scratches his head.

Simple job, my ass! Sean rages to himself. *I've got to get the hell out of here for a while to regroup!* He wades across the room in the ankle-deep diesel, grabs his bag and shoes, and returns to the hallway to dress. "Look at my clothes! They're ruined because of your stupidity!" he yells as he rummages through the half-soaked contents of his bag.

"Man, I'm sure sorry about this." The captain rubs his hand across his mouth. "It's clearly our fault. We'll turn the claim in to our insurance company; they'll reimburse you for the damage."

Too angry to reply, Sean continues his search for something dry to wear.

Meanwhile, on the other side of the river, in the woods west of Melville, a skeleton crew of seismograph workers shows up at their worksite to do some surveying. They notice a car in the nearby bayou and realize that one of their vehicles is gone. They can hear it running in the distance but can't see it because of the woods. The foreman orders one of the workers to climb up an observation tower with a pair of binoculars. As he reaches the top of the tower, the worker lifts the binoculars to his face and begins to scan the forest.

"DAMN! I can't believe it!" the worker yells out suddenly, a shocked expression on his face.

"What is it?" the foreman asks, concern in his voice.

"It looks like an avalanche site!"

"That's impossible! We're on flat land!"

"Well, whoever's on that drill buggy has mowed down about 100 acres! It looks like everything from here to Melville is flattened!"

"I'd better call the law!"

"Hold on, I can see 'em coming up the road right now!"

Just then, a patrol car with two officers, Wax and Wane, pulls up to the worksite. Officer Wax exits the car as the foreman walks up.

"We're looking for a car thief who might be an escaped mental patient," Officer Wax says.

"I was just going to call you guys so you could add equipment theft to your charges!" the foreman exclaims.

"What?" Wax asks.

"You hear that equipment running?" The foreman gestures over his shoulder toward the woods.

"Yeah."

"That's one of our drill buggies, and that's probably the guy you're looking for. He's joy riding on it! He ditched his car in the bayou right over there."

Officer Wane climbs out of the patrol car. "Oh yeah?" he says. "I'd better check that out." He heads to the bayou.

"My guy up in the tower says that maniac has just about flattened everything from here to Melville!" the foreman gestures. "I'm sure he's destroyed all our ground wires and other equipment too."

"Let's have a look." Wax starts climbing the tower.

Officer Wax quickly reaches the top of the tower. The worker in the tower hands him the binoculars. Wax can't believe the amount of destruction as he pans across the landscape. *It's a massacre of at least 100 acres!* Just then, he sees Timmy, still on the buggy, not far from the highway. Wax quick-steps down the tower, hollering out for Officer Wane.

"Wane, let's go!" he yells, racing for the patrol car. They peel out, already on the radio calling for backup, and head toward Timmy and the drill buggy.

Back on the boat, Sean is getting dressed. Part of his suit is wet and darkened with diesel fuel. Large splotches stain the front and back of his jacket and one ass cheek. Fuming, he stomps up the stairs and through the galley, walking on a downhill slope because the boat is listing. Grumbling about *"the friggin' roller coaster boat,"* he nears the door and attempts to slow down. Suddenly, he slips, slides, then falls. His oily, diesel-coated shoes send him flying to a bone-crushing stop against the high threshold at the bottom of the door.

The deckhand, watching TV, sees Sean slip and fall. "Hey man, are you all right?"

Sean doesn't answer. Angrily, he hoists himself up from the floor and steps over the threshold onto the warm, painted deck. Where, once again, the diesel on his shoes and the downward slope of the boat send Sean sliding and stumbling into a rapid descent along the deck. He ricochets off a crate and desperately tries to grab a hold, but he's moving too fast. Arms flailing and feet flying in every direction, he finally slams to a stop against the side of the boat nearest the catwalk.

On the other side of the boat, George is standing next to Roger, who is scanning the shoreline with his binoculars when they hear the crash. They run, zig-zagging through a stack of crates, to reach Sean as he is pulling himself up from the deck. George is about to offer help when he notices that *"License To Maim"* look in Sean's eye and decides not to act. Roger takes his cue from George and stands aside as well. Sean slowly rises and carefully, high-stepping in his diesel-slick shoes, he stalks off and quickly crosses the catwalk, then makes a bee line for his car.

"Wow—do you think he's abandoning the mission?" George worries aloud. "Maybe he's losing it!"

"Sean would *NEVER* abandon a mission! He doesn't lose it either. He's probably just going to take a break." Roger turns and heads to the other side of the boat to scan the western shoreline.

"Doesn't lose it? Wait until he sees his car," George mumbles to himself as he moves over to the end of the catwalk. Readying himself for a confrontation, he sits down on a crate next to the tranquilizer gun and watches as Sean approaches his beloved Aston.

Walking fast and furiously, Sean yanks open the car door and quickly hops in. He doesn't notice he's sitting in cow shit. He grasps the steering wheel with one hand and turns the ignition key with the other as he realizes both hands, the steering wheel, and the key are all covered with shit. Warm, sticky, slimy SHIT!

He looks down at the seat between his legs, down to his feet, over at the stick shift, and EVERYTHING is covered in SHIT!

Then... the smell hits him. He stiffens, takes a sharp, shallow breath, and almost chokes! His eyes begin to burn and tear up! Cow shit and cow piss ammonia that have been baking in the hot car smell just like George's shoes, only magnified a thousand times!

In a fury, Sean grabs the shit-covered door handle and pulls. His hand slips off, and he grabs it again. This time, pushing hard against the door with his shoulder, the door flies open and he flop-tumbles out of the car and slams onto the ground.

Landing on his back, Sean surveys his car from ground level. He's shocked by what he sees. SHIT IS EVERYWHERE! In total disbelief, he sits up, then struggles to his feet. Holding his arms away from his body, he looks at his shitty hands, his pants, his shoes, then back at his car. Stumbling around to the front of the Aston, he can see the shit-coated bumper pulled out into a perfect "V" shape, his 007 license plate so badly mangled it's not even legible! He explodes with a blood-curdling scream!

"I'll *KILL* that son-of-a-bitch!" Sean roars in anger.

George, watching the scene unfold, realizes he's going to have to protect himself. *Here he comes! He's got that look in his eyes! That's a 'License to Maim' look, all right!*

Sean, *consumed* with rage and with an overload of adrenaline flooding his system, goes into AUTO-KILL mode. He is now operating on AUTO-KILL!

George is intently watching Sean's approach when a cop car appears; it slows then drives directly down the ramp, right behind Sean. George nervously jumps up from the crate and knocks over the tranquilizer gun. It goes off with a silent POP, and a tranquilizer dart hits a rubber-coated life ring hanging near the boat cabin. The dart ricochets, and without a sound, hits Roger in the thigh as he stands looking through his binoculars. The impact comes at the precise moment that a gust of wind parts the banana tree leaves to reveal the voodoo-style scarecrow in a garden on the other side of the river.

"I'm HIT!" Roger yells. He thinks he's been hit with a poisonous voodoo dart. He pulls out the dart and throws it overboard. The fast-acting tranquilizer serum causes him to become weak in the knees, and he begins to wobble.

The cop car, responding to a call about pipeline vandalism, turns toward the boat and comes sliding to a screeching stop directly in between George and Sean, stopping Sean in his tracks and stifling the AUTO-KILL mode. With no place for his anger to go, he internalizes it and begins to shake violently. His senses go haywire. Suddenly, everything is silent. He can't hear or speak. Even his sense of smell goes numb, which is a saving grace since he's covered from head to toe in cow shit.

Two cops, Chief Basile and Officer Poole, jump out of their squad car with weapons drawn. They think George was reaching for the tranquilizer gun when it fell.

"*FREEZE!* Hands in the air! Don't move!"

George does as he's told, but Sean doesn't. The chief repeats the order even *louder* as Poole heads for the boat.

"HANDS IN THE AIR!" the chief yells.

Sean doesn't respond. He is shaking violently, his face flushing as his nostrils open and close rapidly with each heavy breath. Beads of sweat run down his forehead, and he stares blankly.

"Are you all right?" the chief, sensing Sean is ill, holsters his gun.

Sean staggers forward a bit, and the chief reaches out and leans him up against the car. Officer Poole strides across the catwalk, going after George. George, watching the exchange on the bank, doesn't say anything. He's trying to process so many things happening at once and, at the same time, trying to recall what action the Double O field manual would call for in such a situation. The song *"Trust Your Heart"* is blaring inside his head, and he decides on silence.

Officer Poole holsters his gun as he steps up to George, turns him around, leans him over the crate, and handcuffs him. The captain comes out of the wheelhouse on the upper deck just as George is being cuffed, and they have eye-to-eye contact. A heartfelt feeling passes between them.

By now, the tranquilizer has taken full effect on Roger, and he slides down the side of the boat and falls to the deck. The deckhand, standing in the doorway, rushes over. The captain is on the lower deck when Roger goes down, and he too runs over to help.

Officer Poole pushes the handcuffed George across the catwalk and leans him against the cop car and begins a body search. The chief is searching Sean.

"Find anything on that one?" the chief asks.

"Not yet. This guy's wearing a skirt. I don't know if he even has pockets."

"Check the front."

"Yeah. Here's an ID," Poole says.

"I've got an ID on this one too." The chief examines the contents of Sean's wallet. "It says James Bond/Universal Exports. That Lincoln Navigator we picked up in Krotz Springs was leased to Universal Exports!"

"I've got a James Bond here, too!" Poole exclaims.

"Photo ID with the *same* name? Hmmmm... interesting."

"Yeah, and this one works for Universal Exports, too!"

"Fake IDs!" the chief says. *That's violation number one right there,* he thinks to himself. "There's something wrong with this guy. He looks like he's having some sort of a seizure or stroke. I think he needs a doctor. Let's get these two in the car and see if there are more suspects, find out what the hell they're transporting!"

They lock Sean and George in the car and head across the catwalk onto the boat. The chief stops to pick up the tranquilizer gun.

"Hmmm... tranquilizer gun with a silencer, rather sophisticated," he says.

Suddenly, they hear a shout for help. They look up, and the deckhand is running toward them.

"Hey, there's a guy down over there!" he yells.

They all rush over to see Roger lying on the deck.

"Is he drunk or drugged?" the chief asks.

"Neither. He was just standing there looking through them binoculars one minute, and the next minute, he starts wobbling and staggering. He leaned up against the boat rail for a few seconds and then went down."

"Let's try leaning him up against the boat here." The chief bends down to Roger and lightly slaps his face. "Hey, wake up! Are you all right? What's your name?" He slaps again.

Mumbling an inaudible, "Bond, James Bond," Roger's eyelids flutter.

"This guy's out of it!" Poole says.

"Maybe he got hit with the tranquilizer gun. When it fell, it might have gone off. Check him for some ID, Poole." The chief turns as the captain comes on the scene. "Does somebody want to tell me what the hell's going on here?"

"I wish somebody would tell *me!*" The captain surveys the situation.

"You missed the best part!" The deckhand says to Chief Basile. "One of those crazy sombitches tried to steal a railroad truck and he drove it right off the trestle!"

"Which one stole the truck?" The chief is thinking, *violation number two: Theft of Railroad Property.*

"The first one you put in the car. He's lucky to be alive!" The deckhand motions toward the squad car.

"The one in the skirt or the other one?" the chief asks.

"The other one. He bailed out of that truck just in time... right before it sunk!"

"Sunk? The vehicle sunk?" *Violation number three,* the chief says to himself. *Destruction of Railroad Property.* "Who ARE these guys anyway?" he inquires.

"I don't know," the captain replies. "They never said much. We picked up their cargo in New Orleans and then picked them up under the 190 Bridge in Krotz Springs. It was the damnedest thing! We never picked up anyone under a bridge before; it's always at the dock. We got over here and they started messing with the pipeline. I thought they were pipeline people."

"So they were messing with the pipeline, huh?" *Violation number four: Tampering With Oil Field Property.* "Yeah. And the next thing you know, they had a hot air balloon out here on the deck!" The captain points.

"Hot air balloon?!"

"Yeah. Then this morning, it got away from them, and that's when they tried to steal the railroad truck. He damned near drowned!"

"There was another guy, too," the deckhand interjects. "A real wild-looking sombitch! But he left last night and never came back."

"What was he driving?" the chief asks.

"A brand new Lincoln Navigator."

"Bingo!" The chief looks over at Poole.

"Chief, look at this. You're not going to believe it!" Poole holds out a card.

"Not another same ID?"

"You got it!"

"There's some crazy shit going on around here! We'd better get these guys over to Dr. Bellefontaine's clinic and have them checked out. Especially the shit-covered one. He looks like he's having a seizure or a stroke or something."

"I *KNEW* it!" The deckhand turns to the captain. "Didn't I tell you he was headed for a stroke!"

The chief and his officer lift Roger by placing his arms over their shoulders, and they head for the catwalk. Roger's feet are dragging; he's pretty much dead weight. They get him across the catwalk and into the squad car.

"Just our luck! It's Sunday and no ferry!" the chief says to Poole. "Well, I'd better get going. It's a long drive over to the other side. Here's the crime scene tape. You stay and tape everything; I'll send backup and a search warrant."

The chief drives up the ramp and turns onto the levee headed for Krotz Springs. As they pull away, George looks through the back window of the car and makes eye contact with the captain once again.

The captain raises his hand in a small, uncertain wave.

The patrol radio goes off.

(SCRRRRR) . . . "Unit Two, to Unit One, come in! Come in, Unit One!"

(SCRRRRR) . . . "This is Unit One. Go ahead," the chief answers.

(SCRRRRR) . . . "We've picked up a suspect on that stolen vehicle out of Krotz Springs. But that's not all he stole!" Officer Wax says.

(SCRRRRR) . . . "Yeah, go ahead."

(SCRRRRR) . . . "It appears he ran the vehicle off the levee into the swamp and then helped himself to a drill buggy belonging to a seismograph outfit working down here."

(SCRRRRR) . . . "Have you got an ID on him?"

(SCRRRRR) . . . "Not yet. Backup just arrived, and Vaughn and Wane are bringing the guy out of the woods right now. From here, he looks to be a white male, mid-40s."

(SCRRRRR) . . . "Did anybody get hurt?"

(SCRRRRR) . . . "No, but we've got a *helluva* lot of damaged property on this end!"

(SCRRRRR) . . . "What kind of damage?"

(SCRRRRR) . . . "Well, for starters, he must have leveled about a hundred acres of wildlife refuge with that buggy! He was probably at it *all* night! We had to fire shots to get him off!" Wax exclaims.

(SCRRRRR) . . . "Damn! That's too bad about the refuge!" *Violation number five: destruction of Federal Land,* the chief says to himself. "What else?"

(SCRRRRR) . . . "Oh, seismograph equipment, tangled cables everywhere, not to mention the stolen car—it's probably totaled! Vaughn and Wane are bringing him up right now. Man, he looks violent! They're about to search him," Wax says. "I'll let you know if we get an ID."

Officer Vaughn shoves Timmy up against the police car. "Hands up, on the car! Let's go, spread 'em! Spread those feet! Anything in your pockets?" Timmy stares straight ahead with a crazed look in his eyes. When he doesn't answer, the officer goes in with both hands. "Oooff . . . ah . . . Damn! You PERVERT!" he yells.

"What?!" Wane's hand goes to his gun.

"This sombitch doesn't have any pockets! Oh, man! Damn!" He yells at Timmy. "I oughta *shoot* you!"

"Easy! Easy!" Officer Wane says.

"*I've got to* wash my hands in the ditch!" The officer heads for the ditch.

"Go ahead. I got him; he's not going nowhere."

(SCRRRRR) . . . "Unit One to Unit Two. Any ID on your guy yet?" the chief inquires.

(SCRRRRR) . . . "Nothing yet, I'll let you know," Wax responds. (SCRRRRR) . . . "As soon as you can, although I've got a pretty good idea what his name is. I'll catch you back at the station."

The chief hangs up his radio and takes a good look at the three Bonds in the back seat. He watches them through the security screen that separates the seats and sees Sean; full of cow shit, covered with diesel, and shaking. Roger; clean as a whistle but passed out and leaning against George, who is sitting quietly in the middle wearing his filthy kilt and ruffled shirt. The chief calls headquarters.

(SCRRRRR) . . . "Unit One to Base."

(SCRRRRR) . . . "This is Base. Go ahead, Unit One," the dispatcher says.

(SCRRRRR) . . . "Ah, Lynette, I need you to contact Dr. Bellefontaine and tell him we're bringing in, ah . . . what could be a couple of emergencies."

(SCRRRRR) . . . "Roger that. Will do. What is going on? Does it have anything to do with that pipeline call we got this morning?"

(SCRRRRR) . . . "All hell's broke loose on the east side of the river! That pipeline call was just the tip of the iceberg. I need you to call in all of our 'Off-Duties' and contact Judge Bordelon for a search warrant."

(SCRRRRR) . . . "ALL?!"

(SCRRRRR) . . . "ALL! We need every available man! There's a boat docked next to the East ramp. That's where I left Officer Poole. Get Officers Hearns and Bates to take our K-9 unit over to that boat and search the cargo. I want the area around the suspect boat, the East ramp, the base of the pipeline, and the railroad trestle thoroughly searched! Get a hold of Officers Taranto and Fertita. I want both our boats in the river. And I want both sides of the riverbanks checked south to Krotz Springs and north to Simmsport!"

(SCRRRRR) . . . "That's a 20-mile stretch! *What* is going on?!"

(SCRRRRR) . . . "We're not sure yet. Also, get a hold of Detective Coco. Have him run a background check on a James Bond and a Universal Exports. Have him start with the rental vehicle that was abandoned in Krotz Springs. There could be a connection."

(SCRRRRR) . . . "Roger that, will do. On an unrelated note, Ms. Rhodes called in and reported that someone tore up about a half-mile or so of her levee. She thinks it may have been cattle rustlers. She's doing a head count now and will get back to us on that."

(SCRRRRR) . . . "We saw that damage on the way up to the east ramp. She can count if she wants, but more than likely it's related to the pipeline, the railroad, Krotz Springs, the boat, and these suspects!" *Violation number six: destruction of private property,* the chief thinks to himself. "God only knows what else has happened out there! I just pray there are no bodies! This could all be terroristic! Go ahead and get busy rounding up those officers, dogs, boats, etcetera. We're pulling out all the stops on this one!"

(SCRRRRR) . . . "That's a *lot* of manpower and expense! It's Sunday. We're starting out on overtime! What about our budget?" the dispatcher queries.

(SCRRRRR) . . . "We've got that grant from Homeland Security we've been sitting on. Now's a good time to use it!"

(SCRRRRR) . . . "Do you want me to contact 'em?"

(SCRRRRR) . . . "Not just yet. Let's give it some time to unfold. The last thing we need right now is a 'boy-who-cried-wolf' scenario. Nonetheless, I want this investigation handled with microscopic scrutiny!"

(SCRRRRR) . . . "Should we attach a terror alert color code to this?" She reaches for the HLS Terror Alert Chart.

(SCRRRRR) . . . "Yeah, go ahead and code it *RAINBOW*. That way, if it escalates into a full-scale launch, we'll be covered! I'm about to cross the 190 Bridge. My E.T.A. is about ten minutes. We've got to move on this!"

(SCRRRRR) . . . "Roger that."

In the back seat, George has been listening to the conversation. *Ten minutes*, he thinks to himself.

They cross the bridge and take the first ramp to the right. Sand blasting and painting equipment at the bottom of the ramp indicate recent work on the bridge. The chief drives past the construction site and onto Hwy 105, which runs parallel to the river and along Melville's eastern levee.

This road's not impassable! George says to himself. *Another glitch in the intelligence!*

The chief approaches a sign that reads: 'MELVILLE twelve Miles.'

(SCRRRRR) . . . "Unit Two to Unit One. Come in, Unit One," Officer Wax says.

(SCRRRRR) . . . "This is Unit One. Go ahead," the chief replies.

(SCRRRRR) . . . "I've got an ID on that suspect."

(SCRRRRR) . . . "Let me guess . . . *JAMES BOND!*"

They've got Timmy! George thinks to himself.

(SCRRRRR) . . . "How'd you know?!" Wax blurts out.

(SCRRRRR) . . . "Because I've got three other suspects right now using that same name! It must be an alias!"

(SCRRRRR) . . . "Four guys using the same alias? You know their rap sheet has got to be a *mile* long!"

(SCRRRRR) . . . "Did your suspect say anything?" the chief inquires.

(SCRRRRR) . . . "No, but one look at him and you can tell he's a criminal!"

(SCRRRRR) . . . "Does he look injured in any way?"

(SCRRRRR) . . . "He's got a black eye and a pretty bad limp," Wax replies.

(SCRRRRR) . . . "I'm gonna run these three through Dr. Bellefontaine's clinic to have them checked out. We'd better do the same with that one you've got. These guys are foreigners. There could be international implications. We need to be very thorough with all of this or it could end up in a media frenzy. We want to cover all the bases and our *asses!* Leave a couple officers out there. I want a full report on all the damages and have the car he stole crime-taped and towed to the station." *Violation number seven, stolen vehicle.* The chief makes a mental note.

(SCRRRRR) . . . "Roger that. My E.T.A. is about eight minutes," Wax says.

(SCRRRRR) . . . "Mine's about the same," the chief responds.

The road is long and winding, but the eight minutes seem to fly by. In no time flat, they pass over the south levee and enter Melville.

Hmmm . . . more levees. At least that piece of intelligence was correct, George observes from his back seat.

The area within the levees is only about two square miles. The first thing George notices is a quaint little school to the left. The next thing that catches his attention is the many different churches in such a small area. There are three or four churches along the main drag, with a dozen more steeples dotting the horizon of the tiny town.

There must be about twenty or thirty churches in this town of maybe a thousand people. It feels so peaceful here, and like there's a spirit of great tolerance toward all the different faiths. George ponders the thought.

Up the road is the clinic, a small brick building equipped to handle minor emergencies but specializing in mental illness. Right next door is the police station. The songs *"Trust Your Heart,"* and *"We Have All the Time in the World"* are playing in George's head as they come to a stop sign. Across the intersection is a Founder's Day tribute billboard proudly proclaiming:

MELVILLE: Founded 1889 . . . Population 1,376

Both squad cars reach the clinic from opposite directions at the same time and pull into the parking area side by side. The chief looks over at the other car, and he and Timmy eyeball each other. The chief is alarmed by the maniacal look on Timmy's face and perceives him as a real threat. All the chief's senses are on heightened alert as he exits the vehicle with his hand on his gun. Officers Wax and Wane exit their cruiser as Officer Cottrell comes out of the station. They all converge on the sidewalk in front of the clinic.

"Damn! He's a criminal, all right!" the chief says, looking back at Timmy.

"We know his type!" Officer Cottrell slaps his blackjack against his palm.

"Man, he sure did a number on those woods!" Wax exclaims. "That sombitch! Some of that refuge was virgin forest!" The chief turns to Wane. "Go see if you can give Lynette a hand calling those volunteer officers."

Some of the clinic staff emerge from the building. A short, heavyset, round-faced white nurse with thick, loud makeup named Debra and a short, heavyset, round-faced black orderly named Mosley are on opposite sides of a gurney being pushed outside. A stern-looking, no-nonsense nurse named Hebert is pushing a wheelchair.

"Y'all might want to use the gurney for the one on the right in the back seat. He can't walk at all," the chief offers. "And use the wheelchair for the guy on the other side. I think he may have had a stroke or something."

"Damn! Sa puew! He sure does stink!" Mosley shakes his head. "What about the one in the other cruiser?" Cottrell points toward Timmy.

"Better put leg irons on that one; keep the cuffs on him, too. He looks like he might try and make a break for it." The chief looks worriedly at Timmy.

"This guy must have fallen in cow shit!" Nurse Hebert says as she helps adjust Sean in the wheelchair. She looks over at George in his kilt. "And him, he's sure dressed kind of strange for these parts," she says, rolling her eyes.

Nurse Debra and Orderly Mosley struggle to lift Roger onto the stretcher. He is semi-conscious and can barely hear or see. Everything is a blur to him. The nurse and orderly crisscross each other several times while positioning Roger on the stretcher and strapping him down. For a moment, they are standing next to each other, and both being round-faced and about the same height and weight, although different skin colors, their images blend in Roger's blurry vision, and

121

he perceives them as one entity, emerging as a *voodoo* figure! Roger suddenly stiffens and jerks; his eyes fly wide open, and he tries to sit up. As the orderly steps away from Nurse Debra, the movement disrupts the blended image, and Roger returns to his tranquilized condition.

"He looks like he's having some sort of panic attack," Nurse Debra observes. "We'd better hurry and get him inside the clinic!" The two begin to push the gurney toward the door.

"Wait!" Nurse Hebert propels Sean in the wheelchair ahead of the gurney. "Let me in first! Doc will want to see this one *right away!* His condition looks more serious than the others!"

The chief holds the door open as the procession into the clinic begins. Nurse Hebert is in the lead with Sean, stroke-like and shaking uncontrollably, handcuffed and covered in cow shit. His face is bright red and his nostrils are flaring. Roger is on the gurney, as Nurse Debra and Orderly Mosley roll him in zig-zag fashion into the clinic. George, handcuffed, in his grimy kilt and wrinkled, ruffled shirt, is hop-walked by Officer Wax holding onto his elbow. Taking up the rear is Timmy in leg irons and handcuffs. In torn, filthy clothes, with a swollen black eye, he limps along, covered in grease and mud from head to toe. Officer Cottrell strongholds him by the arm, leading him through the door and up to the reception desk.

"Is Dr. Bellefontaine on his way up front?" Nurse Hebert asks Anna, the receptionist, also the doctor's daughter.

"Yes. He was making his rounds through the ward. He's on his way."

George and Timmy are told to sit down and directed into chairs apart from each other just as Sean has another *violent* shiver.

"Better page the *doc, NOW! CODE BLUE!* This guy's in bad shape!" Nurse Hebert holds Sean down in the wheelchair.

(SCRRRRR) . . . "Code BLUE in the main lobby! Code BLUE, again!" Anna keys the PA mic.

Suddenly, Timmy leaps from his chair.

"SIT DOWN!" Cottrell says loudly to Timmy.

"But that's my cue!"

"Sit down or it'll be your ASS!"

Timmy sits back down. *That must have been my cue!* he says to himself as he reverts to his agent-like mode, his shifty eyes darting from side to side. Standing near the door, the chief and Wax keep a close eye on him.

"Isn't that the most violent-looking sombitch you've ever seen?" Wax says.

"Criminal to the *core!*" the chief replies. "I'm anxious to see what Detective Coco digs up on him!"

"I wouldn't be surprised if he's on America's Ten Most Wanted list!"

"Oh, I'll guarantee you, he's wanted for something!"

"That one in the skirt looks harmless," Wax surmises.

George sits quietly in his corner, mentally humming along with the tunes playing in his head.

"Oh, I doubt *any* of them are harmless!" the chief voices his concern.

Just then, the doctor comes rushing through the swinging doors. "Do we have a *Code BLUE* here?!" he asks Anna.

"It's this one right here, Doc," Nurse Hebert pushes her charge forward.

The doctor takes a quick look at Sean. "Get him in the exam room, STAT!"

The doc, followed by Nurse Hebert pushing Sean in the wheelchair, Orderly Mosley, and the chief take off down the corridor. Chief Basile yells back to Wax and Cottrell, "You two, stay and keep a close eye on those two! Don't let them outta your sight!"

"Let's get him up here!" The doc gestures toward the exam table. "Damn, he stinks! Where did you find this guy . . . in some barn? He's full of cow shit!"

The orderly, Nurse Hebert, and Chief Basile struggle to lift Sean onto the table as he aggressively thrashes about, his arms and legs shaking uncontrollably. They try to hold him still as the doctor attempts to examine Sean's eyes with a small penlight. "Give me a blood pressure—STAT!" the doctor yells out.

Back in the lobby, the receptionist Anna asks Wax, "Can we get a name on any of these guys?"

"Bond, James Bond," Timmy stands up and announces.

"Yeah, right. SHUT UP! AND SIT DOWN!" Cottrell yells.

"We're having a bit of a problem with names right now," Wax says to Anna.

"That's so strange." Anna leans over to Wax and says softly. "His first name and last name are the same, and the middle name is James. I wonder what his parents were on when they named him?"

In the examination room, Nurse Hebert is desperately trying to wrap a blood pressure cuff around Sean's arm.

"What's the story on that blood pressure?" the doc asks as he places his stethoscope first one place, then another. "Quick, what is it!?"

"I'm trying as best I can!" the nurse replies in frustration. "What do you think, Doc? A stroke or what?"

The doc doesn't answer at first, as he's intently focusing on Sean. He moves his stethoscope around Sean's chest. "I'm just not sure," he says finally.

"Blood pressure, 300 over 220!" Nurse Hebert announces loudly.

"My God, that's off the charts! Let me have that!" The doc frantically grabs the blood pressure pump and rechecks Sean himself. "DAMN! If this ain't a stroke, it ought to be! Quick, give me 20 cc's of Perzonia and 30 cc's of Quintellizine . . . STAT!"

Nurse Hebert quickly fills two syringes and hands them to the doc. He just as quickly injects one after the other in Sean's backside. Immediately, Sean's shaking goes from violent to barely noticeable, and he becomes calmer.

"I never saw anything like that in all my years of medicine!" the doc says, amazed.

"Well, is it a stroke?"

"With all the symptoms he evidenced, you would think so, but I don't see any paralysis." He leans over and speaks to Sean. "Are you feeling any pain?"

Sean does not respond.

Moving his finger back and forth in front of Sean's eyes, the doc sees a slight response. "What's your name? Can you hear me?" The doc snaps his fingers near Sean's ears; still, there's no response.

"We've been having a bit of a problem with identification," the chief offers.

"He can't hear. I don't think he can speak, either. It looks like . . . what was he doing when you apprehended him?" the doc asks.

"He was walking."

"Walking normally?"

"Kind of fast, but straight. He was going downhill, toward the boat ramp on the east side of the river."

"You know, this looks like RRD."

"What's that?" the chief asks.

"RAGE REFLEX DISEASE," the doc answers.

"You mean like Acid Reflux Disease?"

"They sound alike but are quite different. *Reflex* is a bending back, whereas *reflux* is a flowing outward. I think he swallowed a scream!"

"WHAT?!" The chief is incredulous.

"He *swallowed a scream*. It's rare. I've only read about it. I've never seen it. In theory, it's a combination of adrenaline and raging anger flooding the central nervous system and then suddenly stifling and locking up the system. With nowhere to vent, this response is turned inward and internalized, similar to the immune system attacking itself."

"Rage ingestion?" The chief looks puzzled.

"Precisely! It blocks all of the senses and temporarily paralyzes the motor skills, causing temporary problems such as blurred vision and the inability to speak, hear, or smell . . . which in his case is a *good* thing! But he can still comprehend what's going on around him. That's why, when you look in his eyes, you can still see someone home."

"He appeared to have a stroke or seizure," the doc continues.

"Because of the convulsive shaking and combative behavior. But like I said before, with no visible paralysis, I can rule out the stroke side of it. With that high blood pressure, he's lucky he didn't completely blow his stack and have a full-blown stroke or even expire! I've never seen blood pressure that high! I don't know what the record is, but the Guinness people might be interested in this." The doc turns to Nurse Hebert. "What's his BP now, Nurse?"

"It's coming down some . . . 250 over 190."

"That's still *very* high."

"How soon will he be able to talk? I've got a lot of questions for him," the chief asks.

"That's hard to say. When he swallowed that scream, his larynx was temporarily paralyzed. That was probably the first motor skill to go."

"He was sure fighting us when we tried to handle him!"

"He wasn't doing the fighting. The combativeness is a central nervous system reflex. It's a result of the arrested rage pent up inside. Because of the paralyzed larynx, he can't verbalize the scream. In other words, he can't let it out. He internalized it, and it's seeping into his muscular skeletal system, fueled by the overload of adrenaline in his nervous system. The scream is trying to come out any way it can. That accounts for the convulsive combativeness. The symptoms will gradually dissipate in a day or two, and he should return to normal."

"That's a pretty amazing theory, but you know what else it sounds like? A very *violent* criminal backed into a corner! I'd better take him to jail. When he comes out of it, no telling what will happen! He could be *extremely* violent! He'd be better off behind bars when that happens!"

"Are you *CRAZY?!* You can't take him to jail! He needs to be closely monitored. He's coming apart at the seams! Or should I say, he's *SCREAMING* apart at the seams?! Oh no, you can't take him to jail! He *must* be monitored! His blood pressure could continue to spike. His convulsiveness could become contorted. At his age, his bones are very brittle, and the violent shaking could cause multiple fractures! Oh no, you absolutely can't take him to jail! In fact, you need to take these cuffs off him right now!" the doctor says sternly.

"*ARE YOU CRAZY?* He might have some of what you say, but I know criminals and . . ." the chief is adamant.

"*No, I'M not crazy!* Let's compromise and put a straitjacket on him. That way, he can't contort and hurt himself. We'll clean him up and keep him medicated and calm."

"Oh no, Doc. That's where I draw the line. You can't clean him up! You could be destroying crucial DNA evidence. I've got a major crime spree on my hands out there! It could even be terroristic in nature! There could be dead bodies out there! Not no, but *HELL NO!* You will not be allowed to clean him up! He'll have to stay like that until I see how this investigation unfolds!"

"OK. Fair enough. We'll put him in the dayroom where he can be monitored from the nurse's station. We'll give him another shot and put him in the straitjacket." The doc turns to Nurse Hebert. "Nurse, get on the PA and have all of the other patients cleared out of the dayroom, please."

(SCRRRRR) . . . "Clear the dayroom, please. Clear the dayroom immediately!"

Upon hearing Nurse Hebert's PA request, Timmy once again jumps up from his seat.

"SIT DOWN!" Cottrell yells at him.

"That's my . . ." Timmy begins.

Officer Cottrell squeezes the handle on his black jack. "I am WARNING you! There's nothing we'd love more than to tear into a sombitch like you!" He looks over at the office staff. "Pardon my French, ladies." Then back to Timmy. "Go ahead, try something! I'm begging you!"

I'd better do as he says, Timmy thinks to himself. He'd probably really hit me just like that idiot in the bar scene! In these low-budget productions, the actors aren't trained too well! Timmy sits back down and once again drifts back into his Bond-ness.

Meanwhile, back in the examination room, they've managed to get the straitjacket on Sean. Looking like a moth in a cocoon, he's placed back into the wheelchair, and Nurse Hebert wheels him down the hall and into the dayroom.

"I'll park you right over here near the window so you can take in some of the scenery," Nurse Hebert says soothingly. "I've got to go and help the doc. Nurse Ashley is right over there in the nurse's station in case you need anything."

Nurse Hebert was speaking to Sean out of habit rather than actual conversation because she knows he can't hear. Sean's eyesight is beginning to clear, and he slowly surveys the room in true Bond-like fashion. The room is about 20' × 30', with a door on each end and one in the middle for the nurse's station and observation room. Everything is painted a drab institutional green. Windows line the outside wall and the front of the nurse's station. The window glass is thick, double-paned, with diamond-shaped wire mesh between the panes. There's also a large, octagon-shaped steel picnic table with benches all around.

It's all welded together and bolted to the floor, like something you would see in a jail's bullpen. In one corner, high up on the wall, is a TV bolted to a shelf. In the nurse's station is Nurse Ashley, a beautiful young woman who is updating patients' charts. Meanwhile, back in the waiting room, Roger is lying on the gurney and gazing up at Nurse Debra.

"Hey, baby!" Roger moans in a groggy, almost inaudible voice. His vision is blurred, and he tries to focus.

The swinging doors open, and Orderly Mosley tells Nurse Debra to bring Roger to the exam room. She rolls the gurney through the doors and down the hall and into the examination room where the doc is waiting. Nurse Hebert and the chief follow along behind them.

"Roll him over here and let's get him on the table," the doc says. "One, two, three, LIFT! I love this kind of stuff! This is real medicine! It reminds me of my residency days. Unlike psychiatry, there's never a dull moment. OK . . . give me a BP and a temp . . . STAT!"

The doc leans over Roger, checking his pupils. "He's not seeing much! This guy's out of it! He's either drunk or drugged. Do you feel pain anywhere?" he asks Roger, then turns to the chief. "What do you know about him?"

Roger moans and tries to focus. "Hey, baby," he says with a slurred voice.

"I believe he was shot with a tranquilizer gun," the chief says.

"A *what?*" the doc asks.

"A tranquilizer gun misfired just as we arrived. It may have hit him."

"BLOOD PRESSURE is 60 over 35," Nurse Hebert announces.

"That's kind of low." The doc looks concerned

"TEMPERATURE is 96 degrees," she says.

"OK. Let's get him stripped and look for an entry wound." The doc steps back from the table and turns to the chief. "You know, I don't know why I ever went into psychiatry. It can be so boring at times. On the other hand, this kind of action can really get your juices flowing!"

On the exam table, Roger is undressed by Nurse Debra on his right and Nurse Hebert on his left. They remove his safari jacket and belt, then his shirt. They unzip his pants while Orderly Mosley removes his shoes and socks. Roger, even in his semi-conscious condition, realizes two women are removing his clothes. He pours on the *"Oh baby's"* one after the other, but his words are so garbled that it sounds like one continuous moan.

"Sounds like he's in pain! Let's go! Hurry up!" the doc admonishes.

"We're going as fast as we can, Doc!" Nurse Hebert replies. The two nurses, listening to Roger's mumbling, begin to chuckle.

"Listen to this old fart!" Nurse Hebert whispers to Nurse Debra. "Wonder what he thinks is going on."

The nurses have a hard time unzipping Roger's pants, but finally, the zipper comes down and his pants fly open. The nurses can't help themselves, and they both burst into laughter.

"WOW!" Nurse Debra exclaims.

"What's so funny?" the doc turns back to the patient.

"He may be out of it, but one thing's working just fine!" Nurse Hebert laughs.

"Oh b . . . b . . . b . . . baby!" Roger tries to articulate.

"Come on . . . at his age . . . on a tranquilizer? Impossible!" the doc, looking over, exclaims. "He must be a *heavy* Viagra user, or that tranquilizer could carry a Viagra component and it's working in an uptake fashion. Hey, get it? *Uptake!*" He laughs at his joke.

Orderly Mosley, standing alongside the exam table, moves in front of Nurse Debra and into Roger's view. Their faces blend in his blurred vision and turn into a voodoo figure. Roger is so startled his eyes pop open really wide, and he looks scared to death! He sucks in his breath, his heart races, and his body begins to jerk about wildly! The orderly grabs Roger's legs to hold him down.

The doc rushes over. "Calm down! Calm down! It's OK! It's OK!"

Gradually, the blurred image dissipates and Roger drifts back into his semi-conscious state. Once again, his hungry gaze is directed toward the two nurses.

"He had a similar episode when we were taking him out of the cop car. It's like a panic attack," Nurse Debra says.

"He could be having an allergic reaction to the tranquilizer," the doc offers. "We're going to need some blood work on him and an EKG. I just *love* this kind of doctoring. I feel like I'm back in the trenches again, working the ER. Did anyone find that point of entry?"

"Here it is, Doc! Just above the knee!" The orderly points excitedly.

"The wound is indicative of the standard .012 mm small animal dart. The reddish discoloration around the entry site could be an allergic reaction or the beginning of a bruise from being hit at close range," the doc surmises.

"I think it was a ricochet, Doc, from about 20 ft," the chief offers.

"Yeah, well, we need to find out what type of tranquilizer it was. We'll get a urine specimen in case the drug doesn't show up in the blood work. It might be easier to detect in urine, and we'll get a diagnosis quicker."

"Get a urine sample out of him? He's almost passed out!" Nurse Debra says.

"Catheterize him!" The doc gestures toward Roger's private parts. "That shouldn't be a problem. You've got *plenty* to work with!" He laughs.

The chief, standing out of the way, was anxiously waiting for some kind of diagnosis. "Is he going to be all right?" he asks the doc.

"Well, for the time being, all of his vitals seem to be OK, with the exception of a slightly irregular heartbeat. That could be because of the current blood distribution in his body and the excitement associated with the . . . uh . . . erection. I'll know more when I get the results of his EKG and lab work."

The chief gives a sideways glance toward Roger's lower half. "Well, ah, good, then. So, if all his tests pan out, I'll just take him on to jail. He can sleep it off there."

"*Are you CRAZY?!* You can't take him to jail! Didn't you see the reaction he had a few minutes ago? Oh no, he needs to be . . ."

"Let me guess . . . *MONITORED!*" the chief offers with a sneer.

"Exactly! At least until we figure out what kind of tranquilizer he was hit with, the level of the drug in his system, and whether or not he's having an allergic reaction to it. He could go into anaphylactic shock! He could slip into a coma! Or, worst case scenario . . . it could *KILL* him!"

"If none of that happens, how long will it take for him to come out of this condition?"

"Well, that's difficult to say. Depending on the type of tranquilizer, it might contain a timed-release component, and that's another good reason for monitoring him. At his age, his metabolism is slow. The tranquilizer could build up in his system and overload it. I'm sure his detoxification capabilities aren't that great, either."

"*HOW LONG, DOC?*" the chief asks, trying to control his frustration.

"You're probably looking at a day or two, at the very least, before he comes out of it, and the after-effects could linger on for as much as a week."

"Isn't there some kind of antidote you could give him?"

"Sure. But I would have to know the *exact* type of tranquilizer he was hit with. As soon as his lab work comes back, I'll get in touch with the local veterinarian, Dr. Fonteneau. He may have an antidote on hand, or at the very least, he might have access to one. But even if we got an antidote, it wouldn't work right away."

"We've got the tranquilizer gun; we could check for chemical residue and maybe get some idea of what was in the dart. Isn't there *something* you can give him to speed things up?" the chief queries.

"Well . . . there is something that may move the drug more quickly through his system, but it's very risky and could result in heart or liver failure. Tranquilizers are designed to immobilize, and they're pretty powerful. You don't want to *permanently immobilize him*, do you?" the doc asks.

"*NO!* I'll check for residue on that tranquilizer gun and maybe come up with something."

"Go ahead, but you better be *absolutely* sure that you recover the complete chemical composition of the tranquilizer! If he's given the wrong antidote, it could *KILL* him! I think it's best to let him gently ride it out."

"I agree; I just don't know why he can't *gently* ride it out in jail!"

"Why are you so *hell-bent* on taking him to jail? It's just right next door! You could bust a hole in the wall, and he'd be in jail!" The doc shakes his head in exasperation.

"You don't understand, Doc. When criminals find themselves on the wrong side of the bars, they feel like a caged animal! That gives us, in law enforcement, a lot of leverage toward getting a confession and solving crimes. It gives us a *psychological advantage*. It rips at their guts, and they usually spill them! A man in your position, being a shrink and all, surely you can understand that."

"I understand that, but I have a job to do as well. If I release him and you take him to jail and he takes a turn for the worse and dies, you could be setting the city up for a major lawsuit, not to mention what it would do to my malpractice insurance! *I could lose my license!*"

"Yeah," the chief sighs disgustedly. "I guess you're right."

"I *know* I'm right! Look, these guys may have been involved in some major crimes, but considering their medical conditions, they're more patients than prisoners right now."

"Well, I suppose you're right, Doc, but don't forget, they were prisoners *first!* And I'm going to be keeping a 24-hour guard on them."

"I'll put this guy in the dayroom, along with the other one. The windows are double-paned glass with inset wire. They'll be perfectly secure in there. It's not the same as bars, but the effect is along the same lines."

"Are you kidding me, Doc? If it was bulletproof glass, maybe. But to hardened criminals of their caliber, those windows are a *joke!* In fact, I better post Officer Wane outside those windows in case of an attempted escape!"

"You can also position your officers in the nurse's station if you like. They'll have a full view of the patients, er . . . prisoners at all times. We have cameras in the dayroom; we can monitor and document everything. You know, in case anything goes wrong. We can all cover our asses!"

"All right, that sounds good. But as soon as those lab tests come back and they start improving, they're both going to jail!"

"Fair enough, I guess. We'll play it by ear. Now, what about the other two back in the waiting room?"

"The one in the leg irons was in an auto accident. He's got a bad limp and a black eye. The one in the kilt, well, maybe he's just plum crazy!"

"OK. We'll address the one with the medical needs first." The doc turns to leave.

"Oh no, Doc! I'm getting first crack at that one! I've wasted too much time already!" the chief insists.

"But he could be *seriously* injured!"

"He didn't look like he was in too much pain to me. It's important for us to interrogate him fresh from the crime, before he has a chance to start formulating lies and alibis. We can't give him any more time to think!"

"It's your call, but I wouldn't leave the clinic with him," the doc warns.

"Why not?"

"He could have internal injuries. After an auto accident and walking around injured . . . you never know. He could be fine one minute and collapse the next! I've seen it a *thousand* times!"

"Yeah, you're probably right," the chief sighs in resignation.

"You can use my office to interrogate him."

"What color is it? Color and criminals have a connection when it comes to confessions."

"The walls are painted *FIRE ENGINE RED!*" The doc smiles broadly.

"FIRE ENGINE RED?!" the chief exclaims.

"Yeah. A while back, I was writing a paper on aggression, and I purposely had my office painted red. Then I added four 6-foot fluorescent lights. All in an 8' x 10' room! It's quite stimulating, to say the least!"

"Good! Maybe it'll piss him off enough to make 'em crack!"

"What about the one in the skirt?" the doc asks.

"He ought to be right up your alley! He's not injured, just give him a medical once-over, enough to cover our ass and try to determine if he's sane enough to stand trial. A guy like that would try to cop an insanity plea in a heartbeat!"

"Well, I'm ready for number three!" The doc starts to leave.

"OK. Let's go get 'em."

"Hold it a minute." The doc turns to Nurse Hebert and points to Roger. "You'd better strap him down for that catheterization."

"He didn't move a muscle when we took blood samples. He's *really* out of it!"

"Strap him down anyway. Can't be too careful. After you're finished, put him in the dayroom with the other one, and get that blood work to the lab, STAT!"

Roger hears the muffled noises around him, and his vision is still blurred. As he's being strapped down, he's aware of hands touching him.

"Oh yeah, baby! Oh yeah, whatever you like! Come on! Whatever you want! Oh yeah, baby, I'm yours!" Roger begins to moan as the chief and doc leave the exam room and head down the hall toward the waiting room.

The receptionist, Anna, smiles at them as they come through the swinging doors into the room where Officers Wax and Cottrell are guarding George and Timmy. George is fixated on Anna because of her striking resemblance to the actress who played Evangeline in the musical he watched back on the boat with the captain. Timmy is anxiously awaiting his next cue.

"Do you hear something? Do you hear something?" Timmy asks George.

The doc, seeing the intensity on both George and Timmy's faces, recognizes the abnormal behavior of Timmy's repeated question about hearing something. A red flag goes up. *The chief only sees one criminal fraternizing with another!* The chief points toward George. "All right, *YOU!*" he says loudly. "Go with the doc! Cottrell, I want you standing right outside the exam room."

George and the doc enter a small examination room behind the reception area. As they pass through the doorway, Cottrell closes the door behind them and assumes a guard-post stance.

The chief looks over at Timmy and locks eyes with him in a tough, standoff stare.

"*YOU* must be the director!" Timmy declares loudly.

"On your feet!" the chief commands, ignoring Timmy's comment.

"Now, stand right there beside Officer Wax," he instructs.

Angry with himself for forgetting his walkie-talkie, the chief picks up the clinic phone. "This is the chief," he says. "I'm going to be over here at the clinic for a while. As soon as Detective Coco gets any new leads on Operation Rainbow, have him contact me."

"I'll take care of that immediately," the dispatcher says.

"All right, let's go." The chief hangs up the phone and heads for the doorway.

Officer Wax grabs Timmy by the arm, and they follow the chief through the swinging doors and down the hallway.

Finally, they're ready for the next scene. Timmy mumbles to himself.

They pass the exam room where Roger is about to be catheterized. Nurse Debra and Orderly Mosley are on opposite sides of the gurney and have repeatedly tried to insert the catheter but are having problems. Roger continues to moan and groan.

"Oh baby! Oh baby! Oh baby!" Roger says huskily.

Orderly Mosley and Nurse Debra lean over Roger and once again try to insert the catheter. Roger opens his eyes only to see two faces waver above him, then blend into a voodoo monster image.

"Aahhhhhhhhhhhhhh!" he screams in terror. His body stiffens and his eyes fly wide open! Everyone in the clinic hears Roger scream! In the hallway, Timmy stops and hesitates at the exam room door.

"KEEP MOVING!" the chief commands.

The doc and George hear Roger's screams. "Have you ever known your buddy on the gurney to have panic attacks?" the doc asks.

"No, not that I know of," George answers.

The chief, Officer Wax, and Timmy arrive at the doc's office. It looks like the other small office, with one door that has a 2' × 4' window in it and the wire inset glass. The chief opens the door and turns on the light in the RED room. He reels backward from the intensity of the red and the glare of the lights. "DAMN!" he says, stepping aside to let Timmy pass on into the room. "Go ahead and have a seat behind the desk," the chief instructs.

Stepping back into the hallway, the chief closes the door behind Timmy. He and Officer Wax watch through the window in the door and discuss their strategy. The colorful room doesn't seem to bother Timmy at all.

"Man, *that room!*" exclaims Officer Wax. "Who in their right mind paints an office FIRE ENGINE RED and then puts in a million watts of light to bounce off the friggin' walls?"

"I don't know, some bullshit study the doc was doing. When he said it was *FIRE ENGINE RED,* he wasn't shittin'!"

"Have you ever seen a more violent-looking criminal?" Officer Wax muses, looking through the window at Timmy.

"Nope, never!" The chief tightens his lips.

"I've got to admit, he kinda scares me!" Wax offers.

"Well, he don't scare me! I've been wanting a piece of a sombitch like him for a long time. We'll good cop or bad cop him. I'll play the *heavy.* He'll spill his guts or I'll rip *'em out!*" The chief hitches up his pants for emphasis.

The chief and Officer Wax, having finished discussing their *plan of attack,* return to the RED room ready to start the interrogation.

"Hey man, if I'm going to play this scene . . ." Timmy blurts out to the chief.

"*Scene?* What do you mean, *scene?* We don't talk that hippie shit over here!"

"I've got to get to wardrobe," Timmy says, ignoring the chief's comment.

"Oh, don't worry about that. We'll get you fixed up all right . . . maybe something in a nice *ORANGE JUMPSUIT!*" The chief checks over the police report. "I'm more interested in why you were fighting in that bar last night and making verbal threats." He looks up from the report.

"Those people could use a few lessons. They didn't know what the hell they were doing!" Timmy replies.

"And I guess you were just the guy to teach them!"

"Somebody had to. It was mostly improvisational. I had to . . ."

"Carrying a concealed weapon . . ." The chief flips through his papers.

"It was a *PROP!*" Timmy interrupts.

"It was *CONCEALED!* And what about stealing that car?"

"Again, improvisation. It's what the scene called for," Timmy shrugged.

"What'd I tell you about that scene shit?" the chief reminds him. "Hey, just give it to us straight," Officer Wax interjects.

"So that's how you operate. Improvising at any given moment by *'doing or taking'* whatever you want! Whatever the *'scene'* calls for!" the chief glares.

"Well, yeah. When you're in a pinch, it's the only way to keep rolling."

The chief tries to control his anger; he can't believe the casualness of Timmy's comments and his arrogant demeanor.

"I guess that's why after you crashed the stolen car into the swamp, you stole that exploration vehicle and proceeded to mow down the forest!"

The chief's remark about the forest reminds Timmy of his arrest. He looks down at the table, and shifting his eyes back and forth, he drifts back into his Bond mode. Just then, Detective Coco, holding another report in his hand, knocks on the door. The chief goes out into the hall and speaks to Coco, who briefs him about the boat. Meanwhile, George and the doc are in another office talking. The doc is sitting behind his desk with George in front. George keeps turning his head toward the door to look out the window.

"So how are you feeling?" the doc asks in his best clinical fashion. "You look a bit nervous and kind of sad. Are you OK? Are you in any pain? Are you injured anywhere?"

"To tell you the truth, I've been trying to figure out what's real and what's not."

Patient having trouble with reality and the other guy in the waiting room hearing imaginary sounds. Could be schizophrenia. The doc writes in his pad.

"Everything has been happening so fast. And I've got these songs playing in my head, and they just won't stop." George puts his hands to his head for emphasis.

"Songs . . . so there's more than one song?" *Another schizophrenic symptom. Hearing one song is sometimes normal, but not more than one.* The doc makes another notation. "And what are these songs like? Are they loud?" he asks.

"There are two songs, one old and one new. But no, they're not loud. They're nice songs, but they just won't stop. And I'm wrestling with this classification/status problem."

Experiencing delusions of grandeur. The doc writes. "Is there anything else bothering you?" he asks.

"Yes. It seems that I've been questioning myself a lot lately."

"What kind of questions?"

"Oh, nothing specific. Just questions like . . . what if this or maybe that."

"Are these what ifs and maybes of a serious nature?"

George is reluctant to reveal more information than necessary.

Sensing George's reluctance, the doc quickly changes the subject back to the songs. "So, the songs you hear, are they popular ones you've heard lately? You know, it's not uncommon for a person to hear a song early in the morning and carry the tune throughout the day. But two songs playing simultaneously, that's not common." *Another sign of schizophrenia . . . classic case of 'split mind,'* the doc notes.

"Yeah, well, I don't know." George looks around the room in confusion.

"You know, I'm a bit of a music buff myself," the doc offers. "What are the songs you hear? Maybe I know them."

"The old song is, *'We Have All the Time in the World.'*"

"I'm not familiar with that one. How does it go? Can you sing a few words?"

"We have all the time in the world." George begins to sing. *"Time enough for life to unfold all the precious gifts life has in store."*

"I don't think I know that one, but it sounds beautiful. How long has it been playing in your head?"

"About thirty years." George turns to look out the window at the receptionist.

Has no concept of time, another indicator, symptoms stacking up.

The doc hurriedly writes. "And what about the new song?"

"Oh, I heard that one for the first time last night on the boat with the captain. It's very powerful. It makes me feel and think about things like never before."

"What's that song? Maybe I know it."

"It's called *'Trust Your Heart.'* It goes something like this . . . *Sometimes you just cannot trust what you see with your eyes; sometimes your ears only hear mere conjecture and lies. All your senses may betray what's true . . .*"

Doc picks up the next line . . . *"Sometimes to see your way clear and to hear the voice of God, you must turn from your senses and learn to trust your heart."*

"You *KNOW* it! You *KNOW* the song!" George exclaims excitedly.

"Oh yes! It's from the musical Evangeline."

"Yes! I watched it last night on the boat. The captain knows it backwards and forwards! He knows it by heart. He seems so *REAL!*"

"Lots of people around here know the musical, but sadly, there are so many more who have never heard its message. Why do you think *that* song, out of all the songs in the musical, stuck with you? Is it because of this *'real'* aspect that you're trying to figure out? You know, that's exactly what the song is all about. It causes a person to question himself, even if he has no desire to know what is real and what is not. You're right; it's a very powerful song."

George turns again to look out the door window. "Yes, I know," he says softly.

"You keep looking out the window. What do you see?" the doc asks.

"That woman, the receptionist. She looks like the woman who played Evangeline in the musical."

Doc leans over the desk to look through the window. "Yes, come to think of it, she does. That's my daughter Anna; she's studying to be a psychologist."

Just then, Detective Coco stops by Anna's desk for a quick chat before heading back to the station. George is stunned at the resemblance of Detective Coco to Gabriel in the *Evangeline* musical. He begins a mental inventory of all that has been happening: seeing the similarities of Anna/Evangeline and Coco/Gabriel, the two songs playing continuously in his head, the ongoing conflict of Inactive/ Active/Standby, thirty years spent in his garage with the same car, the what-ifs and maybes, and to top it all off, a multitude of mishaps on this mission where everything that could go wrong has gone miserably wrong! He feels a core collapse begin to take place within the depths of his being. It's all too much. He's going down!

The doc, observing George, senses the depth of hurt and anxiety George is experiencing. The doc has seen this phenomenon before . . . this is a *broken man,* he thinks. A man who has come to the end of a long, hard struggle with himself and life as he's known it. This is what happens when ego burns out! The doc watches as George lays his head on the desk in defeat. The doc decides to allow George a little *quiet time* and returns to his writing.

The patient is mentally, physically, and spiritually bankrupt. A mere shell of a man . . . a babe in the woods. Brings to mind the scripture: <u>unless you come as a child, you cannot enter the kingdom of heaven.</u> This is the perfect time for him to surrender and turn from whatever addiction or "ism" has plagued him—alcohol, gambling, sex, religion, etc. Now is a good time for him to give himself over to a higher power and forsake whatever fueled and drove him down this path of isolated narrow-mindedness and ultimate split mind. Whatever has repressed his spirit needs to be replaced with a desire and determination to open up, shift gears, and turn the page.

The doc continues to work up a treatment protocol for George, even though he doesn't anticipate treating him. His suggestions will be used in his report to the chief. He feels that George is definitely in full flight from reality and exhibiting numerous schizophrenic symptoms. He feels that George is being bombarded with what-ifs and maybes, which is a clear indicator of low-grade fear and lack of confidence. Not knowing the true nature of George's holies or isms, the doc is leaning toward a "fits-all" approach.

He continues writing. *Perhaps a twelve-step self-help program of recovery is in order once this patient is stabilized. I've had varying degrees of success in the past using such programs. This form of treatment engages the patient in his own recovery rather than simply medicating.*

Meanwhile, at the end of the hall, the chief has returned to Timmy and Officer Wax in the glaring red office. Before continuing the interrogation, he takes a moment to adjust his eyes, as well as his body, to the room. He is still reeling emotionally from the previous round of questioning and feeling really pissed off!

The chief, trying to remain calm, addresses Timmy. "Let's talk about that boat you guys were on, its cargo, and your company."

"What about it?" Timmy replies in his most Bond-like tone.

"First of all, is that Universal Exports or Imports?"

"Exports."

"And just what are you guys exporting? And don't try to tell me it's that crap in the crates on deck! We checked that out. There's nothing in them but junk! What was the real cargo? Is it still hidden on the boat or have you already made the drop?" He glances down at the police report. "It says here that during the scuffle in the bar last night, you mentioned somebody named Sanchez." The chief suddenly slams his fist on the table! "Is Sanchez your contact?! Who in the hell is Sanchez?!"

Timmy, staring silently at the chief, decides to throw him a morsel. "*Aspic*. That's all I'm telling you," he says.

"What *aspect?* You're not telling me shit! There was something else in those crates, according to the markings on them. They've been to damned near every port on the European side of the Atlantic! I'll tell you what this looks like. It looks like you're in the smuggling business and that junk is just a front for whatever was in those crates! Like maybe, *DRUGS!*" The chief yells.

"*Aspic*. That's all I'm saying." Timmy folds his arms across his chest smugly.

"ASPECT! You're talking out of your ass! What's your real business?! What are you really doing down here?!"

"OK . . . Mardi Gras. We thought we'd take in a New Orleans Mardi Gras," Timmy offers nonchalantly.

"Oh yeah, that's it . . . just a *leisurely* visit! That explains *everything!*

You all are just a bunch of foreign junk dealers on your way to New Orleans. And full of Mardi Gras revelry, y'all just happened to stray 150 miles off course and unleash a vandalistic rampage on my community! Sure, I can see that! All that party spirit had to go somewhere! Right?!" The chief glances over to Officer Wax and rolls his eyes.

Timmy shrugs his shoulders in an *'I don't know'* response.

"Don't give me that shit! What were y'all doing messing with that pipeline?" The chief demands loudly. His face is beet red and he's sweating profusely. With clenched fists, he turns away from Timmy and begins to pace the floor. He looks over to Officer Wax and gives him a *'your turn'* look.

"You know, that can be construed as a potential *terroristic* act," Officer Wax speaks calmly to Timmy. "If we find probable cause to believe that, do you know how many agencies are gonna want a piece of you? To name a few: the CIA, FBI, Homeland Security, and state and local parish authorities. And then, because there's a boat involved, the Coast Guard is gonna want some, too. Then there's the boys at the Forestry Department. They take the environment very seriously! You could get ten years just for destroying land that's part of a protected wildlife sanctuary! It could be a *long* time before you see daylight!"

The chief spins around, still boiling mad. "Hell, I could lock his ass up for 2-3 years just on the misdemeanors, not to mention the felonies . . . car theft, carrying a concealed weapon, and destruction of federal land!"

"The best thing you can do is come clean," Wax says. "Maybe the judge will go easy on you."

Just then, Detective Coco knocks on the door window, trying to get the chief's attention. The chief heads for the door just as Officer Wax leans back in his chair and accidentally keys his radio.

"(SCRRRRR) . . ."

"I guess that's a wrap." Timmy quickly stands up.

"Yeah, that's a wrap I'll pin on your ass! Now SIT DOWN!" the chief yells at Timmy, then goes out in the hallway. Detective Coco is taken aback by the chief's red-faced demeanor.

"Got another report for you. Tough customer, huh?" the detective asks.

"Yeah, you got that right!" the chief grabs the report.

Meanwhile, the doc is still sitting quietly with George, who suddenly raises his head and looks around the room with a lost look in his eyes.

"Are you all right?" the doc asks. "You've been resting there for quite a while."

"Yeah, I guess so. I guess I'm a little tired. No . . . I'm exhausted!"

"Tell me about the classification/status problem," the doc prods gently.

Inactive-Active-Standby. I can't tell him about that. That's CLASSIFIED! George reminds himself. "Oh, that's nothing important," he says to the doc. "What I'm really interested in is this REAL thing. It's eating me up! If I could just put my finger on it."

"Some people say there's no reality, only perception. Technically, that may be true, but there's no substance to that statement. It's more of an excuse for hovering around in a state of limbo. That kind of thinking is not really being grounded. A person's perception can be altered in many ways throughout the course of a day by all sorts of stimuli that can be either helpful or harmful."

"But what is really *REAL?*" George has been listening intently.

"I think perception of reality and truth is in constant flux, and it depends on the collective consciousness of whatever circles you travel in: the people you associate with, their interests, and their level of awareness," the doc offers.

Sean, Roger, and Timmy. One is a control freak, one is a sex maniac, and one is a lunatic. I don't stand a chance! George thinks.

"Most people belong to some sort of business organization, civic group, or church, etc.," the doc continues.

"Church? I don't know about that one, Doc."

"Belonging to a group can provide a reality check. But you've got to watch out that no affiliation becomes extreme. When that happens, the group mentality is more cult-like. Some refer to that as being 'culterized,' and if that's the case, you're facing a false positive."

"Culterized . . . false positive . . . I don't get it . . ."

"You know, *DECEPTION* . . . when a man believes he's 100 percent right but he's actually dead wrong!"

"That sounds like a Catch-22. If a man believes he's 100 percent right, how can he *know* if he's dead wrong?" George looks confused.

"Oh, this reality stuff is tricky business. The veil between what's real and what's not is very thin. The mind is fragile and can be manipulated quite easily. That's why you've got to be on your toes constantly, sober-mindedly aware, *not paranoid,* but aware of *ALL* stimulants! Once you're acquainted with beneficial and detrimental stimulants, you can make clear choices. You do have the power to choose, you know."

"Choose, huh?" George rubs his chin, deep in thought.

"Yes. You take your past experiences and blend them with your present situation and decide what's right for you. That becomes *your* truth."

"What about a young person without a lot of experience to draw upon?"

"Everybody's got to start where they are. The journey of a thousand miles begins with one step. I can't stress enough the importance of examining *ALL* the stimulants in one's environment! It's crucial for the well-being and quality of a full, *real* life. The unexamined life is not worth living! False positives abound everywhere! If you get caught up in one, you're just a hop, skip, and jump away from the gates of insanity!" The doc is adamant.

"What?"

"It's called: *LIVING A LIE!* A false positive usually involves some type of fear, control, and extremism. Together, they produce a distortion, which is the beginning of a full flight from reality! This scenario could very well have been the undoing of many past civilizations!"

"How would you identify a false positive?"

"Most false positives disguise themselves as intellectualism. These false positives project an air of elitism or grandiosity and are practiced by followers who exhibit haughtiness, superiority, and unreasonableness. In other words, *some people are too smart for their own damn good!*"

"Yes, but how do you know . . ."

"Look, if people spend a whole lot of time trying to convince you of something, it's probably because they're not sure of it themselves! Truth is relatively simple and needs little or no convincing. A *real* person lives by example and with a live-and-let-live attitude. Such a person doesn't have to try and force-feed anybody anything! This person's life is based on the concept of attraction. Others want what he has because he is happy, joyous, and free."

"That makes a lot of sense, Doc. But how can you tell if you're in a false positive if you believe you're 100 percent right?"

"Let me try and explain it this way. After a while, a person or group of people living in a false positive begins to live against the natural flow of things, in constant conflict with something or somebody. Nothing seems to work out for them, and they're getting nowhere fast! Eventually, they're defeated. But even in defeat, they stubbornly try to justify their position. It's astounding how some people just don't know how to say . . . *I WAS WRONG!* 'Belief-ism' is so strong that sometimes an individual or group will have to lose *everything* before admitting they were on the wrong path! They can't see until they can see, and they can't hear until they can hear."

Sounds like this mission, George thinks.

"Human beings are multi-dimensional—physical, mental, emotional, and spiritual. Many people operate primarily in the mental and physical realms while paying little or no attention to their spiritual and emotional sides until something bad happens," the doc continues.

"Spiritual and emotional, huh?"

"Yes. By ignoring those two dimensions of our humanity, people are only functioning at half their potential. And potential is that special something that can develop and become actual or *real!*"

"Half-REAL?"

"Yes. Those people are not whole or fully functional human beings.

Of course, none of us will be *complete* until we meet our maker."

"Whole, huh?"

"Yes. When all four aspects—physical, mental, emotional, and spiritual—are working in harmony with the natural flow of things, you have a well-balanced being that can enjoy true freedom of the human spirit. Too much or too little attention paid to one or all of these aspects of our humanity causes a person to become unbalanced."

"It sounds like a tightrope act." George shakes his head.

"Damned near! It's not easy, and for somebody like you, it could get *real* wobbly when you first start out."

"That's it, Doc! REAL! That's what I'm *after . . . REAL!*" George exclaims.

"If I were your physician and treating a malady like yours, I would have to recommend something like a twelve-step program of recovery along with vitamin and nutritional therapy before taking a pharmaceutical approach to your problems. I'm not entirely ruling out medication, but only if necessary."

"Yeah, well, ah . . . aren't those twelve-step programs just for drunks?"

"Oh, those steps are for more than alcoholics. They have been successfully used for drug addicts, sexaholics, gambling addicts, the religiously intoxicated, workaholics, shopaholics, and any other 'holic' that overcomes a person!"

"I don't know, Doc . . . *self-help?*"

"I'm a fair judge of character, and I'd say you're a guy who's done his share of carousing. You know . . . drinking, gambling, women, etc."

"Well, yeah, Doc, but . . ."

"The twelve-step program will help you examine those indulgences and determine whether or not they're mere 'tendencies' or full-blown 'isms.'"

"Isms?" George asks.

"A little too technical for you? How about 'holic' as in alcoholic? Surely, you're some kind of 'holic?' Everybody is some sort of 'holic.'"

"I don't know, Doc."

"I don't know your *'holic'* either. Self-help is about helping yourself through self-examination and self-diagnosis. You'll be the judge of both. But you'll have to ask yourself REAL questions and answer them honestly! Questions like: *Am I doing things in moderation for pleasure or to fill some deep-seated need?* You'll have to take yourself apart and put yourself back together again. It's all about finding the truth about *YOU*."

"It sounds like an overhaul!"

"It could be just what you need. To use an automotive analogy, you're tired, worn out, exhausted. You've gone a lot of miles; your rings are shot, you're losing compression, your clutch is slipping, and all of your what-ifs and maybes are like loose bearings."

"Well, ah . . ."

"Clearly, you're at some turning point in your life. Self-help could be just what you need. A life lived without soul-searching or self-examination is a life not fully lived. That's my professional opinion."

"What about church? You mentioned that a lot of people go to church to find reality or truth."

"Yes. But more often than not, people go to church because of social pressure or they're riddled with guilt because of bad behavior. Many times, they end up stagnantly arguing over what belief is right or wrong for the collective group as opposed to what is right for the individual. This kind of behavior leads to years of little or no spiritual growth! If you go into a church without some sense of self and with all the desperation of a drowning man, you could find yourself sinking in a sea of scriptural controversy! You could end up *beached in belief,* caught up in the teachings of one person whose opinions and understandings of the truth could create a false joy in you if you don't have a REAL sense of yourself. You would be like a little kid who's whistling in the dark and pretending not to be afraid when he's really scared to death! On the other hand, church is just the ticket for some people. It's a gamble. You know all about gambling . . . right?"

"Well, ah, yeah, sure . . ."

"In church, you've got one person . . . preacher, priest, rabbi, etc. leading the flock. Everybody is dependent on the leader's interpretation of scripture. The followers may say that they rely on their own interpretation, and the leader may seemingly encourage them to search the scriptures on their own, but to a great degree, they are being opiated by the leader's doctrine. I'm sure you've heard the quote: *'Religion is the opiate of the masses.'"*

"And what if that person leading the flock is wrong?'"

"Precisely my point! It's a hell of a gamble! And in some of those mega-churches, there are *thousands* of people looking to that one leader for guidance and godliness!"

"I don't think I would want to be in their shoes!"

"You're telling me! In a twelve-step program, there may be ten to twenty-five people, maybe a few more, in a group. The chairperson, a volunteer, varies each week, and no one is paid anything, and everyone has an *equal* voice. All of the twelve steps come out of the Bible, and there is the benefit of many helpful interpretations because of group participation."

"That sounds a lot more democratic."

"It does, doesn't it? Its very structure exemplifies democracy. A no-nonsense guy like you might fit right in. You'll find they're striving for spiritual progress rather than spiritual perfection! It's more relaxed and less regimented than religion. Personally, I've always believed that religion is man-made and that spirituality is God-given."

"That's an interesting thought . . . religion is man-made and spirituality is God-given. Hmmm . . ."

"In my opinion, it's best to keep these matters simple rather than complicated."

"Yeah, sure. What about *'New Age'* thinking? Couldn't I . . ."

"What?! Create your own reality? With a mind and malady like yours, I wouldn't recommend *'New Age.'* In fact, I would strongly advise against it! You would be setting up *permanent residency in your head!"*

"You think so?"

"If some of my suspicions about your condition are correct, living in your head is the reason you're in this trouble now. Professionally speaking, I would have to say that your best bet is with those 12 steps. Your problems aren't unique. They cut across all segments of our society, and sadly, they're part of the very fabric of humanity."

"I just want what's *REAL!*" George beseeches.

"God helps those who help themselves. Give self-help a chance. And if you work the program, you will develop a *vital sixth sense,* discover the *Great Reality* within yourself, and enjoy true freedom of the human spirit."

"Great Reality?! True freedom of the human spirit?!"

"Yes, within yourself. It's right under your ego. You'll find it as soon as you surrender."

"*SURRENDER?!* You didn't say anything about *surrender!* I thought this would be simple!"

"Simple, but not easy. Reality requires surrender. And you need humility to achieve surrender. It's humility that brings you down to earth."

"I don't know, Doc. I don't even know how or where to begin."

"Start with writing. Dig down into every crook and cranny of your being and admit the truth about yourself and spell it out on paper. It's like cleaning house. Discover and discard. This is a fact-finding and fact-facing mission."

"That's a pretty tough assignment."

"It's the start of ego deflation. You want REAL, don't you?"

"Well, yeah . . . but surrender . . . how can that lead to *REAL?*"

"It is through weakness that we gain strength. And that's where faith comes in."

"You didn't say anything about *faith!*"

"Faith is what will help carry you through the self-leveling process. You will gain greater measures of faith through learning truth. And the proof of having acquired faith will come when you 'step out' on faith."

"What do you mean, step out on *faith?*"

"Imagine yourself on a ship headed for home. It's a long journey. When you almost reach land, the ship drops anchor, and you have to swim the final mile."

"That sounds treacherous!"

"Faith is what gives you the courage and stamina to keep going. And after having 'cleaned your spiritual house' and discarded the extra baggage of ego, you're not weighted down and can swim the final mile."

"Do you think Evangeline surrendered? Do you think she found what was *REAL* by stepping out on faith?"

"Definitely! She attained faith, hope, and love . . . three key elements in living a *REAL* life. By the way—we have the *Evangeline* musical in our library if you'd like to watch it and be further inspired. I'll have the nurse bring it up to the dayroom for you. Officer Cottrell will take you there. I need to check on your buddy who was in the auto accident."

Out in the hallway, Chief Basile has finished reading the updated report from Detective Coco and instructs him to keep digging for more info on the Bonds and to have the K-9 dogs sniff out the Lincoln Navigator that was picked up in Krotz Springs. Ready to resume Timmy's interrogation, the chief reenters the "RED" room. Once again, he's startled by the room's glaring red interior and sucks in his breath. With a pained look on his face, he approaches the desk where Timmy and Officer Wax are sitting. He lays the report down on the desk and leans toward Timmy.

"We did some checking on a James Bond, if that's really your name. The only thing we came up with was an attorney in Florida named James Bond. You don't look like an attorney to me. You look like someone who needs an attorney! And a damned good one at that! Have you ever even been to Florida?"

"Yeah," Timmy says, recalling the License to Maim mission in Florida.

"And just *what* exactly were you involved in there?"

Timmy, still cuffed and in rusty leg irons, filthy dirty and covered with grease and mud and sporting a swollen black eye, still manages to maintain his arrogance. "I help people with problems," he says with an air of superiority.

"So you're a *PROBLEM SOLVER,* huh?" the chief spits out.

Timmy's condescending attitude is like a slap in the face to the chief. "More of a *PROBLEM ELIMINATOR*," Timmy says calmly.

Timmy's cocky answer damn near pushes the chief over the edge! "What are you . . . some kind of *ASSASSIN?!*"

"No. I have a *LICENSE TO MAIM!*"

The chief slams his fist onto the desk and lunges at Timmy! Officer Wax jumps between them and manages to wrestle the chief to the door and out into the hallway.

"C'mon, Chief, calm down! Calm down!" Wax says.

"FREAKIN' ANIMAL! He has a *LICENSE TO MAIM!* Have you ever heard such shit?! Well, I have a license to lock his ass up!"

Just then, the doc walks up. He's shocked at the chief's appearance. "What the hell is going on? Are you all right? You look like you're about to go into cardiac arrest! And look at your hand, it's bleeding." The doc takes the chief's hand to examine it and quickly checks his pulse.

"I'm fine, it's that sombitch in there! He won't crack!" The chief yanks his hand away from the doc.

"What the hell happened in there?" The doc gestures toward the red room. "You'd better watch your temper, chief; your blood pressure is probably way up there."

"I'll *CRACK* that sombitch! He'll spill his guts or I'll *RIP* 'em out!" The chief tries to push Wax aside. "FRIGGIN MONSTER, that's what he is!"

"Chief, CALM DOWN! CALM DOWN!" the doc warns. "He's not worth having a heart attack over! Now, take a deep breath, calm yourself."

The chief takes a deep, shaky breath and tries to regain his composure.

"You're right, Doc . . . he's not worth it!"

"Why don't I take him back to the exam room, give him a 'once over,' ask a few questions, and see what I can find out for you?"

"He's a mean one, Doc! He could be dangerous!" Officer Wax warns.

"Doc, you're no match for his maniacal mentality!" the chief says. "He uses an insane slang! I can't understand half of what he says!"

"Could be a head injury! He was in a car crash!" The doc looks through the window at Timmy, completely disheveled, still sitting calmly at the desk.

"He's got a head injury, all right, but it's *not* from a crash!" the chief exclaims angrily. "He was born with it! In all my years, I've *never* come across such a diabolical criminal! Doc, I'm warning you, if you try to climb inside his mind, he'll twist your brain into a pretzel, and *you'll* be the one needing a shrink!"

"Well, you let me worry about that. I'm a trained professional. The important thing is to check out his physical injuries first."

"Maybe Doc *can* get something out of him," Officer Wax offers.

"If you're looking for a confession, you might want to start with the one in the skirt," the doc suggests. "He seems lost, searching for something . . ."

"Oh, he's looking for something, all right . . . his next big heist!"

"No, he doesn't strike me as a hardened criminal."

"Why? Just because he's wearing a skirt, he appears innocent? That could be part of his MO! You need to wake up, Doc! You've been cooped up in the clinic too long! Come on . . . if the guy in the skirt is a friend of the maniac in there, then he's no saint! You know, 'birds of a feather' and all that!"

"Okay, maybe you're right. But I need to examine him now. He could be injured, could have a concussion. He could keel over at any minute!"

"At least that would save the taxpayers a lot of money!" the chief snorts.

"I know you're angry, but you really can't mean that!"

"Yeah, you're right. Even a beast like him deserves due process. OK, check him out. But the cuffs and leg irons are staying on him!" As the chief turns to leave the room, he points his finger at Officer Wax. "And I want you in the exam room the whole time! We'll interrogate the guy in the skirt as soon as I get back from the station."

"Try to take it easy! Don't forget your blood pressure!" the doc shouts at his back as the chief heads out into the hallway.

"Yeah, yeah . . ." the chief mutters under his breath.

As soon as he enters the station, the dispatcher, Lynette, calls out to him. "Hey chief, Jagneaux's been calling and wants his car back."

"You tell him that his car is part of a major crime scene investigation and it'll be released to him as soon as it's cleared!"

The chief steps into Detective Coco's office, where he finds Coco on the computer. "How are the boys coming along with the search of that boat?"

"Officer Poole just called in and said they haven't found anything more than those crates of junk."

"Whatever they were smuggling, those Bond guys could have thrown it overboard when they saw us coming. Better get the drag boat to search the river around the crew boat. Tell them to be careful, in case there are explosives, dirty bombs—no telling *what's* in that water!" Hollering down the hallway, he adds, "Lynette, get an officer over there to run that drag boat."

"I'm on it," she replies.

The chief looks over Coco's shoulder as he types on the keyboard.

"Did you find out anything else on that alias, Bond James Bond?"

"No, not yet. This computer is so slow."

"What about the car hidden in the bushes? Have you run the plates? Do you have a make on them?"

"I'm working on it. Poole said the configuration on the rear plate was a little strange, unlike anything around here. And the plate on the front was too mangled to make sense of. The vehicle appeared to have been in an accident."

"Considering the caliber of criminal we're dealing with, it was probably a hit and run!" The chief walks to the doorway and calls out.

"Lynette, check on any hit-and-run accidents that occurred between Melville and New Orleans in the past 24 to 72 hours."

"Sure thing, chief," she replies.

"Coco, I want the Lincoln that was abandoned in Krotz Springs and Jagneaux's stolen car both dusted for prints."

"That Lincoln's a rental. It's bound to have a slew of prints," Coco offers.

"I don't care! Get it done! Call in some extra help if you have to."

"Aye, aye, captain! Will do!" Coco replies enthusiastically.

"And get another K-9 unit over there to search the boat and surrounding area."

"We've already got two units on it now!"

"Just add another one. These guys are from abroad, and you can bet there are going to be some international implications. The name of the game is: COVER YOUR ASS! There's got to be *something* on that boat, unless they already made the drop-off! They were up to no good, and I'm determined to figure it out! Maybe they set a chemical catastrophe plan into action, and this whole area of Melville could be littered with timed-release devices! Have you heard from the pipeline people yet?"

"Yes. One of their reps called in; there's no damage to the pipeline."

"What?"

"No damage. All they found was a pig trapdoor open with an older model 'T' type pipeline pig in pieces on the ground."

"I'll bet they were really PISSED OFF!"

"No, quite the contrary! They said they got a big laugh out of it!"

"WHAT? A big laugh?!"

"They said that thing was an obsolete relic, and even if it would have run, there was no pressure in the line."

"I can't believe they weren't pissed off. What about the railroad vehicle and the seismograph equipment? They're no laughing matter!"

"Yeah, you're right about that. The railroad official told me that vehicle was a highly sophisticated X-ray unit used to examine the tracks for weaknesses in the rails."

"How sophisticated was it? Can they put a price on it?"

"Oh, it was loaded with high-tech gadgets, like a GPS capable of transmitting those X-rays from the tracks via satellite to railroad technicians for analysis."

"How much is it worth?"

"Take a guess!"

"I don't know! How much?" the chief snaps in irritation.

"Go ahead, take a guess!" Coco urges.

"I don't know! Just tell me *HOW MUCH* is the damn thing worth?!"

"In excess of a million dollars!"

"DAMN!" The chief shakes his head in disbelief.

"The railroad people are considering it a total loss and saying that even if they could retrieve it from the river, the instrumentation couldn't be salvaged."

"These criminals are going to pay out the ass!"

"Don't you mean through the nose?"

"BOTH! And what about the seismograph people?"

"They're still tallying up the damage, but a preliminary estimate is in the five to six figure range."

"DAMN!"

"Yeah!" Coco struggles with the computer. "Damn this computer!"

"Here, let me give it a try. I want you to radio Officer Wax and tell him I'll be over to the clinic soon. Ask him to put that prisoner in the dayroom with the others when the doc is through with him."

Meanwhile, at the clinic, Timmy is on the table being examined by the doc. The doc is checking his eyes, ears, nose, etc. Officer Wax is standing at the door watching when his radio goes off. At the sound, Timmy shifts back into actor mode.

"Are you the director?" Timmy asks the doc.

"Yes, you could call me that." The doc is puzzled by the question. "I understand you were in an auto accident."

"Yeah, that was a hell of a stunt! I missed my mark because of lousy lighting and a shitty location."

Concerned that Timmy's response indicates a head injury, the doc continues, "That's a nasty-looking bruised eye. Did you get that in the accident?"

"Nah, I got it from some idiot who didn't know what the hell he was doing!"

"We may have to apply something to that swelling and those bruises."

"MAKE-UP!" Timmy shouts loudly.

"No, I was thinking more on the order of an ice pack."

"Oh."

"Do you have any blurred vision?"

"No."

"How about your ears? Any ringing, anything like that?"

"Not at the moment."

Recalling the incident in the waiting room when Timmy asked George if he heard something, the doc thinks. *Hmmm . . . he must be experiencing intermittent audio transference.*

The doc decides to check out his schizophrenia hunch. Unsure if he's on to something or not, the doc proceeds with the questioning.

"Do you like music?"

"Yeah, sure. I've been known to carry around a tune or two."

Immediately, another red flag goes up. Knowing that George carried around a couple of songs in his head and that Timmy and George are friends, acquaintances, co-workers, or whatever, the doc drifts into deep thought for a moment to construct a schizophrenia scenario. *Could it be possible that their schizophrenic worlds are running parallel?*

The doc turns his attention back to Timmy's exam. "Why are you limping? Is your leg injured?"

"It's my knee. I must have hurt it in that last scene."

Scene? Could this guy be an old hippie or beatnik talking like that? "Well, let's have a look at it."

"Do you do any casting?" Timmy asks.

"Oh, I don't think your knee is going to need a cast."

"I know that!" Timmy chuckles. "Man, I've got to call my agent."

The doc is again puzzled by Timmy's comment but concentrates on piecing together a diagnosis.

"You'll get your phone call," Officer Wax says just as his radio goes off again, sending Timmy back into his Bond mode.

(SCRRRRR) . . . "This is Coco. The chief wants to know if the doc is finished with that last prisoner's exam?"

"Are you about through, Doc?"

"Well, for the time being. Physically, he seems to be OK."

(SCRRRRR) . . . "Yeah, he's finished."

(SCRRRRR) . . . "OK, the chief says just put him in the dayroom with the others for now. He'll be back over there soon."

(SCRRRRR) . . . "Roger that. You heard him, let's go." Wax gestures toward Timmy, then the door.

With a real tough-guy persona about him, Timmy gets off the exam table. The doc tries to help him by taking hold of his arm, but Timmy pulls away with an angry, mumbling growl.

"Watch it, Doc! This sombitch could be dangerous!" Wax rushes to stand beside Timmy.

The doc is amazed at how quickly Timmy's demeanor changed and steps aside so Officer Wax can escort Timmy out of the room. As the doc observes Timmy's body language, he thinks to himself, *That was a clear-cut shift of personality. Definitely split-minded schizophrenic behavior!*

SCENE . . . CASTING . . . AGENT . . . MAKEUP . . . With a burst of enthusiasm and full understanding, the doc shouts, *"That's it! That's it! He's an ACTOR! Either he is actually an actor by profession or schizophrenically, he imagines himself to be an actor."*

Doc follows after Officer Wax and Timmy and watches as they enter the nurse's station and approach the door to the dayroom. Officer Cottrell, who's been guarding the other Bonds, opens the door and gruffly orders Timmy inside. The doc steps up to the observation window and watches all four Bonds together.

There's the first one I examined, in the straitjacket. He's out of the wheelchair now and leaning against the windowsill. Looks like a general surveying his troops. The fact that he's standing at the far left of the room indicates a need to distance himself in order to create a sense of authority. Even in his filthy condition and in a straitjacket, he has an air of superiority.

In reality, he's a cross between a cowboy and a mechanic who's had a bad day. He exhibits a severe case of RRD, Rage Reflex Disease, which is very rare. I feel privileged to be in the presence of such a disorder! I am quite certain that my diagnosis of schizophrenia for those other two is correct, and I wonder if this guy in the straitjacket is also schizophrenic.

In some cases, schizophrenics can display very violent outbursts of anger, but when that anger is turned inward, it becomes an internalized outburst of rage, RRD. Both expressions of anger appear to be from similar but opposite polars. I wonder if RRD is a component of schizophrenia or vice versa? Could it be possible that this patient's Rage Reflex occurred at the precise moment his worlds shifted from real to schizophrenic?

A transformation interruption caused this patient to be suspended in a schizophrenic purgatory. He is in a neutral position. Maybe that's the answer for schizophrenic patients . . . to form an identity from their split-mindedness and assume a neutral personality.

But then, what's wrong with neutral? As long as it's socially acceptable, it shouldn't be a problem. My people, the Acadians, were French neutrals for over 150 years. Before the exile, ours was an identity forged out of neutrality, and it had served us well for over 400 years. Neutrality allowed the Cajun people to survive the forces of assimilation.

The doc turns his attention to Roger, lying on the gurney, rolling his head from side to side. The noticeable bulge in his hospital gown causes the doc to wonder.

Could that one be a heavy Viagra user? And could the tranquilizer have contained an ingredient that, combined with Viagra, is causing a perpetual erection? That might explain his being able to maintain the erection while being semi-conscious. But what I can't understand is his periodic frightful reactions, while under such a powerful tranquilizer, to seemingly non-threatening circumstances. Is it possible that he is also a schizophrenic and has experienced an interrupted transformation? Maybe his frightfulness is the result of his shifting worlds, and he's feeling trapped! Poor soul . . . he's caught between levels of existence.

As the doc looks over at George, he feels torn between keeping a professional distance and a heartfelt connection. Of the four Bonds, George is the one the doc has truly "bonded" with. Maybe because of George's country bumpkin persona or his sincere search for truth, whatever it is, the doc feels a kinship with this fella from the *other side of the pond.*

That guy in the skirt is struggling so hard to find the Great Reality, the doc thinks. He's like a babe in the woods. He must have suffered a traumatic event somewhere along the line that caused him to break with what's REAL and what's not. His schizophrenia has bogged him down and forced him to live in the past for so long now that he has no concept of present day. How pathetic! But I give him credit for seeking the truth with such urgency and devotion and being open to change. He is tenacious and tenderhearted like most Cajun people. I can't help but like him.

Finally, the doc focuses on temperamental Timmy.

And that wild-looking one in the corner that we just brought in. The elusive criminal/actor. Whether or not he's a real actor or is just aspiring to be one, the very art of acting is about transforming oneself into different characters, much like schizophrenia. Maybe pretending pushes the human heart, mind, and spirit to more rewarding levels of performance. This guy is no doubt a schizophrenic, but his spirit of creativity allows him to forge ahead.

The common denominator of these four Bonds is that they are united in their disconnectedness. They all seem to be from different walks of life, with one wearing an expensive suit, one in a safari outfit, another in a kilt, and the other in ragged casual clothes. Yet they all claim the same identity. Is it possible that they really believe they are all the same guy? Could their individual split-minded episodes have blended into a like-minded migration that brought them here? Birds of a feather flock together.

Perhaps by combining their split minds, they have created a whole consciousness. Their worlds collided and resulted in chaotic order. Each of them contributed valuable qualities to their shared schizophrenia . . . Authority, Sexuality, Sincerity, and Creativity!

This is the first documented case of: GROUP SCHIZOPHRENIA! The implications are mind-boggling! This could be the New Order! Imagine if schizophrenia was treated as an order rather than a disorder! If it was viewed as an ability and not a disability!

"Man, look at these misfits!" Officer Wax says to Officer Cottrell as they stand watch at the doorway.

"Yeah, they sure don't look like a typical gang!"

"They look like they all come from different places."

"I'll tell you what they look like . . . something straight out of *One Flew Over the Cuckoo's Nest!*" *The two officers laugh out loud.*

"I'll have you know, this is a respected mental facility!" the doc admonishes the officers.

"Sorry, Doc. We didn't mean anything disrespectful. We were just kidding around," Wax says.

"Yeah, Doc, we didn't mean to sound insulting. On second thought, they look like that movie, *The Dream Team!*" Cottrell and Wax both start laughing again and can't stop!

"This is *NO* laughing matter!" The doc is adamant.

Wax and Cottrell try to restrain their laughter but can't help grinning and chuckling to themselves. Just then, the chief walks in and they quickly become straight-faced cops!

"What's the story? How's everything going over here?"

"All the prisoners are in one room there, chief. We were just looking them over," Wax says.

"That's a sorry sight, ain't it?" The chief shakes his head sadly.

"Yeah, we were just . . ." Cottrell starts to speak.

"We were just about to get some coffee . . . want a cup, Chief?" Wax elbows Cottrell to shut him up.

"Nah. You guys go ahead and take a break."

"Doc . . . coffee?" Wax asks.

"No thanks."

"We'll be right down the hall if you need us," Wax says as the two officers take their leave.

"Well, Doc, what about that Cagney clone?"

"What?"

"You know, like the movie, White Heat with James Cagney. The guy was a real monster. Reminds me of that crazy sombitch in the corner. Did he have any major injuries?"

"His knee is causing him a lot of pain and it's swelling pretty bad. That shiner looks awful nasty with the scrapes and bruising, and his eye has a broken blood vessel that's going to take some time to heal. But what I'm more concerned with is a possible head injury. He speaks in an interesting slang."

"Did he pull that 'aspect' shit on you? He tried the same thing with me. He's just trying to con you. Aspect this and aspect that! Hell, everything I asked him about, all he would say was 'aspect.'"

"He talks like an actor. I'm surprised you didn't pick up on that when you interrogated him," the doc says smugly.

"That could all be part of his MO. A criminal of his caliber has got a long sleeve, and no telling what's up it! He might act like an actor, but that's just what it is . . . an ACT! Believe me, Doc, thirty years on the Force and I've honed my instincts real sharp. He's criminal to the core! There's only one place for a monster like him."

"You're *NOT* taking him to jail!"

"Him and that other one in the skirt! There's *nothing* wrong with them!"

"I told you, he could have a head injury!"

"Like I said before, he's got a head injury all right, but not from any accident!"

"You don't know that! It's too early to tell."

"Let me guess . . . he needs to be *MONITORED!*" The chief smirks.

"Well, he did admit to hearing non-existent sounds, and this could be indicative of schizophrenia or a head injury."

"Schizo, my ass! *Psycho* is more like it! Look at him! That sombitch could run ten miles through a swamp with a bullet in him, a pack of dogs on his ass, and never even breathe hard! A sombitch like him operates on pure adrenaline! I'm telling you, Doc, he's conning you!"

"Well, I have reason to believe, based on sound clinical observations, that he may be schizophrenic. It will be extremely difficult to tell where the head injury ends and the schizophrenia begins. If he's an actor by profession, that compounds the problem! And to differentiate between the three could take some time."

"When I make all these charges stick, he and the prison shrink will have plenty of time to figure it all out."

"You know, they may *all* be schizophrenic."

"Come on, Doc."

"Consider the evidence. They all use the same name and identity. At least two of them, the one in the kilt and the one with the head injury, have auditory delusions and other schizophrenic indicators."

"*Indicators?*" The chief raises his brows.

"Symptoms. Such as fearfulness, which is seen in the one who was hit with the tranquilizer. Something keeps startling him. It could be triggered by audio or visual phenomena."

"Come on, Doc! What about the one covered in the cow shit? You said he couldn't hear anything at all!"

"No, he can't hear anything at the moment, and that's because of RRD, Rage Reflex Disease. But you said that when you arrested him, he was quite intense and walking very fast down the boat ramp."

"Yeah, and I also said I didn't think he was hurrying to take a piss, either. He had *criminal* intentions!"

"Well, you interrupted that intention. And what happens in the schizophrenic patient is a triggering mechanism that is activated in the brain. Sight, sound, smell, taste, or any number of things can set off this mechanism. The patient's perception is then shifted or altered, and he is sometimes transported to another time, place, or dimension. He often operates on a completely different audio link or frequency compared to a normal individual. Sometimes I think our acceptance of what we term normal is actually hindering our greater understanding of *abnormal.*"

"That's some heavy stuff, Doc! But back to his hearing . . . he has no audio. You said he couldn't hear!"

"Exactly. My guess is that when you arrested him, he was in mid-shift, and right now, he's caught between perceptions. He's all blocked up."

"You said he swallowed a scream or an outburst."

"Yes. That happened at the precise moment he was shifting perceptions or dimensions, and some of those dimensions run deep. This is what leads me to believe he is also schizophrenic."

"The only thing deep about these guys is their criminality. Take a good look at that Cagney guy. He's as criminal as they come."

"Or he's a warped schizophrenic actor."

"So what you are suggesting, Doc, is *gang schizophrenia?*"

"Well, ah . . . I have to admit, some of this is theorization on my part, and my imagination might be working overtime," the doc says.

"Then that's all it is . . . theory!"

"No! Most of what I have told you is based on sound clinical observation and what is already known and accepted about schizophrenia. The fact that they all go by the same name indicates that they may have simultaneously morphed into the same identity of this Bond James Bond, whoever he is, and there could be more of them!"

"That's a stretch, Doc! A *'Bond invasion!'* Nah, my guess is that Bond James Bond is an alias that they're using as a terroristic tactic to confuse law enforcement in the event of a capture."

"Well, until we have more information, I'd like to keep all of them here. I know this: they are sick and maybe even insane!"

"Yeah, I agree with you on that . . . *CRIMINALLY INSANE!* Like I said before, there ain't but one place for an animal like that Cagney character, and that's *JAIL!* And the one in the skirt, too. I have yet to interrogate him, but you can see there's nothing wrong with him! He's watching TV!"

"You can't take *him* to jail! He may be the only link they have to reconnect to *our* reality!"

"I'll tell you what, Doc . . . why don't you line them up and we'll have our own version of *To Tell the Truth* and we'll ask the *real* Bond James Bond to stand up!"

"Very funny! Look, the best way to deal with a schizophrenic is to go along with them until you discover the depth of their delusions, and then determine an appropriate dose of medication. But lately I've had some different thoughts about that approach. Next, you therapeutically guide them back into reality, our reality. I think that by keeping them all together and watching them interact with one another and using the one in the kilt as the vehicle to carry the other three back toward *acceptable* reality, it would be better for your investigation."

"Better for *my* investigation or *your* theories?" the chief asks.

"For both of us. I've got surveillance cameras here and . . ."

"Hell, the jail's got SURVEILLANCE CAMERAS!"

"But this could be medical history in the making! Look, it's always been believed that the schizophrenic patient lived in his own little world with his own audio link. To learn that it's possible to share that world with other schizophrenic patients in similar worlds . . . why, that knowledge would *REVOLUTIONIZE* the way we treat schizophrenia and other brain disorders!"

"Think of it! One connects with another who connects with another who connects with another, and so on and so forth! Together, with God's help, they would emerge into a state of consciousness or a new dimension in which they could all function on the broad highway of the universe. It's the same way Alcoholics Anonymous was started, along with the twelve-step programs. Imagine twelve steps for the schizophrenic . . . once they're stabilized, of course! When one patient discovers another with the same malady and realizes he's not *alone,* that in itself is soothing and reassuring. There is strength in numbers."

"Doc, aren't we getting a little off the subject?"

"That's it!" the doc suddenly exclaims. "Instead of treating them individually, maybe we should be treating them as a group and give them some means of unifying themselves. We can't underestimate the power of unity! It could cut years of therapy and medication in half, or in some cases, down to nothing! Who knows . . . they may be able to cure themselves one day!"

"That's all fine and dandy, but we need to stick to the task at hand, and I've got work to do." The chief checks his watch.

"Yeah, I may be getting a little carried away . . . but I just thought . . . I mean, the second step of the twelve-step program just came to mind. The one about believing a power greater than ourselves could restore us to sanity. Isn't that what these patients need the most? It sure couldn't hurt!"

"Well, I wouldn't know about all that. You might have something there, Doc. But what I do KNOW is that I've got a *major crime spree* on my hands!"

"Well, I don't know for sure, either. But I am sure this whole experience will yield great things for both of us! And maybe for them also, if they stay here!"

"Yeah, and there are some types of insanity that require incarceration, such as: CRIMINAL INSANITY! I ain't got time for all this analytical bullshit! They're *criminals*, pure and simple, and they damned near destroyed our whole community! You can't deny that!"

"Well, ah . . ."

"Look, let me interrogate the one in the skirt and we'll see what unfolds and take it from there."

"Fair enough. You can use my office."

"The *STROKE CHAMBER?!* No way! I'll use that small office up front."

"Be my guest. I'll observe the other three in the meantime."

Just then, Wax and Cottrell return from their coffee break.

"Wax, let's get that one in the skirt out of the dayroom and take him up front. I want to question him. Cottrell, you stay here. I want an officer in front of this door, at *ALL* times!"

The chief taps on the window trying to get George's attention, but he's glued to the TV, mesmerized by the *Evangeline* musical. The chief taps louder

"Is he deaf or what?" the chief asks Doc.

"Let me turn off that TV."

When the TV goes off, George turns toward the nurse's station with a questioning expression. The chief gestures for him to come over to the window. George slowly spins around in his seat as if he doesn't quite understand, then points to himself as if to ask . . . *who, me?* Angrily, Officer Cottrell grabs the PA microphone.

(SCRRRRR) . . . "YES YOU—in the skirt, get over to the door, *NOW!*" Cottrell points his finger toward George, and Timmy immediately springs into his actor mode.

George gets up and goes to the door, followed by Timmy.

"*NOT* YOU!" Cottrell yells at Timmy. "Just the one in the skirt!"

"I thought I heard my cue . . ." Timmy looks confused.

"MOVE BACK! BACK AWAY FROM THE DOOR!" Cottrell shouts.

"See what I mean?" The doc nudges the chief. "He said *CUE* . . . I believe he must think . . ."

"O-P-Q . . . I don't know what the hell it means, but he thinks he's going to make a break for it; that's exactly what he thinks!"

"No . . . not the letter 'Q' but C-U-E . . . it's actors' terminology! I tell you, he's an ACTOR! Or he *thinks* he's an actor."

"Actor, my ass! He's a cold-blooded killer! He admitted it!"

With a hand on his blackjack, Cottrell opens the door and allows George to pass through, then closes the door behind him. He gives Timmy an *'I dare you! Don't even think about it'* stare, and Timmy steps back away from the door.

Sean is watching the proceedings. *They're probably taking George to a torture chamber. I hope he doesn't negotiate with them. Surely, he'll remember the first rule of interrogation: NEVER NEGOTIATE WITH THE TERRORISTS! But his habit of spitting out 'what-ifs, maybes, and benefits-of-a-doubt' makes him a good candidate for Stockholm syndrome! He may be only an interrogation or two away, in fact!*

CHAPTER IV

*G*eorge is led away by the chief and Officer Wax, the songs from the musical *Evangeline* playing in his head. He's taken to the same office behind the receptionist area where he'd talked with the doc earlier. Once inside, he takes a seat at the desk and waits while the chief and Officer Wax talk outside the closed door.

"Do you want to good cop/bad cop him?" Wax asks.

"Nah. No need to be heavy with him. Doc said this one is somewhat sensitive. He might be ready to crack. Let's try to let him do most of the talking. If the doc's right, this guy will spill his guts!"

The chief and Officer Wax enter the room. George, looking confused, is sitting at the desk, his head nervously bobbing up and down then side to side. The chief sits down, more pleased to see this kind of behavior during an interrogation rather than a criminal who is cool and calm.

"How are you feeling?" the chief asks.

"I feel like I'm going to *BURST!* Like I'm about to *ERUPT!*" George stares down at the desk.

"Well, just feel free to spit it out, then!" The chief looks over at Wax with a confident grin.

"Yeah, man, get it off your chest!" Wax encourages.

"Just take your time and tell us what's on your mind," the chief says.

"You want to know what's on my mind? You really want to know what's on my mind?" George stands up and spreads his arms. "Well, I'll tell you what's on my mind! I'm being bombarded with all these opposing comparatives: Inactive/Active, Passion/Obsession, Reality/

Romance, Positive/False-Positive, Life Imitates Art/Art Imitates Life. I'm trying to sort them out with a fragile mind, subject to manipulation, trickery, deception, and engulfed in stimulants of every kind and coming from every direction. It's all too much or too little to take in with a head that can't hear the heart and a heart that won't hear the head!"

"I'm debating about accepting a belief system at the risk of being opiated, with the truth about deception being what it is. I could be headed for a stagnated false joy! The only way to avoid that happening is to be true to thyself, by incorporating all aspects of the mental, physical, spiritual, and emotional. And then embarking on a fact-finding mission of self-leveling ego deflation through surrender, which is something I never dreamed of, but is the way of being transported to a new dimension of existence! I could develop a vital sixth sense and enjoy true freedom of the human spirit! But you can't always trust your senses because they may betray what's true, so you must turn from your senses and learn to trust your heart! But I'm not sure if learning to trust your heart is part of the vital sixth sense or not. At any rate, I think the trick is not to let your head outrun your heart. As I told the doc, that's a lot to accomplish in order to feel and be *REAL!*" George slumps back into his chair, exhausted.

The chief's smug grin has disintegrated into an expression of dumbfounded, jaw-dropping awe. *This guy is a friggin' goose in a rainstorm! He couldn't grab his own ass with both hands if he tried!*

Wax is also stunned by George's outburst. *What insight! Who would think, looking at this guy, that he would have such a profound perspective on life?*

"I don't think you understand what's going on here," the chief tries to make eye contact with George. "You and your buddies are in *deep* shit! We're not interested in your personal insights! We want to know about the boat, its cargo, the pipeline, and how that railroad maintenance truck got to the bottom of the river."

I KNEW that was a maintenance vehicle! But no, MR. PERFECT knew better! George mumbles under his breath.

"Let's start with first things first . . . what's your *real* name?" The chief takes out his pen.

"Ja . . . Ja . . . Ja . . . Jor . . . Jor . . . Jor . . ." George hears a faint voice from within—*be true to thyself.*

"Your ID says James Bond. The same as your buddies. Or is it Bond James Bond? With all of you using the same name, it's got to be an alias. This smacks of something that was hatched in the *Big House!*" The chief slams his palm down on the desk.

"Have you ever been in the pen?" Wax glares at George.

"Have you and your buddies done time together?" The chief leans in.

"No, I ah . . . I . . . I . . ."

"You can't tell me your buddy with the black eye and leg irons has never done any time!" The chief demands.

"Ah, I . . . I . . . I . . ."

"I take it you work for Universal Exports, also?" Wax asks.

"That's right."

"And where is that located?"

"Well . . . we're universal."

"You *must* have a home base!" The chief interjects.

"That would be London."

"I hope your company has deep pockets, 'cause we've got a helluva lot of damage here that someone's going to pay for!" Wax clenches his teeth.

"Not to mention the criminal charges! You boys are going to need a *damn* good lawyer! And that's gonna be costly!" the chief adds.

At the mention of a lawyer, George immediately thinks of Warren Perrin and the apology aspect of their mission. The wheels in his mind begin turning. Silently, he stares down at the desk, and his eyes roll back as he drifts into deep thought and reviews the mission thus far.

It looks like he's pondering something important. He might be a genius! I wonder how deep his well of wisdom goes? Too bad a guy that smart has wasted his life on crime! Wax muses.

Talk about being in the right place at the right time . . . if anybody belongs in a lunatic bin, it's this guy! He's a basket case! the chief thinks.

George is deep in thought. Sean and Roger are basically out of it, incapacitated! And with Timmy, there's no telling what's going on!

"Why'd y'all try to steal that railroad truck?" Wax demands.

"Were you after the electronics?"

"Why'd y'all mess with the pipeline? What was the real cargo on that boat? Have you already made the drop?" The chief throws out questions rapid-fire. "And who the hell is Sanchez? You guys are a long ways from New Orleans . . . so don't give me that Mardi Gras shit! What's the *real* reason you're here?"

George is so deep in thought, his hearing switched off, that he doesn't respond to the questions. *By now, the yacht must have been seized, the Navigator has been found, Sean's car has been discovered, the balloon is up, up, and away, and we've all been arrested. Everything that could go wrong has gone wrong! It's obvious that our intelligence was flawed and therefore, inactionable. When I take into account everything I learned from the captain, and he was probably on the level, I believe all he really wants is an apology for the Cajun people; and since the apology was part of our mission, why not compromise and at least salvage what we can of this mission? Sure, Sean will be pissed off and he'll think I negotiated with the terrorists and the mission is a failure. But I see now, these people aren't terrorists! We might have been wrong about Primeaux and his operation, too. I believe the captain is sincere, the doc seems genuine, and these cops are just trying to do their job. We did tear up a lot of property.*

"Do you even hear anything we're saying?" the chief shouts.

"You need to come clean; we've got you dead to rights. Hell, we've got enough on all four of you to put y'all in jail for a long, long time!" Wax adds.

"I'm surprised you're not screaming for a lawyer!" the chief interjects. "Usually, that's the first thing I hear: I want to call my lawyer!"

Yeah, a compromise seems like the smartest way to go, and if we can hire Warren Perrin as our lawyer, maybe we could kill two birds with one stone. Perrin could help us out of this jam and we could help him get the Cajun apology. Yeah, a compromise is the best deal . . . maybe the only deal! With the rest of the unit out of it, the outcome of this mission is up to me. It's MY turn to run the show! George looks up at the chief. "Can I make a phone call?"

The chief picks up the phone and slams it down in front of George.

"Sure, you're allowed *one* call! Go ahead, knock yourself out!"

"Do you mind? I'd like a little privacy."

The chief and Officer Wax look at each other as if they can't believe the nerve of this guy. But they leave the room to let George make his call in private.

"I'm going to touch base with Detective Coco; I'll be back in a bit. Stay in front of this door. Call me if you need anything."

"Sure thing, Chief."

George dials the number to HQ in England. Ms. Munynickle answers the phone.

"HQ."

"Ms. Munynickle, this is George. Let me talk to 'N,' quick!"

"So how's Roger? Is he OK?"

"Yes, he's fine. I haven't got time for that now! Patch me through to 'N,' please!"

"Sure. Right away!" she says sarcastically while taking her time to beep 'N'. *George is probably jealous because I'm going with Roger! But he doesn't have to be so rude!*

"Yes, Ms. Munynickle?" 'N' answers the phone.

"I've got one of the Double Os on the phone . . . it's George. He says he needs to talk to you. Sounds like he's in a big hurry!"

"Patch him through."

"'N,' is that you?" George asks.

"Double O, how's New Orleans?"

"We're still in Melville."

"WHAT?! The last time I spoke with Sean, he said it was all systems go! He was ready to execute the mission! Where is he?"

"He's here. We've all been arrested!"

"WHAT?"

"We've all been arrested and we're being held in some sort of country clinic. I believe it's a mental institute. It's very old, but clean. It's painted that institutional green from the 1930s."

"Let me talk to Sean," 'N' tries to remain calm.

"He's in another part of the clinic right now, but even if he was here, he couldn't talk."

"Is he gagged?"

"No . . . he's just in a straitjacket. That's part of the reason we're in this clinic instead of the jail."

"WHAT? Is Sean OK? If he's not gagged, then why can't he talk?"

"Well, the doc here thinks Sean had some sort of stroke."

"A STROKE?"

"They say it was a stroke, but I don't believe it."

"If not a stroke, then what happened?"

"Ah . . . well, there was a series of unfortunate events that took place, and they were, ah . . . counterproductive to the, ah . . . mission. It really pissed him off."

"Tell me more . . ."

"Well . . . there was a little mishap with Sean's car."

"Oh no! Not his *CAR!*" 'N' leans back and lets out a sharp breath.

"I think that's what sent him over the edge!"

"Over the edge? You don't mean that he . . ."

"AUTO KILL! He had that *License To Maim* look in his eyes when he got arrested!"

"Arrested in AUTO KILL . . . how long ago?"

"A few hours ago."

"What's his demeanor like now?"

"Very stiff, unyielding. You might say he's wearing a psychological straitjacket, as well."

"And the look in his eye . . . has it subsided at all?"

"Not yet."

"This could be a case of MISSION MADNESS!"

"Well, I've never seen him so mission-minded as he's been on this mission! He kept insisting that *everyone* we encountered was working for Primeaux! You know, as well as I do, we always engage at least one ally per mission! He refused to take *anything* at face value! He was reading a deeper meaning into everything and linking it to Primeaux's plan for a ONE WORLD TASTE!"

"Sounds like MISSION MADNESS, coupled with the AUTO KILL. If the situation shifts enough, he could come out of it, if he doesn't crack first."

"Well, he doesn't look too good right now."

"And what about Roger?"

"Well, ah . . . he was accidentally shot with the tranquilizer gun. He's sort of out of it!"

"WHAT?"

"He keeps drifting in and out of consciousness. And then sometimes he'll have some sort of attack. It looks like something is startling him; he stiffens up and his eyes bug out and roll around. I overheard some of the staff say they thought he was having panic attacks."

"I've got an idea what that's all about. He's going to need desensitizing. Now, what about Timmy? Is he still in one piece?"

"Well, . . . that all depends. Has he ever had any hearing problems?"

"Not that I know of."

"He keeps asking me if I hear something and he keeps talking about his 'Q,' whatever that means."

"I know what it means."

"What's it mean?"

"It's a long story. Look, I'll put it this way . . . with Sean and Roger out of commission, I wouldn't expect too much help from Timmy. His participation relied heavily on their functioning input. Do you see a way out?"

"From this facility?"

"Do you have any gadgetry with you or access to any?"

"No, it's all on the boat."

"You mean the yacht?"

"Ah, yeah . . . the *yacht!*"

"Look, I'm expecting Pierce in here any moment. Maybe he can help."

"With me being the only one functioning, I kind of doubt it."

"What is your best assessment of the situation? And what do you recommend should be done?"

"Well, it looks pretty hopeless with respect to obtaining the Aspic data."

"Are you suggesting what I think you're suggesting?"

"Well, I . . . uh . . ."

"*ABANDON THE MISSION?* The Queen's NOT going to like this!" 'N' sets jaw tightly.

"Well, I don't think we have to abandon the entire mission. There's another angle besides the Aspic data that I believe we can salvage."

"And what's that?"

"The Apology."

"Ah yes. Sean mentioned that all of you had stumbled across a great deal of information about that matter."

"Yes. The captain and I talked for quite some time when I was on the *yacht.* It all sounds legit. That captain has sure done his homework on the Cajun issue. It's been his life's mission to right this wrong!"

"Provided a wrong really was committed!" 'N' reminds.

"An apology could serve as a vehicle to get us the hell out of here! It'd be a good-faith offering and could sugar-coat some of this mess we're in!"

"Why, Double O, that sounds like the double talk of a manipulating opportunist. You're saying we should use the apology as a bargaining chip!"

"No, that's not what I meant! When I say good faith, I mean good *faith!*"

"Just what are you proposing?"

"Well, we found a series of newspaper articles written by a local attorney named Warren Perrin. And it appears that he's been leading the effort to obtain this apology for the Cajun people. Of course, Sean thought that this Perrin guy is a front man for Primeaux and maybe even a diversionary expert!"

"That makes sense . . . a diversionary expert. Maybe so."

"Well, anything is *possible* but not always probable, and I think Mr. Perrin is just what he appears to be . . . a Cajun attorney committed to obtaining an apology from the Queen for the terrible things done to the Cajun people by the British! And this is another example of Sean linking everything to Primeaux's plan for ONE WORLD TASTE!"

"What did you say that attorney's name is?"

"Perrin . . . Warren Perrin."

"Let me check my database real quick and see exactly what we've got on this Mr. Perrin. Hold please."

Just then, Wax opens the door and leans into the room. "Hey, you can't stay on that phone all day, ya know!"

"They've got me on hold right now. I won't be much longer."

"You'd better hurry it up!" Wax returns to his post, closing the door behind him.

"Are you there, Double O?" 'N' returns to the line.

"Yes."

"Well, your intelligence gathering was right on the money! It seems a number of newspaper articles were written by Warren Perrin or about Perrin in the past fifteen years or so, concerning this apology. He's an eloquent, passionate spokesman for the Cajun people and the need for this apology. I don't understand the Queen's reluctance to deliver an apology unless it's unjustified."

"It could be her pride . . . not wanting to admit to such a shameful deed by the British."

"Double O, that's quite a strong statement!"

"Strong, but maybe true. The cruelty of the British toward the Acadian people during the exile and their suffering for years afterward is documented on court records and preserved on microfilm at a university and cultural center in Louisiana. I'm sure it can all be easily verified."

"It will have to be if the Queen is going to apologize."

Ms. Munynickle interrupts on the intercom.

"Yes, Ms. Munynickle?" 'N' responds.

"Pierce is here to see you."

"Good. Send him in, please."

"Well, do you want me to contact Mr. Perrin?" George asks.

"Call him and ask him to call me. I'll contact Tony Blair and let him know what's happening and will be back in touch with you, if necessary. Good work, Double O."

"OK. Thanks." George hangs up just as Wax comes back into the room.

"It's about time! Where'd you call? Some other dimension?" Wax asks.

"Actually, I called London."

"*OVERSEAS?!* That's going to cost a *fortune!*"

"Can I make another call?"

"OVERSEAS?!"

"No, a local call."

"I don't think so. You're only allowed *one* call! I'll check with the chief when he gets back, so just sit tight."

Meanwhile, back at the London office. "Ms. Munynickle, get Tony Blair on the phone for me, will you please?"

"I'll get on it right away, but it may not be easy contacting him. He's taking some R & R on the Queen's yacht somewhere in the Caribbean."

"Yes, I know. Do what you can, please. Thank you." 'N' replaces the phone as Pierce walks in and closes the door behind him.

"That Munynickle is sure on edge lately! Must be the *change of life* or something!" Pierce shakes his head. "So what's going on?" he asks.

"We're pulling out of OPERATION ASPIC."

"WHAT? ABANDON A MISSION?" Pierce's jaw drops.

"No, we're not abandoning the mission, we're *revising* it."

"Revising? Why?"

"Some of our intelligence proved to be inactionable."

"What went wrong?"

"The Double Os have been arrested and are being held at a clinic in Melville, Louisiana!"

"A detention center?"

"No, a *clinic.*"

"Why don't they bust out?"

"It's not that simple."

"How complicated can it be? We've got *four* Double Os over there! With Sean at the helm and a yacht load of gadgetry . . . piece of cake!"

"You don't understand. There are political implications, and the fallout could be catastrophic! We could be disqualified from the Culinary Olympics, and it would be disastrous to our world image!"

"Look, our first objective has always been to complete the mission at hand! The 'political implications' have always been secondary! We don't have to 'revise' anything! Send me over there, I'll bust them out, and we'll execute the mission as planned!"

"You don't understand. This is about *damage* control!"

"Damage control, my ass!" Pierce begins to pace the floor. "I know I can get them out of there! Have you tried contacting Sean through his watch, an audio homing device?"

"It's my understanding that all the equipment is on the yacht, and they have no access to any of it!"

"There's GOT to be some way to—"

"THEY'VE GOT SEAN IN A STRAITJACKET!" 'N' shouts out in frustration.

"WHAT?" Pierce replies in shock. "They must be trying to torture it out of him!"

"Torture what out of him?"

"What in the hell are Roger and the rest of them doing to help him?"

"Roger is having some acclimation difficulties associated with certain triggering aspects of the environment and a past mission."

"What do you mean? What mission? What aspects?"

"That *Live and Let Live* mission. The voodoo factor."

"Voodoo, my ass! Didn't he go through desensitization after that mission?"

"Yes, he did. But he was accidentally hit with a tranquilizer gun loaded with a fast-acting serum, and he's been having what appear to be panic attacks. I believe he thinks he was hit with a voodoo dart!"

"DAMN!"

"The combination of past mission reassociation, environmental triggers, and serum was probably too much for his system. More than likely, it has rendered all desensitization null and void!"

"Surely, he'll snap out of it when the tranquilizer wears off!"

"That could take a couple of days, and then he'd still have to contend with the reassociation factor and environmental triggers. I could touch base with the boys in the Psych Department, but I know exactly what they'd say! They'd just insist that the serum reactivated his receptor sites to the voodoo saturation and that Roger needs to be brought in for detoxing and desensitization!"

"Voodoo AND a tranquilizer—what are the odds? DAMN!" Pierce shakes his head in disgust.

"I tried to tell Sean how powerful this ancient stuff is. He minimized it! He thought Roger could handle it."

"And the others, what about them?"

"Well, you know Timmy's an avid Shakespeare fan."

"Yes, so what?"

"Well, he was on stage in a Shakespearean play when we reactivated him, and he never really snapped out of it!"

"How can you justify sending a Double O in his *condition* out on a mission? Isn't that the reason he was deactivated?"

"Well, yes, but we thought once the mission was underway, he'd adapt. We consulted with the boys in the Psych Department, and they felt certain that with Sean leading the operation, along with the influence of the other agents, Timmy would become fully engaged and focused on the mission."

"That was a hell of a gamble! You can't rely on those Psych recommendations. They've got the slowest revolving door in the whole damn agency! I bet they just *LOVE* analyzing Timmy!"

"Well, we *had* to include him just like we had to include George! It was at the Queen's insistence."

"What about George?"

"Well, George just called in and informed me about everything."

"So that means he has access to a phone. And that also means he's being moved around. Why the hell doesn't he make a move to free Sean so they can bust the hell out of there?"

"Right now, George is checking into the possibility of a compromise."

"COMPROMISE? That's NOT revision—that's negotiation! I thought our policy was *NEVER NEGOTIATE WITH TERRORISTS!*"

"It's a tough call. Some of our intelligence may have been flawed. I don't like it any more than you, but we have to put the situation into perspective! There's a huge PR factor at stake here! And aside from being banned from the Culinary Olympics, we could lose our funding for future missions of AMALGA!"

"The hell with the Culinary Olympics and the PR! They've got Sean in a straitjacket!" Pierce slams his fist on the desk and begins to pace the floor. "Is Sean being held in solitary confinement? Is there a way for George to get to him and remove the straitjacket?"

"The jacket is for his own safety."

"WHAT?"

"I didn't want to tell you this, but we have good reason to believe that Sean is stuck in AUTO KILL!"

This horrifying news brings Pierce's agitated pacing to a sudden stop. Facing the wall, he takes a slow, deep breath and contemplates what Sean must be going through; AUTO KILL in a *straitjacket!* Wanting to rip someone limb from limb while your own are in a vice. Pierce locks his arms tightly around his chest and lets out a beast-like howl . . .

"AAARRRGGGGHHHHHHH!"

"Calm yourself, Pierce . . . there's more."

"There's *MORE!*" The veins pop out on Pierce's neck. "So what else?"

"Maybe you should sit down," 'N' says in a somber voice.

"Just tell me!"

"Well . . . uh . . . uh . . . Sean is exhibiting signs of *MISSION MADNESS!* He could crack!"

"NOT SEAN! SEAN *NEVER CRACKS!* Other Double O's might crack, but SEAN *WILL NEVER CRACK!*"

Pierce storms out, slams the door behind him, and rushes through the outer office to the parking lot. Once in his car, he immediately turns on his GPS.

I know he's upset about Roger and me, but . . . Ms. Munynickle thinks as Pierce rushes by. Just then her phone rings, and Tony Blair asks to speak to 'N'.

Back at the clinic, the chief arrives to find George and Officer Wax discussing the need for a second phone call.

"He wants to make another call. He already made a call to England!" Wax complains loudly.

"Oh yeah . . . you want another holler across the pond, huh?" The chief looks at George.

"No, he said this second call would be a local one."

"Yeah, well, you know by law you're only allowed one call!"

"I realize that," George says.

"Well, just to show you what a decent guy I am, and since your buddies are in La-La land, I'm gonna let you make a call on their behalf. So who do you want to call this time?"

"A local attorney by the name of Warren Perrin."

"I was wondering when you were going to start screaming for a lawyer!"

"Do you know Mr. Perrin?"

"Sure do. Around here, everybody knows Warren Perrin!"

"Have you got his number?"

"It's in the phone book."

"I'll look it up for you." Officer Wax grabs the phone book.

"You know it's Sunday, and he's probably not at his office, but who knows? If he's not there, you can try him at home," the chief offers.

"Here's the number," Wax says.

George dials and is quickly rewarded with an answer. "Warren Perrin's office, Darylin speaking."

"Hey, somebody's there! Uh . . . I mean, may I speak with Warren Perrin?"

"Who's calling, please?" the secretary asks.

George covers the mouthpiece. "Do you mind?" he asks.

"No, no, yeah . . . OK . . . we'll be right outside." Both the chief and Officer Wax mumble as they leave.

"Hello? Are you still there?" Darylin asks.

"Yes. Sorry about that."

"Who's calling, please?"

"I'm a representative for the Queen of England," George says importantly.

"Hold, please." Pushing the hold button. "Mr. Perrin! Mr. Perrin! It's a representative for the *Queen of England* on line one!" She calls out loudly, so excited she forgets to use the intercom.

Well! Maybe all the years I've spent advocating for the Cajuns has finally produced an apology! Mentally crossing his fingers, he picks up the phone. "This is Warren Perrin. How may I help you?"

"Hello! Is this Warren Perrin, the Cajun attorney?" George asks.

"Yes."

"The one seeking an apology for the Cajun people from the Queen of England?"

"Yes, that's me."

"My name is Jor . . . Jor . . . Jor . . . Ja . . . Ja . . . Bond, James Bond." George shakes his head, trying to unscramble his thoughts. "I represent her Royal Majesty, the Queen of England. Are you still interested in that apology?"

Could be a prank, but still . . . "Yes, of course! Now, who is this again?"

"The name is Bond, James Bond."

"This call doesn't sound long distance. Where are you calling from? Is this some sort of joke?"

"I'm calling from Melville. My colleagues and I have been arrested and are being held in a mental institute."

"Ah . . . this is a joke, right?" Perrin chuckles.

"This is NO joke!" George realizes he's not being taken seriously. "We are in need of an attorney, and I am authorized to act on behalf of the Crown!" He motions for the chief to come in. "Here, you can talk to the chief, and he will verify what I'm telling you!"

"Yes, uh . . . Hello, Mr. Perrin?" The chief takes the phone.

"Who are you?"

"Chief Basile with the Melville Police Department. How are you, sir?"

"I'm trying to figure out if this is a joke or not. Who was the person I was just speaking with?"

"Well, he's one of four suspects we arrested earlier today. They all have the same name—Bond James Bond. They're all foreigners from England, and they've been on a crime spree reigning down terror on our community! We have them in custody here in Melville at Dr. Bellefontaine's clinic."

"*Terror?* Is it really that serious?"

"Well, what would you call stolen vehicles, over a million dollars in property damage, tampering with pipelines, concealed weapons, and making bodily threats to people? And that's just for starters. I've had to call in all my off-duty officers and every available volunteer to search for additional suspects and damage! We've *never* seen anything like this before! These four suspects were on a boat down at the East ramp in Melville with a load of crates filled with God-knows-what! I'm convinced they're trafficking in something illegal! They may have a contact in New Orleans because that's where they were headed."

"Sounds pretty bad! And only *four* suspects are responsible for all that damage? That's a lot of activity for just four guys!"

"Exactly, that's why we're combing the area for more suspects!"

"Have they confessed to anything yet?" Perrin asks curiously.

"They haven't talked—ah, yet."

"So they're refusing to talk?"

"No. They *CAN'T* talk, except for two of them, and everything that comes out of their mouths sounds like it's coming out of their *ass!* One looks like he had a stroke, the other was drugged by a tranquilizer dart. The third one was in an auto accident and may have a head injury, and when he talks it's all threats or nonsense. He's a real maniac! And the fourth one is the guy you were just talking to, not that he makes much sense, either."

"I guess that explains why they're all in a mental institute and not in jail."

"Well, for the time being. As soon as they're able, they'll be transferred!"

"Are they under arrest?"

"You bet your ass they're under arrest!"

"What are they accused of doing?"

"Tampering with the pipeline, stealing vehicles, and destroying railroad property, carrying a firearm, damaging private property, damaging seismograph property, damaging Federal land, and a possible hit and run, and on and on and on!"

"Can you give me specifics?"

"In broad daylight, they stole a railroad maintenance X-ray truck and ended up destroying it! It's at the bottom of the Atchafalaya River because the stroke guy drove it off the tracks and into the water! The maniac guy stole a private auto after abandoning a rental vehicle and then drove the stolen vehicle into the swamp. He then proceeded to steal a seismograph drill buggy, and after destroying thousands of dollars of seismograph wires and equipment, he trampled hundreds of acres of a Federal wildlife refuge! That was after he'd been in a barroom brawl and was carrying a gun! We're not sure who tore up Ms. Rhodes' levee, and we found a car hidden in some bushes all bashed up like it'd been in an accident! The pipeline was pried open, and some trash was left beside it. Tampering with the pipeline is a Federal offense! There could be some maritime violations concerning the boat and its cargo, and I've not even mentioned all the misdemeanors!"

"Well, ah . . ."

"And . . . then there are the FAA charges pending for flying a hot air balloon in a no-fly zone!"

"That's a sizeable list of charges!"

"Those old boys are in a world of shit! They're gonna need a damn good lawyer; hell, they may need a team of lawyers! They did a lot of damage! And when it's all tallied up, I wouldn't be surprised if it's in the millions!"

"MILLIONS?"

"You're not grasping the magnitude of this! Yes, millions . . . and they're liable for every penny!"

"Allegedly liable!"

"Oh, they're guilty, all right! And *legally* liable!"

"You say that nobody's confessed to anything . . . right?"

"That's right, but we've got dozens of eyewitnesses!"

"Well, thank you very much for all the information. Could I talk to that Bond fellow again?"

"Sure thing." The chief hands the phone back to George.

"Mr. Perrin?" George asks.

"You're right! You and your colleagues are in a horrible mess!"

"Do you think you can help us?"

"I don't know, but I'd like to try. I understand you're from England. Have you contacted anyone over there for legal help?"

"No. I called my employer in London to obtain authorization for the apology you're seeking."

"And who gave you this authorization?"

"Why, the Queen, of course."

"And the Queen of England is authorizing *you* to administer the apology?"

"Oh no. Tony will do that when he gets here."

"*TONY . . . as in TONY BLAIR?*" Perrin asks skeptically. "Hmmm . . . I'll tell you what . . . why don't you call Tony Blair and have him call me? In the meantime, I'll be thinking about your situation," Perrin offers.

"I'll have to call HQ, and they'll relay the message to Tony."

"Who?"

"My employer."

"Sure, you do that. I'll be waiting right here." Perrin hangs up the phone and sits staring at it, not sure whether to believe what has just transpired.

"I've got to make one more call," George tells the chief. "To London."

The chief debates a moment before answering. "OK, go ahead. Your first one was free, but we're billing you for this one! We're not running a long-distance phone charity here!" he says tersely.

"Universal Exports will pick up the tab." George dials the phone as he waves the chief out of the room.

"HQ," Ms. Munynickle answers.

"Ms. Munynickle, patch me through to 'N' . . . *quick!*"

"He's on another line with Tony Blair just now."

"That's perfect! Patch me through!"

"Yes, George, I've got Tony on the other line. How's it shaping up over there?" 'N' asks.

"I just talked to Perrin. He's willing to help us, but he definitely wants that apology. He wants to speak to Tony; I don't think he believes me."

"I can't say that I blame him. He's been working and waiting more than a dozen years for this apology, and when the call comes, it's from a guy who's under arrest in a mental hospital! Have you got his number?"

"Yes . . . 337-555-1212."

"OK, George, hold on a minute." 'N' switches over to Tony. "Hello, Tony?"

"Yes," Blair replies.

"OK. Warren Perrin is willing to help our guys. You need to contact him at 337-555-1212 to arrange a meeting and presentation of the apology and to secure the release of the Double Os."

"That sounds good. I'll get back to you."

'N' switches back to George. "George? Everything's arranged. Tony will be calling Perrin."

"Great!"

"George, look, ah . . ."

Just then, Pierce barges into the room.

"George, hold on a minute," 'N' says.

"I've been studying some topographical satellite surveillance of Melville, and I'm convinced that a westerly approach via the railroad would be a success. I can use a handcar if I have to!" Pierce offers excitedly.

"According to a new media report, there was a derailment a few years ago, and when the tracks were rebuilt, they installed special sensors. They'd pick you up in a minute, especially on a handcar!"

"*Hrumph! Media reports!* They're shoddy, at best! You can't believe everything you read in the newspapers or see on TV!"

"Look, I've got George on the line here. Tony will be talking to the Melville contacts. We've already agreed to go with a compromise."

"*TERRORISTIC NEGOTIATIONS!!??*" Pierce is aghast!

"It's an *arranged compromise*. And at this point, it's our best and only option. If all goes well, we will be able to classify the mission a success! And then the appropriations committee will authorize money for our new division, AMALGA. The Cajuns will get their apology, and everybody WINS!"

"What about the Queen's Chefs and the gold medal?"

"Let's be honest. Even with the Aspic data, there's no guarantee they could win. Look at the competition they'd be up against. That U.S. team with Primeaux would cream them! Aspic or no aspic. There are three years till the next Culinary Olympics after this one, so maybe the chefs can work on their recipes and win the old-fashioned way—by earning it!"

"Sean's not going to like this! But if it'll get him out of that hellhole, I guess it's OK," Pierce concedes.

"We've got to accept this solution. It's the best we can do."

"It's just that it reeks of *DEFEAT!*"

"Why don't you go out, have a few martinis, chase a couple skirts, and check back with me tomorrow? I'm sure things will be better by then," 'N' offers.

"Yeah, . . . a few martinis and a couple skirts sounds like a *winner!* See you tomorrow!" Suddenly brighter, Pierce hurries off.

'N' picks up the phone. "Sorry about that, George—are you still there?"

"Yes, but I'm pushing it! We need to wrap this up."

"Sure. Here's the deal. With Sean and the others out of commission and no possibility of obtaining the Aspic data, we're scrapping OPERATION ASPIC. We'll consider it collateral. I'm putting you in charge of the remaining mission."

"*Me*—in charge?" George swallows loudly.

"That's correct. You're at the helm. It's your show . . . your mission. Let's see, we'll call it . . . uh, uh . . ."

"RIGHT THE WRONG!" George exclaims.

"Yes, that's it! RIGHT THE WRONG! Very fitting. I'll have Munynickle type up some authorization codes. With Tony working the political front, it looks like we're in business!"

"Wow! I don't know what to say. Thanks, thanks a lot! Well, I better get going. I've been on the phone too long, and these guys are getting pissed!"

"Congratulations, 0028! We'll be in touch!"

George hangs up and stares in amazement at the phone. A huge grin spreads across his face as the chief enters the room.

"Well, it's about time! NO MORE CALLS! Let's go, I've got work to do!"

Officer Wax and the chief hustle George back to the dayroom.

Meanwhile, Tony Blair has had some time to contemplate what he will say to Warren Perrin. He takes a deep breath, picks up the phone, and dials Perrin's number. Normally, he would have his secretary place the call, but he realizes that this case warrants his special attention.

Darylin answers the phone. "Warren Perrin's office," she says.

"Tony Blair calling for Mr. Perrin."

"Hold, please." Darylin pushes the hold button and gushes loudly into the intercom. "It's him! It's him! It's *TONY BLAIR!*"

"Warren Perrin, speaking."

"Hello, Mr. Perrin! Tony Blair, Prime Minister of England. How are you?"

"Just fine, thanks."

"I understand a few of our boys have gotten themselves into a predicament over there in Louisiana."

"Well, from what I understand, that's putting it mildly!"

"Yes, well, we would like to clear this up as soon as possible and as *discreetly* as possible."

"Are you requesting my services as an attorney?"

"Yes. There's also another matter we would like to take care of, as well."

"And what would that be?"

"I am aware that you've been petitioning the Queen for an apology because of the British expulsion in 1755 of the Acadians in Nova Scotia."

"That's correct. I've been petitioning for fifteen years now. And it's ironic that you should call today because I'm in my office today working on yet another petition!"

"Well, no need for that. The Queen has authorized me to officially recognize your past petitions and to present the apology with her deepest, heartfelt regrets."

"When?"

"Well, it just so happens that I'm vacationing on the Queen's yacht in the nearby Caribbean, and if the weather cooperates, I could be in Melville within twenty-four hours or less."

"That's a hell of a coincidence, isn't it?" Perrin smiles into the phone.

"I know what this must look like. The truth is, it really is a hell of a coincidence! But believe me, the Cajun apology has been on our agenda. Recently we've been extending apologies for past deeds around the world. The Cajuns were on the list, and given the current situation, we've placed this case at the *top* of that list."

"You mean because of your boys over here in a bind?"

"Yes, and the fact that I'm so close by . . . there's no time like the present!"

"I have to tell you, I feel stunned by everything that's happening! I mean, after fifteen years of petitioning and countless trips to your embassy in Dallas, it seems hard to believe that the apology is about to become a reality!"

"Your efforts have not been in vain, Warren, and your requests have not gone unheard. It's all been under advisement for some time now."

"If this is all true and on the level, then on behalf of the Cajun people, I am grateful for your acknowledgment and apology for one of the worst atrocities ever committed. But this apology must *NOT HAVE ANY STRINGS ATTACHED* to it! The apology will *NOT* be a trade-off for the mess your 'boys' are in! The apology will stand on its own well-deserved merit. And the legal situation we have here will be handled within the limits of the law, with as much skill as I am capable of. Are we in agreement?"

"Absolutely, *NO STRINGS* attached! I feel certain that you're a fine attorney and can resolve this predicament for us."

"I'll do all I can to helpyour boys. But they are going to have to face the music, whatever that may be. And from what I've heard, the band is playing pretty damn loud!"

"Just how serious is it?"

"Well, I won't know all the details until I get over to the clinic in Melville. I've had a short conversation with the chief of police there, and he informed me that local, state, and Federal laws have been broken. There's quite a lot of property damage, and it's also possible that some maritime violations have been committed as well. In today's tense climate, the pipeline intrusion alone could easily be viewed as an act of terrorism!"

"That sounds like a full plate."

"I'd say it's more of a buffet!"

"The British government will make *full financial restitution for all damages!*"

"Well, that's a step in the right direction and may satisfy the locals, but the Federal charges may not be so easily taken care of."

"Yes, well, we do have friends in high places."

"I'm sure you do, but that's not what I was suggesting! Crimes at the Federal level will require full disclosure of the accused. If I'm going to help your boys, I'm going to need full disclosure."

"Well, ah . . ." Blair rubs his chin thoughtfully. "I can only disclose certain information, and that information is revealed on a 'need-to-know' basis. And any disclosures are to be held in strictest confidence!"

"Of course," Perrin responds. "I'm bound by attorney/client privilege, and what is said to me stays with me. Now tell me, exactly what are your boys doing here?"

"They are a specialized Elite Unit working out of MI-6 on a covert mission."

"Hmmm . . . I understand they were headed for New Orleans. How did they end up in Melville?"

"Yes, they were. That's part of it. They were acting on what turned out to be *inactionable intelligence* based on faulty satellite surveillance."

"New Orleans is 150 miles from here! I'd say you need a new satellite."

"Let's just say they were in the wrong place at the wrong time."

"What's the other part of it?"

"That would be a 'need-to-know' disclosure. Once we reviewed the intelligence, it may turn out to be quite embarrassing."

"Embarrassment is the least of your problems. And being in the wrong place at the wrong time is not exactly a good defense in a court of law."

"Perhaps some diplomatic immunity is applicable here."

"Maybe . . . maybe not. But with the Patriot Act in effect, even though they're employed by the British government, diplomatic immunity may not be a viable solution."

"As I said before, we have friends in high places. However, I would prefer to handle all of this as quietly as possible."

"I'm well aware of your friends, and you're free to pull those strings if you prefer. Just don't get them tangled up in the apology. Remember, . . . *NO STRINGS ATTACHED.*"

"Oh, absolutely. No strings attached."

"So what about the apology?" Perrin asks.

"As I said, I can be there in twenty-four hours or less."

"OK. Where should we meet?"

"Well, I was thinking about that. And I remembered that the Japanese Emperor had signed the WWII surrender on the deck of the U.S. battleship, Missouri. Why don't we have the apology presentation on the deck of the Queen's yacht? It would be very symbolic and befitting for the apology."

"Yes, I agree."

"And if you're willing to assemble the appropriate politicians, dignitaries, and the press, we'll handle the rest of the details on this end."

"It's short notice, but given the circumstances, it can be arranged."

"Fine. Is there anything else I can do?"

"Yes, there is. In my previous petitions, I made it clear that we were NOT seeking monetary damages, but were requesting a monument be erected in honor of all who were exiled."

"Sure. No problem."

"There is also the matter of the expulsion order that has never been lifted."

"That will be rescinded immediately. The paperwork will be ready to sign at the ceremony."

"Hopefully, everything will go as planned."

"I'm sure it will. We'll see you tomorrow at this time."

"OK. But I can't guarantee your boys will be ready for release that soon. I'll leave right now for Melville and will do everything I can."

"I'm confident that you'll succeed, Warren! And I trust you'll be discreet about the disclosures and protect the identities of my boys. When you obtain all the details of the damages and charges, you can reach me at 007-007-0007. I'll be waiting to hear from you."

"I'll talk to you as soon as possible. I'm on my way to Melville."

Warren Perrin hangs up the phone and sits for a moment in silence. A rush of emotions washes over him, and he feels united with the shattered lives of 1755 that have been his inspiration for such a long time. He walks slowly into Darylin's office. "I can't believe it! I just can't believe it!" he exclaims.

"What?" She's amazed at the look on Warren's face.

"After all these years . . ." Perrin smiles broadly.

"So tell me . . . what did Mr. Blair say?"

"We're getting the apology! Can you believe it?"

"That's *WONDERFUL!* So, it's really going to happen?"

"It looks that way! Tony Blair said so! And along with the apology, the expulsion is being lifted, and the monument will be erected!"

"Oh, Mr. Perrin, that's great! When is this all taking place?"

"Tomorrow afternoon. Tony Blair will be arriving within twenty-four hours on the Queen's yacht. We'll have the ceremony on deck where we'll sign the documents and receive the apology."

"Wow, this will really be something!"

"I've got to hurry over to Melville right now, and I need you to notify Governor Blanco, CODOFIL, and the local press to attend the ceremonies tomorrow afternoon. Tell them we'll call later with more specifics.

"Sure thing." Darylin picks up the phone.

Meanwhile, at the clinic, George is back in the dayroom with the other Bonds. The TV is on, and George is mesmerized watching the *Evangeline* musical. Sean, still unable to hear, speak, or smell, is leaning on the windowsill watching George.

There must be subliminal messages coming through that TV! George is glued to it! It's got to be another one of Primeaux's diversionary tactics! Sean thinks.

Roger is lying on the gurney with a bulge beneath the sheet, while Timmy, sitting in a chair on the opposite side of the room from Sean, is staring at the wall and nervously awaiting his cue. Doc, Nurse Ashley, Officers Wax, and Cottrell are all in the nurse's station watching the Bonds while the doc is making notes on his observations. Meanwhile, the chief is at the station with Detective Coco and Lynette, the dispatcher.

"Any reports in yet about criminal activity in our outlying areas?" the chief asks Coco.

"So far, nothing has come in."

"What about those extra dogs we have searching the boat? Have they sniffed out anything?"

"No, not yet."

"Ah, Lynette, anything from the FAA on that balloon?"

"No, chief. It must have blown away. No one called in any sighting."

"What about the local airports?"

"No, they didn't see anything."

"Damn! I was sure they'd be screaming about a no-fly zone penetration! Well, so much for Homeland Security," he says sarcastically. "Coco, have you notified the Coast Guard about the situation with that boat?"

"Yes. They claimed their resources were already strained and they couldn't investigate unless the vessel had been in a collision while navigating or if a proven crime had been committed on board. And even then, they'd need a federal search warrant. They said if the situation develops into something more concrete, to call them next week."

"*CONCRETE?* What the hell do they want? If a plane was out there that even smelled suspicious, there'd be a slew of government agencies all over it like stink on shit!"

"The Coast Guard was familiar with that boat. It had recently been inspected and was flagged for a number of infractions and granted a thirty-day temporary permit to operate. So they're within the law."

"Yeah, yeah! What about the pipeline people? I guarantee you, they are *REALLY PISSED OFF!*"

"Well, chief... actually, it's quite the opposite. They claim the line that was tampered with was dead at the time and that no real damage was done, so they decided not to press charges."

"That shouldn't have *anything* to do with it! It was still an act of vandalism and maybe terrorism, too!"

"I got the impression that they just didn't want to deal with the paperwork."

"Damn! What about the railroad and seismograph people? I know they've got to be pissed!" The chief grits his teeth in agitation.

"You're absolutely right!" Coco responds. "They've filed charges and are in the process of tallying up the damages."

"Chief, do we need to get the cells ready for the prisoners?" Lynette asks.

"Nooooooo! I don't know how I let that damn doc talk me into this shit! Here I am with a *major* crime spree on my hands, a community in shambles, and my jail sits empty while his clinic is full of MY prisoners! He always has to run the show! Ever since we were kids, he *always* got his way! Sombitchin', piss-ant, weekend *E.R.M.D.* trying to live out the glory days of his residency! I ought to *ARREST* him and throw his ass in jail for obstruction of justice!"

The chief and Detective Coco return to Coco's office. A moment later, Warren Perrin arrives.

"Hello. I'm Warren Perrin. I'm looking for Chief Basile."

"Just go down the hallway, and he's in that room on the right," Lynette points toward the hall.

"Thank you." Perrin walks down the hall and looks into the room. "Excuse me, Chief Basile? I'm Warren Perrin. We spoke on the phone."

"Yes." The chief turns in surprise. "Oh sure! We've never met, but I've heard a lot of good things about you and your efforts with that apology." He shakes Perrin's hand.

"Thank you, I appreciate that. The reason I'm here is to represent those English guys."

"Well, like I told you on the phone, they're gonna need a good lawyer... a *damn good* lawyer!"

"Are they still next door at the clinic?"

"Yeah."

"Are they all right?"

"You mean aside from being *criminally insane?*"

"You don't know that for sure."

"I've been on this beat long enough to know a criminal when I see one, and with all that's been going on around here the past eighteen hours or so, adding insanity to the mix is no stretch!"

"What I meant was, are they *physically* OK?"

"Yeah, they're OK."

"If they're OK, then why are they still at the clinic and not in jail?"

"I've been asking myself that very question!"

"And?"

"Well, when we arrested them, one guy was having some sort of stroke and definitely needed medical attention, and the one hit with the tranquilizer dart is sleeping it off right now. But he could have slept it off just as well over here!"

"A tranquilizer dart... now that sounds serious."

"Nah, he looks like he's enjoying himself. Another one of them crashed a car—oops... I mean a *stolen car*—in the swamp, and he's got a busted-up knee and a swollen black eye. Doc wanted to keep them over there for *observation.*"

"Well, ah..."

"Hold this one for observation! Hold that one for observation! How many times have you heard a doctor... HOLD *HIM FOR OBSERVATION!* If ya sneeze in front of doc, that sombitch will hold you for OBSERVATION!"

"Maybe he's just doing his job."

"Yeah, and he's also trying to cover his ass because of lawyers!"

"No need to get..."

"Sorry, nothing personal... I'm just telling it like it is! The medical and legal communities are always locking horns. One of the reasons I allowed doc to *observe* was because I didn't want my department to get in a legal bind."

"Yeah, well, what about the other guy? The one who called me?"

"Ah yes... the best for last! He's the only one who truly belongs in that cuckoo's nest! He's either crazy for real or crazy like a fox!"

"So you think he's insane?"

"Like I told you over the phone, he doesn't make much sense! He's like a friggin' goose in a rainstorm! But Doc thinks he's the only one of the four who is sane enough to be *in jail!*"

"What exactly are they charged with?"

"*Four* counts of false identity, *one* count of carrying a concealed weapon, one count of fighting in public and making bodily threats, *three* counts of stolen vehicles, two counts of destruction of stolen vehicles, two counts of destruction of private property, one count of destruction of federal land, one count of tampering with private oil field property, and pending charges from the FAA and Coast Guard, along with a multitude of misdemeanors!"

"Are the crime scenes still intact?" Perrin asks.

"Of course."

"I'd like to take a look at them, if you don't mind."

"Be my guest."

"Is the east side of the river considered part of your city limits?"

"Yes. Melville annexed the dock and surrounding area several years ago when we got a new ferry. I know what you're getting at. Unlike the Coast Guard, we had every right to go aboard that boat. It's within our jurisdiction."

"Sounds like a gray area to me. There could be overlapping technicalities involved. I'll have to check on that."

"Go ahead, but I can assure you that we covered *all* the bases! We obtained a search warrant from Judge Bordelon, and the captain gave us permission to come aboard and search his vessel."

"Well, I guess that takes care of that."

"It sure does!" the chief states confidently.

"I'd like to go over to the clinic and meet my clients."

"I'll give you a personal escort right now."

The chief and Perrin leave the police station and walk into the clinic, past the receptionist, through the swinging doors, and into the hallway.

"Brace yourself," the chief warns. "What you're about to see is not a pretty sight!"

As they approach the nurse's station, Perrin gets his first look at the Bonds through the wire mesh glass. His pace slows and his jaw drops!

Sean, in a straitjacket, still covered in cow shit, is leaning on the windowsill with that *License to Maim* look. Roger is lying on the gurney with a bulge beneath the sheet and seems to be asleep. A greasy, mud-smeared Timmy, in handcuffs and leg irons, is limping around in a circle. And George, with his filthy, ruffled shirt hanging out of his kilt, is gazing up at the TV, lost in the music, his head tilted back and his mouth agape.

Perrin is so stunned by the sight, he hardly notices anyone else as they enter the room. The chief introduces Perrin.

"Doc, this is Warren Perrin. Mr. Perrin, this is Doctor Bellefontaine."

Still stunned and without taking his eyes off the Bonds, Perrin offers the doc a limp handshake while Tony Blair's words echo in his mind... *SPECIALIZED ELITE UNIT!* Specialized in what? he asks himself. These are the boys Tony Blair talked about? In a cloud of doubt, he begins to fear that the apology offer may be a cruel hoax.

At that very moment, Perrin notices the *Evangeline* musical is on the TV. Although he can't hear the sound, he's familiar with this part of the musical and the song that's being sung, "Trust Your Heart," and he recalls the powerful words.

Sometimes you just cannot trust what you see with your eyes; sometimes your ears only hear mere conjecture and lies.

All your senses may betray what's true.

Sometimes you need more than reason when faced with a choice.

Sometimes to see your way clear and to hear the voice of God, you must turn from your senses and learn to trust your heart.

Perrin decides to shake off the doubt and fear and embrace faith, hope, and love.

"Well, what are we looking at here, Doc?" Perrin asks.

"That all depends on what perspective you want," the doc replies.

"Chief, mind if Cottrell and I take another coffee break?" Officer Wax asks.

"Sure. Go ahead."

"Are they all right?" Perrin asks. "The chief said one of them had a stroke."

"That's him over there." The doc points toward Sean. "It wasn't really a stroke, but similar. It's a rare condition called RRD or Rage Reflex Disease. In laymen's terms, he was so angry, he swallowed a scream and paralyzed himself. But the paralysis is temporary and confined to his senses, voice box, and some muscular skeletal effects."

"Are you sure he's all right?"

"Oh yeah! His blood pressure was through the roof when they brought him in, but we stabilized him with medication. To tell you the truth, I don't know how the old fart is still in one piece! He must be made out of steel!"

"Man, that look he has could bore a hole right through you! I wouldn't want to get on his bad side!" Perrin says.

"There's no good side to a guy like that . . . they're both *BAD* sides!" the chief offers.

"What about the one on the gurney?" Perrin asks the doc.

"He was hit with a tranquilizer dart. It should wear off in a day or two. He's also got a secondary condition of panic attacks, which may be related to the tranquilizer, or it could be preexisting. He's resting right now."

"Resting, maybe, but judging by the bulge under the sheet, I'd say he was having a pretty good dream!" Perrin chuckles.

"It could end up wet!" the doc laughs. "But, in all seriousness, although his vitals are within normal range, he still needs to be monitored in case of a severe allergic reaction!"

"Doc, do you think they should be in the hospital?" Perrin asks.

"I know this is just a small clinic, but are you questioning our medical expertise?"

"Oh no! Not at all! I just thought they might recover more quickly if they were in a full-service facility. What about the guy who's limping? He's got a hell of a shiner!"

"Well, he was in an automobile accident, but I've examined him thoroughly. Nothing is broken. Sure, he's bruised quite badly, and I was concerned about a head injury because his pupils were dilated, but his vitals are just fine. If necessary, we'll put some ice packs on him and monitor him around the clock."

"Ah, chief . . . don't you think the leg irons and cuffs are overkill for a man in his condition?" Perrin asks.

"*HELL NO!* He's *NOT* a man! He's a violent *MONSTER!* And if he was in my jail, he'd be chained to the floor!"

"What's with the one in the kilt?" Perrin shifts his attention to George.

"Physically, he's fine. Mentally, he's got some problems," Doc says.

"PROBLEM? That's the *understatement* of the year!" The chief taps on the glass to get George's attention. "He's the one who called you. Do you want to talk to him?"

George looks over to the window, and Perrin gives him a thumbs-up, which George hesitantly returns.

Sean, noticing the motion, says to himself . . . *Look at that, a thumbs-up to the enemy! Clearly, the Stockholm syndrome is taking root in him. And after only one interrogation!*

"If you don't mind, I'd like to see those crime scenes now . . . I mean, *alleged* crime scenes." Perrin turns from the window.

"Would you like one of my officers to accompany you?" the chief asks just as Cottrell and Wax walk up, returning from their break.

"No thanks.

"Well, the least I can do is get you through the caution tape. Wax, get on the horn and tell Officer Poole that Mr. Perrin is coming over there to nose around, and I'm giving him full access to the crime scenes."

"Thanks, chief. I appreciate that. I'll see you guys later." Perrin heads off.

"Can you believe that guy?" The chief shakes his head. "Typical lawyer with the *alleged!* They love to throw that word around! My officers had to *pull* that maniac off a stolen vehicle! There's nothing *alleged* about that! He was caught in the act! And Mr. Stroke victim there . . . I've got eye witnesses that saw him steal and drive a railroad truck off the tracks and into the river!"

"You didn't tell me that. Did you tell me that?" The doc scratches his head.

"I told you that. I think I told you that."

"Well, that changes everything! That adds post-traumatic stress to the mix. *Very* interesting! Hmmm . . . unlike most schizophrenic patients who usually display a confused, disoriented look and a fearful demeanor, Mr. Straitjacket projects confidence, strength, and intelligence. Despite the addition of post-traumatic stress, he doesn't seem to be diminished at all. That's amazing!"

"That's not amazing! A criminal of *his* caliber IS always scheming!"

"Underneath that 'look-to-kill' expression is a suave, sophisticated intellectual."

"Oh yeah . . . he's real *sophisticated* . . . caked in cow shit and strapped into a straitjacket!"

"Still, there's something about him that I just can't put my finger on."

"Well, there's plenty about him that I could put my cuffs on! Just because he's a white-collar criminal doesn't make him any less guilty! They're all *CRIMINALS!* I've had enough of this shit! I'm going to recheck the *Ten Most Wanted* list, and if one of them is on it, he's going next door!"

"You can't do that!" the doc yells.

"I sure can do that!" the chief yells back. "I saw the way you were covering your ass around that lawyer. Saying they weren't sick enough for a hospital but too sick to go to jail! What was that all about?"

"*A fine line!* That's what it's about! This is the level of care they require right now, and it's *my call!*"

"Oh yeah . . . well, a *Ten Most Wanted* will have the Feds storming in here! Then we'll see whose call it is! And the patients will immediately become prisoners!"

The two officers have been playing cards over at a corner table, and hearing the conversation getting louder and more heated, they get up and walk over to where Doc and the chief are arguing.

"What was that about the Feds?" Wax asks.

"Oh, nothing. But I've just about had enough of this manipulating shit!" The chief is red-faced angry. "This is no way to house *CRIMINALS!* Look, you two man your posts, *stay extra alert,* and notify me *immediately* if anything comes up! I'm going next door!" The chief storms off.

"Don't worry, Chief!" Cottrell hollers after him and affectionately taps his blackjack. "Between the two of us and Mr. Coldcocker here, we've got everything under control!"

"I wouldn't piss him off if I were you, Doc," Wax says. "He's under a lot of pressure right now. You know, you guys have been friends since y'all were kids, and you have to put the friendship ahead of petty disagreement!"

"Yeah, you're right. And he's got that high blood pressure that doesn't need to be aggravated. Thanks for your words of wisdom, kid."

The doc turns back to the window to watch Sean. *I'd love to know his inner dialogue! Unlike having a patient who can talk and you know where they're at, this is, well . . . suspenseful! If only I had a hint of what's behind that look of his!*

Simple job . . . in and out. Sean stares back at the doc. Simple job, my ass! Look at this shit! It's like I'm here by myself . . . with the other three out of it! Timmy's caught between being audiologically tortured one minute and living in Shakespeareville the next. George is only a benefit-of-the-doubt or two away from full-blown Stockholm syndrome, and poor Roger . . . the boys in the Psych Department sure did a number on his mind! Hell, he's scared of his own shadow now! And coupled with whatever kind of drug cocktail he's been given, he's like dead weight to the mission! FRIGGIN' MONOPOLIZERS! They'll go to any lengths to dominate! Maybe by morning, the drugs will have worn off, Primeaux's brutes will be operating on a skeleton crew, and we'll be able to make a break for it! We'll get the Aspic data and get the hell out of Melville!

Just then, Nurse Hebert walks into the nurse's station/observation room. She's returning from her supper break. "Are all of these guys going to be with us for the night?" she asks.

"Yes, it looks that way," the doc answers.

"Do you want me to notify the kitchen that we'll be having extras?"

"Good idea! I'd forgotten about feeding them! They must be getting hungry!"

Meanwhile, Perrin has been at the *so-called* crime scenes. The police officers and volunteers that have been searching the boat, the river, and riverbanks have found nothing. No bodies, no drug paraphernalia, no signs of smuggling, no terroristic tampering . . . nothing. Perrin speaks to the boat crew, and the only criminal activity they can attest to is the stealing of the railroad truck and its demise in the Atchafalaya. With an attitude of great concern, the captain asks Perrin about George. Perrin talks to the pipeline officials, and they agree not to press any charges in order to avoid the time and hassle of all the paperwork, and besides, no damage was done.

Perrin then talks to the railroad representatives, who also agree not to press charges if *full* restitution is done promptly. The railroad wants to avoid extended legal battles and is more interested in having their X-ray unit vehicle replaced quickly. Perrin leaves the east bank area and drives over to the Federal wildlife refuge, where he meets with the seismograph crew and the Forestry Department, who are surveying the damage done to the wildlife refuge and the seismograph equipment. Perrin convinces the seismograph people, without much arm-twisting, that it would be in their best interest to accept full restitution instead of a long drawn-out legal battle with an uncertain outcome. But the US Forestry Department is not so easily persuaded and is taking a *zero-tolerance* stand.

"It's your choice to pursue legal action, but I must caution you to consider the miles of red tape ahead of you," Perrin points out. "Your own Forestry Department will throw in a few miles because of the sanctuary status, the state Wildlife and Fisheries Department will add more miles, environmental groups will contribute their miles to the mix, and the courts will combine *even more miles of red tape along with years of court cases* before any settlement is reached. The person or persons 'allegedly' responsible for this devastation are from a foreign country and may be eligible for diplomatic immunity. They could be long gone before the legal nightmare is ended and any restitution is made. And the forest is the one that would suffer. It needs to be restored NOW—not 5, 10, or 20 years down the road!"

Although the forestry officials are not happy with the idea of a compromise, they understand the importance of restoring the forest as soon as possible. And like the pipeline, railroad, and seismograph people, they reluctantly agree *not* to press charges. As Perrin drives back to the police station, he mulls over his investigations, conversations, and persuasions with all the parties involved. He feels a sense of success. Arriving at the clinic, he's told that the chief is at the police station. Perrin walks over to the station and finds the chief fighting with the computer.

"Well, Mr. Perrin, what'd you find?"

"A whole bunch of nothing."

"What? *NOTHING? Are you BLIND?! ALL* that destruction and devastation . . . that's one hell of a crime spree! And you call it *NOTHING?!*"

"It looks more like a vandalistic rampage to me."

Holding back an urge to scream, the chief spits out, *"Vandalistic rampage?* To say these guys are mere vandals is putting it mildly! Are you out of your mind?"

"It appears to be nothing more than a case of attempted joyriding on whatever they could get their hands on . . . a pig, a truck, a buggy, a balloon, whatever."

"You make it sound like a bunch of adolescent high jinks! These are *mature* men, and they were up to something! And no doubt, *terroristic* in nature! Come on, you can't tell me that tampering with a pipeline isn't an attempt to cripple or destroy energy systems!"

"With no solid evidence found on the boat, such as explosives, there's no basis to assume any terroristic plot to sabotage our energy systems or anything else. I tell you, it all reeks of revelry."

"REVELRY?!" the chief shouts. "What kind of reveler, vandal, or even criminal drags his own pig halfway around the world to go joyriding in somebody else's pipeline? Gimme a break, Perrin!"

"That can easily be explained," Perrin offers.

"Oh, I can't wait to hear this!" he says sarcastically.

"I overheard a couple of your officers discussing the possibility that these guys were junk dealers headed for New Orleans to sell their cargo and enjoy the Mardi Gras, and they decided to take the pig for one last spin."

"Yeah, right! And I suppose they just decided to take one last spin on a railroad truck and seismograph buggy, too! Oh, and don't forget the joyride on the stolen car from Krotz Springs and the fun of crashing it into the swamp!"

"Well, I'm sure there are explanations . . ."

"And it really was the *last spin* for that very expensive railroad X-ray truck that's now at the bottom of the Atchafalaya!"

"Look, you know how people behave when they come down here this time of year. They think they can just let it all hang out. That's the reason they come to Mardi Gras . . . to take part in *unrestrained* festivities. And sometimes it gets a little out of hand . . . but for the most part, it's all in fun."

"You make it sound like a case of *Brits Gone Wild!* This is not revelry . . . this is *mayhem!* Those guys had a specific intention, and they were hell-bent on achieving it!"

"Yeah, the intention of having a good time . . . just like everybody else."

"Bullshit! There's millions of dollars worth of damage out there! A *good time*, my ass!"

"I can guarantee you that not only do they have the resources to pay for the damage, *but full restitution* for all damages will be made."

"I don't care how deep their pockets are; they're still going to have to answer to these charges!"

"I've spoken to all the parties involved, and they've chosen restitution instead of lengthy court battles."

"That just makes me sick!" the chief snaps in disgust. "Some people think they can do whatever they want! Commit any crime they choose and then just buy their way out of the mess with nothing more than a slap on the wrist!"

"Well now, that's not necessarily . . ."

"What about the Forestry Department? I *know* they're pissed! You can't buy them off! How do you put a price on a protected forest that's been destroyed?"

"They *were* pissed, all right, and they definitely wanted to pursue legal action, but they agreed to full restitution when they realized the red tape involved."

"*DAMN!* They can all back down and drop the charges, but that doesn't mean our district attorney is going to back down and drop anything! In fact, if I know him, he's going to push this all the way to the Supreme Court if he has to! He *thrives* on red tape!"

"Have you talked to him?"

"No. He and the mayor are both in New Orleans."

"Well, I'm going to go next door and check on my clients."

"I'll be over as soon as I get this damn computer working." The chief whacks the keyboard. "I'm trying to pull up the *Ten Most Wanted list*."

"Ten Most Wanted?" Perrin asks.

"That's right! The one in the leg irons . . . he ain't no reveling *Brit Gone Wild!* I bet my left nut on a chopping block, he's wanted for something, somewhere! He is 100 percent pure *CRIMINAL!*" The chief pounds the keys in exasperation.

"I heard the doc say that guy was more than likely an actor."

"No! That's all an act! I'm telling you . . . he's a *CRIMINAL!*"

"Well, whatever you say, but I have to go now." Perrin turns to leave.

"CRIMINAL! 100 percent CRIMINAL!" The chief shouts at his back.

Perrin walks out the front door of the station and over into the clinic. He passes the receptionist's desk and down the hallway to the observation room, where he finds the doc and a nurse watching the Bonds. Officers Wax and Cottrell are at a corner table playing cards.

"How's it going, Doc?" Perrin asks.

"Very good, thanks. Just working up a few notes here."

"That guy in the straitjacket . . . how long is he going to have to stay in those stinking filthy clothes before you clean him up?"

"I wanted to clean him up right away, but the chief said not to. He said we had to preserve DNA evidence." The doc shrugs.

"Don't you think that's a little inhumane?"

"Yeah, but he can't smell anyway."

"But the others in there can smell! And it's beginning to seep in here! In fact, it's spreading throughout the building! I could smell it as soon as I walked in the door!"

"I guess we're acclimating to it. I'm sure when the chief is finished with his investigation, we'll be able to clean all of them up."

"I hope that's *soon!* Look, I know you briefed me on their physical condition, but what about their state of mind? What's your professional opinion?"

"Well, my initial opinion, based solely on preliminary clinical observation, would be a diagnosis of schizophrenia. Your clients are exhibiting several symptoms associated with this disorder."

"You mean *all* of them?"

"I'm afraid so."

"Are you sure?"

"Of course I'm sure!" The doc responds huffily. "They run the whole spectrum of schizophrenic indicators!"

"In what way?"

"Schizophrenia is a psychotic mental illness that is characterized by a twisted view of the world. This disorder makes it impossible to differentiate between what's real and what's imagined. There are four basic types of schizophrenia—*Catatonic, Disorganized, Paranoid, and Undifferentiated.*"

"Yes."

"Take that one in the straitjacket, for instance." The doc points at Sean. "He's tense, lethargic, capable of violent outbursts, or in his case, *inbursts.* All classic symptoms. His body language is also a strong indicator."

"Come on, Doc! How much *body language* can a guy exhibit in a straitjacket?"

"It's his *rigid stance* . . . that's the indicator."

"Ah, I understand."

"And see that one on the gurney?" Doc points toward Roger. "He's having dramatic behavioral disturbances, and I don't think they're related to the tranquilizer. These disturbances are more like *panic attacks*. They could even be *hallucinations* triggered by an audio disruption. These are *all* telltale signs of schizophrenia."

"Well, I wouldn't . . ."

"And the guy in the kilt watching TV . . . we had a long talk, and he outright admitted to me that he was having trouble with knowing what was real and what wasn't. Clearly, a sign of disordered thinking!"

"He *voluntarily* admitted it?" Perrin asks.

"Yes! It was voluntary—he wasn't *forced* to admit anything!" He points at Timmy. "And that one in the leg irons, he's extremely anxious and irritable; he looks as if he's capable of violent behavior. Although he hasn't acted upon that capability since he's been here. Speaking of acting, he may be a professional actor—that's my guess. He'll be the most difficult to treat. The chief believes he's an assassin! Who knows?" The doc shrugs. "He could be a carpenter! But he sure has some very dramatic shifts in personality. I can turn him on and off like a light switch with that PA microphone. Watch this!"

SCRRRRR . . . The doc flips on the mic.

Timmy snaps out of his circular pacing and into the personification of Bond . . . suave, cool, sharp, and shifty-eyed! He walks over to the corner and sits on a chair.

"That doesn't prove anything."

"Oh yeah? Well, watch this." The doc smugly flips the switch again. Timmy springs into action! He sprints over to George and asks if he hears something. When George shakes his head 'no,' Timmy hurries over to Roger, who barely responds, then he heads to Sean and asks the same question. Sean is unable to respond, but he can read Timmy's lips and sense his urgency.

I was RIGHT! Sean thinks. *They're trying to drive Timmy crazy through some type of audio torture! Poor bastard!*

"Yes, I see what you mean," Perrin comments from the window.

"He's lost his hold on reality. Hell, they're all in full flight from reality!" the doc says, shaking his head sadly.

"So would you go so far as to say their condition or conditions fall within the legal definition of insanity?"

"Well, in varying degrees, based on the *clinical* definition of insanity, I would have to say that they meet the criteria needed to declare them mentally unfit."

"So you wouldn't have any problem signing a statement to that effect?"

"No. And that's exactly what the chief is afraid of, that these guys will get off on an insanity plea, but I've got to call it like I see it!"

"That's good. Well, I've got to make a call. Do you have an office where I could have some privacy to talk?"

"Sure. Just use my office down the hall—last door on the right."

"Thanks, Doc," Perrin says. Down the hall, he opens the door to the doc's office. He flips the light switch and is almost blinded by the intensity of the glaring lights and *FIRE ENGINE RED* walls! *DAMN! What kind of craziness is this?! DAMN!* I think I'll make my call outside! He turns off the light and shuts the door. *Man, that room could melt your contacts!*

As Perrin steps outside, the chief is just entering. "You leaving?" the chief asks.

"No. I'm just going to make a call. It shouldn't take long," Perrin replies.

"Whatever." The chief mutters and goes inside.

Perrin opens his phone and punches in Tony Blair's private number.

"Hello, Tony?"

"Speaking. So how is everything there? What's the damage?"

"Well, at least at this point I'm happy to report that it's mostly repairable damage, although it will cost the British government a great deal. Luckily, no one was killed or badly hurt."

"Any idea of costs yet?"

"Well, the damages involve private and public property including a privately owned levee, protected wildlife refuge, seismograph equipment, railroad X-ray vehicle, and stolen vehicles that were destroyed. The US Forestry Department was determined to press charges, but when they realized the extensive court case that would result, they agreed to drop the charges and accept a *reasonable* settlement. As you can well imagine, restoring the forest will be a monumental task and an ongoing one for many years to come."

"Yes, I can certainly understand that."

"Since all of the parties involved agreed to drop the charges against your *boys,* I assured them that restitution would be made within thirty days. You'll have an estimate of the costs within two weeks. Do you agree to those terms?"

"Absolutely! Good job, Warren!"

"Well, before you go congratulating me, you need to hear the rest of it. I realize this is no Exxon Valdez oil spill and that it is a small forest that was damaged, but nevertheless, it has been protected and cared for and loved. *It is not insignificant!* And one of your boys thoughtlessly violated that forest! Multitudes of wildlife have now lost their homes and possibly some of their young as a result of the rampage, and the consequences of this action will be far-reaching! After everyone involved, I expect the costs to be in the *millions!* Is the British government prepared to pay such a huge settlement?"

"Well, that is a substantial sum, but under the circumstances, we have no choice but to honor our offer for full restitution and to pay up! As Prime Minister of Great Britain, I guarantee *everything* will be paid for, regardless of the amount! So it's settled!"

"Not so fast! Some of the other charges are very *incriminating,* and the local district attorney may want to pursue legal action! He could pick up the charges dropped by the other injured parties. That's his prerogative, you know."

"Hmmm . . . I see."

"The doc here at the clinic seems to think your *boys* have cruised a little too far down *Belleview Boulevard.*"

"Belleview Boulevard? What do you mean?"

"In other words, they're out in *left field!*"

"Left field!"

"*Yes. WAY OUT* in left field! And if that's the case, I could obtain their release with an insanity plea. Doctor Bellefontaine is willing to sign the necessary papers."

"*INSANITY!*" Blair is stunned. "That would be quite embarrassing!"

"I'm sure. However, that's calling it what it is, according to the experts."

We've already got a black eye because of this incident, and we don't need a bloody nose, too! If we're going to save face, we have to . . .

"Tony? Are you still there?" Perrin interrupts Blair's thoughts.

"Yes. I was just thinking that the best thing to do is file for Diplomatic Immunity. I didn't want to play that card, but this thing could get ugly."

"Yes, yes, it could. It's unfortunate that in this day and age, with all we're learning about the human mind, there still exists a stigma attached to mental illness."

"I agree. I have a political friend with some mental problems."

"I have to ask this . . . are these guys government employees? I mean, are they even eligible for Diplomatic Immunity?"

"We prefer to say that they're in the *Queen's Service.*"

"Well, the police chief in Melville said they work for Universal Exports."

"Yes, they do."

"So Universal Exports is . . ."

"You're getting into a *need-to-know* area now," Tony interrupts.

"I understand. Nevertheless, if we're going to file for Diplomatic Immunity, we need to provide proof of governmental status."

"Of course. Our embassy representatives from Texas will be in Louisiana early tomorrow morning with the appropriate documents."

"If everything is in order by then, your boys will be released into your custody by tomorrow afternoon."

"That's just what I want to hear!"

"Now what about the apology? Do we still have a green light on that?"

"Absolutely! I have all the documents and certificates in hand, and the additional paperwork on the restitutions will be drawn up before morning. I'm looking forward to the ceremony and meeting you. Have you notified the politicians, media, etc.?"

"Yes. That's happening as we speak."

"Good. And will I be presenting the apology to you or to Governor Blanco?"

"To the Governor. I'll be standing next to her."

"Governor Kathleen Blanco—is that correct?"

"That's right."

"I guess that wraps everything up until tomorrow afternoon, then time permitting, we may be able to have a pot of tea."

"I'm sure some of our expectations will exceed a pot of tea!"

"Oh, you mean the old *bubblee?*"

"Or a Bud or two!"

"Good enough! Our captain informs me we will be entering the mouth of the Atchafalaya River by daybreak and should be docking in Melville by noon."

"You're sure making good time."

"We've got a pretty hefty tailwind helping us along."

"Well, it all sounds like a winner."

"Yes, it certainly does. This is a win-win situation for everyone. Well, I must be going now. I'll touch base with you in the morning."

"I'll talk to you then."

Perrin disconnects and calls his office.

"Hello, Darylin. Have you made those contacts we discussed? Is everybody lined up?"

"Yes, all but the press."

"Let's hold off on notifying them until morning. We don't want to create a media frenzy! What did Governor Blanco have to say?"

"She was very excited and said that she wouldn't miss this for the world! She had a prior engagement that she's rescheduling so she can attend the ceremony. She almost couldn't believe the apology was about to become a reality. She said *it's only two and a half centuries overdue!* And she said to congratulate you on achieving such a monumental success! She is so proud of you!"

"I almost can't believe it, myself! I keep pinching myself to make sure I'm not dreaming!"

"All the hours, days, months, and years that you worked for this apology have now paid off, and I'm so happy for you!"

"We've *all* worked long and hard on this, Darylin! I appreciate the time and energy you devoted to this apology."

"Well, I'm just glad that you never quit believing that the apology would come and that you continued to work to turn hope into reality."

"Thanks, Darylin. Now what about the CODOFIL board members . . . can they make it?"

"No. They're still on that hunting trip in Nova Scotia and miles from the nearest airport. There's no way they can make it back here by noon tomorrow."

"Well . . . c'est la vie! We'll be representing them. You'd better go on home now and get some rest. Tomorrow will be a busy day! I've got some more work to do here before I call it a day."

"I will. But remember, you need your rest, too!"

"OK." Perrin disconnects, then pausing for a moment, he looks up at the trees, sky, and birds, and gives thanks to God for this wonderful day. When he opens the door to the clinic, he can hear arguing. As he hurries down the hall, the voices get louder. He realizes the yelling is coming from the observation room.

"They're MY prisoners!" the chief yells.

"They're MY patients!" the doc yells back, spreading his arms across the door to the observation room.

"I apprehended them!"

"They're my patients now—and possession is nine-tenths of the law! You ought to know that!"

"Don't give me that shit! Don't start telling *me* about the law!"

"If you think you're moving these patients out of here, you'd better get a *COURT ORDER!* You're not the only one around here with authority! Being the director of this clinic gives me rights and authority . . . much like the captain of a ship!"

"*COURT ORDER?* What the hell are you two going on about?" Perrin approaches the melee.

"This sombitch is trying to tell me what to do with my prisoners! I only brought them here to have them CHECKED OUT, not IN!"

"They're MY patients!" the doc says adamantly.

"They're MY prisoners!" the chief insists, red in the face.

"THEY'RE MY CLIENTS!" Perrin states with authority.

As if yanked by a cord, both the chief and the doc quickly turn their heads to stare, gape-mouthed, at Perrin. The yelling comes to a sudden stop.

"Wha—what?" the chief spits out.

"Have you gentlemen ever heard of a little thing called Diplomatic *Immunity?*" Perrin says calmly.

"You're NOT pulling that shit over here! These are real criminals who committed real crimes that need to be accounted for!"

"Diplomatic Immunity? I studied *immunology,* but . . ." the doc ponders.

"Man, Doc, you've been cooped up in this clinic too damn long! Diplomatic Immunity is a nice way of saying *POLITICAL ESCAPE!*"

"Oh sure! What was I thinking?" the doc replies.

"Well, Diplomatic Immunity is actually more of a pardon," Perrin interjects. "The British government will be here tomorrow afternoon to secure the release of these guys. And that British representative will be none other than Tony Blair himself!"

"DAMN . . . Tomorrow?!" the chief asks, stunned. "Hold it just a minute! How do we even know they work for the British government? My investigation revealed that they're employed by Universal Exports!"

"Universal Exports must be owned by or is an extension of their government. Or, as the British like to say . . . *in the Queen's service!*" Perrin explains.

"It's not going to be that easy! I don't care if it's Tony Blair or the Queen herself . . . they better have *proof* that those guys work for the British government!"

"I didn't even get to observe them long enough to even work up a treatment protocol!" the doc mumbles.

"Tony Blair is sending an embassy representative from Dallas over here tomorrow morning with the necessary documents."

"I guess I could continue to observe them through the night and formulate a report with a few recommendations about schizophrenia," the doc offers.

Both the chief and Perrin ignore the doc's comments.

"Those documents damn well better be in order or those sombitches aren't going anywhere!"

"I'm sorry to steal your thunder, chief, but it's a done deal! You can't fight City Hall . . . or, in this case, Downing Street! And you sure as hell can't fight Diplomatic Immunity!"

"Yeah, well, I wouldn't be so sure if I were you! With the Patriot Act in effect, Diplomatic Immunity isn't the free pass it used to be! My boys are still out there combing the crime scenes. If they start digging up bodies, that could change everything!"

"That may be. But in the meantime, we've got to get these guys cleaned up."

"It's not my fault! I wanted to clean them up right away after I examined them, but Sherlock Holmes here said nooooooo!" the doc says defensively.

"I told you that I was preserving critical DNA evidence! Like I said, there could be dead bodies out there! The one in the leg irons all but confessed to being an assassin! And now, according to Perrin here, he's quite possibly a British mercenary!"

"I still say he's an actor!"

"Yeah, right! An actor working for the English government!"

"He could be moonlighting!"

"A 'moonlighting mercenary!' Just when I think I've heard it all, you come up with shit like that! Gimme a break, Doc!"

"It's possible! Anything is possible! Schizophrenically speaking, he could have many professions!"

Perrin interrupts. "Whatever you think, the priority right now is to get those guys cleaned up!" he says with authority.

"Absolutely!" the doc agrees.

"Oh, all right." The chief sighs reluctantly. "But until things around here start adding up and my investigation is completed, I'm confiscating their clothes for my evidence room!"

"Fair enough," Perrin says.

"We can dress them in hospital gowns," the doc offers.

Just then, Nurse Debra and Orderly Mosley show up with the food cart.

"I wish we could have cleaned them up before we fed them. But their food will get cold if we wait. Go ahead and feed them now and bathe them later," the doc instructs.

"I have to be going," Perrin addresses the doc. "Let me have your number, and I'll touch base with you later tonight."

"Sure." The doc hands Perrin his card.

"I've got to get going too," the chief says. "But my officers will stay 'til their replacements arrive." He turns to Cottrell. "If any of them give you any trouble, especially the one in the leg irons, blackjack the hell out of him!"

"I wouldn't do that if I were you!" Perrin says.

"If he acts up, he's getting it! I don't give a damn what kind of political connections he's got! Got it? Ta-ton?" The chief speaks Cajun to his officer, meaning 'you hear?'

"Don't worry, Perrin. Everything will be fine. There won't be any unnecessary force used in my clinic! We have plenty of straitjackets if patients get out of control."

Outside the clinic, Perrin walks toward his car while the chief heads for the station.

"See you tomorrow, Chief!" Perrin says cheerily.

"Yeah, right!" the chief mumbles under his breath.

Back inside the clinic, Nurse Debra and Orderly Mosley are ready to serve dinner to the Bonds in the dayroom, and the doc is giving them instructions.

"That's a heck of a sight! We've got our own private Mardi Gras right here!" Nurse Debra says, looking through the window.

"Yes, they do look like revelers . . . very hungry revelers," the doc agrees. "Now, Debra, you do the serving, and Mosley, you just stand nearby like you're on guard. Your job will be to protect Debra, and they need to sense that. You'll go in and set the food on the table, and the one in the kilt and the one in the leg irons can feed themselves. They'll probably come right over to the table. The one in the straitjacket may not be hungry because of his meds."

The two officers at the corner table begin to laugh. "Sounds like they're talking about feeding time at the zoo!" Wax says.

"That sombitch looks like he wants to kill somebody," Mosley whispers to Nurse Debra.

"He really is scary-looking, isn't he?" she replies.

"At this point, he's only a danger to himself," the doc informs. "I'm sure he's having some trust issues with all of us being here. At any rate, don't approach him—let him come to you. And if he does, you'll have to feed him."

Wax and Cottrell both snicker under their breath and try to muffle their laughter.

"What about that guy on the gurney with the big bulge under the blanket?" Nurse Debra giggles and points at Roger.

"That's probably just a side effect of his meds. He continues to phase in and out. Now, after the others have started eating, try to interact with him. He may not be able to chew, so you might want to liquefy something he could drink through a straw."

As Debra and Mosley approach the door, Wax and Cottrell stand up and come over to stand guard at the door. Wax, with his hand on his weapon, and Cottrell has a grip on his blackjack.

"You want us to go in with them, Doc?" Wax asks.

"Oh no, definitely not! Your uniforms could trigger a flight response. We're trying to keep them calm."

"Better watch the one in the leg irons and cuffs! He still has the capability to overpower someone!" Cottrell warns.

Mosley gets a wide-eyed, worried look on his face.

"And be on your best bedside manner . . . but not too plastic. Those guys are rough, and they'll see through any phony behavior. Now, are you both ready?" the doc asks, his hand on the button to open the door.

Nurse Debra and Orderly Mosley both give the doc a nod, and he presses the electronic button to unlock the door. With a soft *whish,* the doors part, and the nurse and the orderly pass into the dayroom, pulling and pushing a parade of carts loaded with enough food to feed twenty men! All Cajuns love to feed their guests, and it looks like a feast!

Immediately, red flags go up in Sean's mind. *Here it comes . . . reverse psychology! Normally, captors would start with intense torturous interrogation followed by prolonged periods of starvation and sleep deprivation, he thinks. But not these guys . . . they're doing it ass backwards! They've changed the rules of the game! But I guess if you're striving for ONE WORLD TASTE, you start with the food!*

Nurse Debra tries to sound cheerful. "You boys are in for a treat! Come on over here, sit down, and dig in!" she says as she begins to ready the table.

Unlike George, still glued to the TV, Timmy is so hungry he rushes over to the table in his clanking leg irons. Mosley, alarmed by Timmy's speed and noise, perceives it as a potential attack. Wide-eyed with clenched fists, Mosley hurries over to the table and stands near Debra. His movement and sheer size startle Timmy, and he halts his beeline to the table. With his back to Sean, Timmy stands there for a moment gazing at the food.

Nurse Debra looks over her shoulder at George. "Come on, sit down, and eat some of this fine Cajun cuisine!" she says soothingly.

George responds by taking a quick peek at the food, and the wonderful aromas begin to draw him away from the TV. He is torn between Evangeline and étouffée as he walks backward toward the table, his eyes still on the musical. He doesn't want to miss a thing, but the call of hunger is getting louder and louder! Mosley, in an awkward position, can see Sean at the windowsill and Timmy sitting at the table, but he's in the path of George approaching from behind, so he moves to the side, away from Debra, and stands near the foot of Roger's gurney. From this vantage point, he has a bird's-eye view of everyone.

Debra continues to dish out the food and avoids looking up at Sean. She is following the doc's orders and allowing Sean to come to her. She is a little scared of him even though he's securely straitjacketed. By now, George has backed his way to the table and sits down next to Timmy with his back to Sean. He looks down at his plate of food and is anxious to eat but can't seem to tear himself away from the musical. He looks at the food, back at the TV, turns around to the food, and back again at the TV. Timmy is wolfing down his meal, and finally, George can resist no longer—he eagerly starts eating!

"Now, this is *real* Cajun food you boys are eating! Help yourselves to as much as you want!" Nurse Debra says.

"*REAL*, huh? Cajun, huh? Man, this stuff is *GOOD!*" George says heartily.

With his mouth full and cheeks bulging, Timmy is eating like a wild animal that's been without food for weeks. He grunts his agreement to George's comment.

"That's right, honey! This is as *real* as it gets! In fact, the sausage and tasso are prepared right here in Melville at Primeaux's," Nurse Debra offers.

Sean reads her lips. "You may have heard of him . . . he's a world-renowned chef, Paul Primeaux."

Sean reads the words that fall from her lips with such clarity, it explodes in his head like a bullhorn! He immediately hollers out loud from deep within his being, and without making a sound, he screams.

"IT'S A TRAP!"

Sean tries to throw himself forward, but his body refuses to move. He struggles mightily but only manages a slight quiver. Making eye contact with Debra, she senses the fury he holds within and immediately looks away.

Trying to focus on Timmy and George, Nurse Debra is filled with fear, and her heart is racing; still, she tries to appear calm and friendly. Mosley has noticed Sean's intensity and feels the same fear as Debra. He takes a deep breath and a slow step backward, bumping into Roger's gurney, scaring himself and momentarily awakening Roger. Mosley's eyes are wide with fear, and he's sweating profusely.

Sean, still struggling to move, thinks to himself. *The food is probably laced with truth serum, and judging by the way George is stuffing his face, he'll be verbally vomiting in no time! What an idiot! What a buffoon!*

(SCRRRRR) . . . The doc turns on the PA mic to give further instructions. "Ah . . . Nurse Debra . . ."

Timmy throws his fork down violently and immediately goes into Bond mode—a suspicious, shifty-eyed look spreads across his features.

Good! Sean thinks. *Timmy's wise to their tactics!*

Timmy's sudden change in behavior causes Nurse Debra to jump back from the table. Mosley's defenses go up; he clenches his fists so tightly that his knuckles turn white.

Outside the observation window, Cottrell asks, "Doc, do you want me and *Mr. Coldcocker* here to go in there and straighten him out?" He pats the blackjack at his side. The doc ignores Cottrell and keys the mic. "Nurse Debra, is everything all right in there?" he asks.

The keying of the mic shifts Timmy out of Bond mode, and he heartily resumes eating. George blissfully continues eating and watching TV.

Sean resumes his observations. *Timmy must be too weak and hungry to resist! Wait a minute! Maybe it's too good to resist because they're actually eating . . . ONE WORLD TASTE!*

Now that Timmy is eating again and seems settled down, Mosley relaxes a little but remains cautious. Nurse Debra looks over at the doc and nods her head to acknowledge that everything is OK. The doc, on the other hand, realizes he'd forgotten that it was the mic that literally switches Timmy on and off! He decides to lay off the PA system and motions for Debra to offer Sean something to drink. Debra picks up the coffee pot and a cup and makes an offering gesture toward Sean.

I fell for that shit once before on the Dr. Yes mission. Let's see her drink it! Sean says to himself.

Debra looks over at the doc and shrugs her shoulders at Sean's lack of response. The doc points to Roger and motions for Debra to offer him a drink. Debra sets the coffee pot and cup on the table and brushes past Mosley to talk with Roger.

Hmmm . . . he's kind of cute. Debra gently shakes the sleeping Roger. Getting no response, she repeats her question a little louder. "Would you like a drink?"

Roger, still very groggy with blurred vision, turns his head to look into her eyes and lets out a barely audible, "Hey, baby!" he says.

"What's that? I can't understand what you're saying! Are you hungry?" Roger mumbles again. Still, Nurse Debra can't understand. She turns to Mosley. "I just can't make out what he's trying to say."

Mosley comes over, and together they lean closer to Roger's face to listen. Again, Roger's eyes are shut, and they gently shake him.

Roger opens his eyes to a blurry, blended version of the two faces hovering over him as they become one, a horrifying voodoo demon!

"Aaaarrrrgggghhhhhhhhhhhhh!" Roger flings his arms across his face and lets out a fear-filled scream. His blood-curdling outburst scares the hell out of Mosley and Debra. They jump back from the gurney so quickly they almost lose their balance.

"Damn! Something is freaking him out!" Nurse Debra says.

"You can say that again! There's some scary shit going on around here!" Mosley adds.

Sean sees Roger's reaction. *The boys in the Psych Department sure did a number on Roger! STEALTH EXAMINATION, my ass! Poor bastard! He's scared of daylight!*

The doc, still observing from the window, witnesses Roger's action. Hmmm . . . there he goes with that frightful reaction again. But reaction to what? I would think that under such a strong tranquilizer, a response like that would be impossible! His behavior is definitely symptomatic of schizophrenia! If I could just put my finger on the triggering mechanism. Perhaps he's shifting worlds in his sleep and he's waking up in an unfamiliar one, and that's what scares him. Hopefully, by morning, he will have slept off the tranquilizer's effects, and I'll be able to get a few good baseline observations.

Nurse Debra approaches the window and speaks loudly to the doc.

"Do you want us to try again?"

"NO!" He shakes his head adamantly. "But we need to get these guys cleaned up. Bathe *Gurney Guy* first while the others are still eating." Nurse Debra and Mosley return to Roger's gurney and wheel him into the bathroom. Wax, watching the activity in the dayroom, jumps to his feet.

"Hold it a minute! Where are they taking him?"

"Just into the bathroom to clean him up," the doc assures him.

"Is there another door to that bathroom?"

"No, not even a window. There's only one way in and one way out."

"Is there anything in that room that could be used as a weapon?"

"Of course not! The only thing behind that door is a full-size handicap-accessible bath/shower combination, a linen closet filled with towels, washcloths, hospital gowns, and extra straitjackets, and a large table in the middle of the room. The door has an electronic lock that can be controlled from here. I guarantee you, he's not going anywhere! Relax, go back to your card game."

"What about that other door?"

"It has the same electronic lock as this one. These locks are heavy-duty, psychiatrically approved, and come with a fifty-year warranty. We installed the system a couple of years ago. This is just like jail without the bars. Just relax. These guys couldn't get out if they tried."

Nurse Debra and Orderly Mosley roll the gurney over to the table and transfer Roger onto it.

"You go ahead and bathe him," Mosley says. "I'll be right outside the door. I wouldn't want one of those maniacs to corner us in here!"

Mosley leaves the bathroom and stands guard in front of the door. Nervously, he pulls a handkerchief from his back pocket to wipe his sweat-drenched face. *Man, I'll sure be glad when this is over!* "Shouldn't Mosley be in the bathroom with them?" Wax asks the doc.

"She's only giving him a sponge bath," the doc replies.

"Don't forget, we're going to need their clothes, and they have to be kept separate for identification," Cottrell speaks up.

"That's standard procedure here," the doc assures. "We *never* mix a patient's clothing. There are plenty of laundry bags in that linen closet, and I'm sure Nurse Debra will do a good job of bagging everything."

Wax looks over at Cottrell. "Man, this will be a first! How will we tag all those *rags* for evidence? They're all gonna be labeled: BOND and BOND . . ."

"And BOND . . ." Cottrell laughs.

". . . And BOND!" Wax adds with a chuckle.

"C'mon boys, show a little respect! These guys are SICK!" the doc admonishes.

"I guess we'll have to tag the evidence according to the suspect's description," Wax offers, trying to regain his composure.

"That looks like the only way. Man, that's gonna take a long time to write all that up!" Cottrell shakes his head.

"Why not use the nicknames we've been using?" the doc suggests. "For instance, the guy in the straitjacket is called *Mr. Straitjacket,* the fella on the gurney is Gurney Guy, the one in the skirt is *Kilt Man,* and the last, but certainly not least, is *Wild One.*"

"GREAT IDEA, Doc!" Wax and Cottrell reply in unison.

"Now all jokes aside, what about Mr. Straitjacket?" Wax asks. "How are we . . ."

"Right!" Cottrell interrupts. "There's a lot of shit under that jacket! Maybe we should put him in the cruiser and take him over to the car wash!" Cottrell bursts out laughing.

"Good idea!" Wax joins in the laughter, then looks over at the doc's straight face. "OK, OK—all kidding aside. Now seriously, Doc, when you bathe him, you're gonna have to remove that jacket, right?"

"Yes, we have to, but that won't be a problem."

"But will he be a problem once the jacket comes off?" Wax counters.

"Well, if he is, we'll just let my little buddy here handle it! That's what the chief said to do!" Cottrell pats the handle at his side.

"That *won't* be necessary! He's heavily medicated . . . but I was surprised to see him pull himself up from the wheelchair. The straitjacket is just for his protection, not ours. The nurse will remove it for his sponge bath."

"Sponge bath? That sombitch needs to be water blasted! You can smell him from the lobby! I'm serious about taking him to the car wash!" Cottrell wrinkles his nose.

"We've got very powerful soap here, and he should clean up just fine."

"And the *Wild One* . . . how are you going to take off his clothes with the cuffs and leg irons?" Wax asks seriously.

"Well, I guess we'll just have to remove them, at least long enough for him to shower and get dressed."

"I don't think so! The chief said to *KEEP HIM IN RESTRAINTS!*" Cottrell jumps up from his chair.

"Well, surely we can make an exception here," Wax offers. "After all, he's got to be cleaned up. We'll give Mosley the key, and he can take the cuffs off, but the leg irons are staying on! When we get ready to transport him, we'll recuff him. Don't worry, the guy's not going anywhere."

"Yeah, I guess the chief will buy that. Besides, if there's any trouble, 'we' can pick up the slack." Cottrell rubs the butt of the blackjack.

Inside the dayroom, Nurse Debra opens the bathroom door and asks Mosley to help put Roger on the gurney. They do so and then wheel him over to a window against the wall. The doc notices that the bulge beneath the sheet is gone and makes a note that the tranquilizer may be wearing off.

Mosley, still nervous about being in the dayroom, is anxious to get out. He takes the bag of clothes over to the door, opens it slightly, and hands the smelly bag out to Officer Cottrell. *I can't wait until my shift is over!* he mutters to himself and closes the door.

Sean watches as the nurse wheels Roger over to the window. *Baths, huh? They sure are putting a lot of stock in that Stockholm syndrome!* His eyes widen as she approaches with Mosley at her side. Acting very professional but avoiding eye contact, she speaks softly.

"You're next. We're going to give you a nice bath. Here, let me help you into the wheelchair."

Sean can read her lips, and knowing he could use a bath, offers no resistance. Nurse Debra and Mosley get him settled into the wheelchair and head to the bathroom.

It's going to take more than cleaning up a little cow shit to get me to talk! Sean thinks as they enter the bathroom. Mosley helps Debra lift Sean onto the big table, then he removes the straitjacket and puts it in a clothes bag. He starts to leave to resume his position outside the door.

"Hey, you're not leaving me alone with this one!" Debra protests.

"I've got to watch the others. It's OK. I'll be right here."

"Well, all right," she hesitates. "But leave the door open . . . wide open. And stand right there." She points. "Oh, and take this dirty wheelchair with you; we'll need a clean one."

Mosley rolls the chair out of the bathroom as Debra begins Sean's bath.

She's not the type of woman I prefer to get naked with. Sean cringes at Debra's touch. Frankly, I'm disappointed in Primeaux. I would have thought he'd use raving Southern beauties for breaking down our defenses! Roger's lucky to be out of it and unable to witness this!

Sean's bath doesn't take long. Debra dresses him in a clean gown and calls Mosley in to strap Sean into a clean straitjacket. They put him in the new wheelchair, and Mosley picks up the bag containing the shitty clothes and the old straitjacket. Nurse Debra pushes Sean over to the wall and places him next to Roger as Mosley rolls the dirty wheelchair and the bag of clothes over to the door and hands it off to Cottrell.

"What now?" Mosley asks the doc.

The doc turns to Wax. "Do you have the key for the cuffs? We're going to let the *Wild One* bathe himself."

"Here you go, Mosley. It's the small key on the end. Uncuff him near the bathroom door. That way, he'll be less likely to try and make a break for it! But leave those leg irons on!"

Mosley is caught off guard when he's asked to uncuff the maniac! It's the last thing he expected! This surprise makes him even more nervous. Reluctantly, he takes the key ring, and they jingle in his shaking hand.

"I . . . I . . . I . . ." Mosley stutters.

"Hey, don't worry, Mosley!" Cottrell speaks up. "If he tries anything, just yell, and Mr. Coldcocker here will be all over his ass like stink on shit!"

And speaking of shit, man does this stuff stink! Cottrell mutters as he picks up the stinky bag and quickly writes on it: MR. STRAITJACKET. He then places it next to the first bag he labeled: GURNEY GUY.

Why in the hell am I doing this? This ain't part of my job description! Mosley mumbles as he nears the bathroom. He stands in front of the bathroom door and in a weak, crackly voice calls Timmy over.

"Hey, YOU, over there!" Mosley raises his arm and motions to Timmy. "Will you please come over here?"

Timmy doesn't move. He looks through the window at the doc and then over to Mosley . . . then back at the doc. Again, Mosley calls Timmy to come over to the bathroom.

"Hey, YOU over there! Come on over here and take a bath!" *If he doesn't walk over here, I'm damn sure NOT going to get him! I don't want to do this shit in the first place! This just ain't my job!*

Again, Timmy looks at the doc, then to Mosley. The doc makes a gesture to Timmy to go ahead over to the bathroom. *Why doesn't that director say "action" or give me a cue?* Timmy is confused.

"Hmmmm . . . let me try something." He keys the PA mic.

(SCRRRRR) . . .

Timmy springs into action and in Bond mode, he heads over to Mosley! He is walking as fast as his leg irons will let him. Although the doc is still piecing together the puzzle of Timmy's bizarre behavior, he is proud of himself for discovering the triggering mechanism.

"Just as I thought!" he says, speaking into the PA mic.

"That's some crazy shit, Doc!" Wax says in astonishment.

"Crazy like a cuckoo's nest!" Cottrell adds.

Mosley has dreaded a face-to-face confrontation with the *Wild One*; now here he comes, hobble-hopping across the room. The rusted leg irons, shiny handcuffs, swollen black eye, dirt and grease smeared on his torn shirt and pants, the two-day beard stubble, the limp, and the creepy sound of the heavy chains dragging on the floor, along with the intimidating demeanor of his Bond mode, is scaring Mosley to death! Even with all of Timmy's restraints, Mosley feels out-manned and up against what he perceives as a *violent* force!

As Timmy gets closer, Mosley begins to feel like a trapped rat! His instincts are screaming, *RETREAT!* But all he can manage is a half-step backward when his heel bumps against the bottom of the closed bathroom door. Mosley fumbles with one hand for the doorknob behind him, while his other hand is shaking uncontrollably and rattling the keys in a symphony of clinking, jingle-jangles. With his back pressed against the bathroom door and Timmy almost to him, Mosley brings his fumbling hand from behind, raising it waist-level in a halting gesture to Timmy.

This is it! Mosley is sweating profusely.

The doc keys the PA mic, and the sound stops Timmy in his tracks. Shifting out of Bond mode, he looks back over his shoulder at the doc in the observation room.

Timmy slowly turns his attention to Mosley. *I hope this guy knows his lines.*

Mosley seizes the moment by grabbing Timmy's cuffs, and in a split second, he unlocks one cuff. He steps away and walks rapidly to the exit, leaving Timmy standing there with one cuff locked to his wrist and the other dangling by his side. As Mosley gets closer to the *escape hatch,* he starts to calm down and breathes a sigh of relief.

"OK, *boy . . . go* ahead in there and take a bath!" Mosley hollers out in an authoritative voice.

Nurse Debra, finishing up with the dinner table, shouts to Timmy.

"You'll find a towel, washcloth, and gown in the closet."

Timmy goes into the bathroom and closes the door, while the doc buzzes the observation door open. Mosley passes through the door and walks over to a chair next to Wax and Cottrell. He sits down, pulls out his handkerchief, and begins to wipe his face.

"Damn, man! You're wringing wet!" Cottrell exclaims.

"Yeah. It's hot in there." Mosley takes a shaky breath and looks at his watch. *Man, I'm glad that shit is over! Only ten minutes till the end of my shift!*

In the bathroom, Timmy is getting undressed. He unzips his pants and starts to pull them down when he suddenly realizes there's no way to take them off with the leg irons on! He debates his dilemma . . . *To undress or not to undress? To undress or not to undress? To undress or not to undress? That is the question.*

Deciding to call for help, and with his pants down around the leg irons, Timmy shuffles over to the door, opens it, and pokes his head out.

"WARDROBE!" Timmy hollers out into the dayroom.

His shout startles Nurse Debra. She turns around to see what Timmy is yelling about. She immediately understands that his problem is removing the pants, and although she's busy cleaning up the table and wants to hurry up and get home, she knows she has to help him. Agitated, she quickly walks over to Timmy, shoves him down in a nearby chair, and rips apart his pants with her bare hands! It wasn't very difficult because the pants were already badly torn.

Everyone in the observation room watches in amazement as this fleshy, irritated woman shreds Timmy's clothes. She then helps him out of the chair and hands him his shredded pants. She returns to the table to finish cleaning up, and Timmy waddles back to the bathroom, removing his shirt as he goes.

Debra loads everything onto the carts and pulls them over to the observation room door. The doc opens the door and helps her move the heavy carts through the narrow doorway.

"That was quite a show of strength ripping his pants off him like that!" he chuckles. "I should have cut them off earlier; I completely forgot. You are a remarkably resourceful nurse!"

"Thanks, Doc. But I was just doing my job."

"I noticed *Gurney Guy* seems a little more, er . . . relaxed."

"Yes, he does, doesn't he?"

"Did he have any frightful episodes during his bath? Was he combative in any way?"

"No. He was just fine."

"Also, I noticed he's lost his . . . ah . . ."

"He just needed a cool sponge bath!" she responds with a smile.

"Yes, I suppose it could be that. On the other hand, it could be that the tranquilizer is wearing off. We'll just have to wait and see if anything else comes up! In the meantime, we've got to bring some beds into the dayroom."

"We've only got two available beds on the whole unit. They're in rooms 17 and 18 and are already made up."

"Good! But we need . . ."

"We've got extra cots over at the jail, Doc. I could call the chief and have him bring one over," Wax offers.

"That sounds like a winner!" the doc says.

(SCRRRRR) . . . "Unit two to base."

(SCRRRRR) . . . "This is base. Go ahead."

(SCRRRRR) . . . "Lynette, could you have the chief bring over one of those spare cots we have in cell one before he goes home?" Wax asks.

(SCRRRRR) . . . "Will do." Lynette replies. "But I doubt he's going home. He's pretty wound up."

(SCRRRRR) . . . "Roger that . . . over and out."

"OK. Let's see here," the doc says. "It's pushing 7:00 p.m. and . . ."

"I've got to get going and pick up my kids," Nurse Debra interjects.

"Well, OK. You take these carts back to the kitchen, and Mosley can get the beds."

"I gotta feed my dogs!" Mosley speaks up.

"It won't take long," the doc assures him.

Nurse Debra heads off to the kitchen, and Mosley goes to get the beds.

Meanwhile, Timmy is standing naked in the bathroom, in his Shakespeare mode, in front of the mirror.

"To shower or not to shower? To shower or not to shower? To shower or not to shower? That is the question," he says aloud to the mirror. *Since I'm here anyway, I may as well go ahead and shower, but I'll make it quick! I want to get back on the set.*

Timmy grabs the soap and quickly goes through the motions of washing. He rinses off and pulls back the curtain.

"This isn't much of a dressing room!" he yells out.

He opens the closet, grabs a towel, and sees the stack of hospital gowns. *Not much in the way of wardrobe, either! These low-budget productions are pathetic! My agent's going to hear about this!*

Timmy dries off and puts on a clean gown. On his way out of the bathroom, he notices the toilet.

"To shit or not to shit? To shit or not to shit? That is the . . . UUGGGHHH!" He's suddenly hit with a cramp. *I think I'll shit! But I have to be quick and get back on the set!*

The shit and shower didn't even take fifteen minutes, and Timmy emerges from the bathroom just as Mosley is returning with the first bed.

"Go ahead and put the bed next to the gurney. Maybe *Mr. Straitjacket* will take the hint and try to get some rest," the doc says. "Oh, and get the *Wild One's* clothes out of the bathroom while you're in there," he adds.

Mosley, feeling nervous about returning to the dayroom, is also pissed off because he's working late. He glances out the observation room window to get a fix on all the Bonds. Timmy is sitting on a chair at the far right of the room, Sean is leaning against the windowsill to the far left, and George, near the center of the room, is glued to a chair watching TV.

Mosley wheels the bed into the dayroom and hurriedly places it next to Roger. He quickly rechecks everyone's position before turning his back and opening the bathroom door. A blast of *out-of-this-world* odor hits him in the face.

"*DAMN!* What the shit?!" he exclaims loudly.

Mosley grabs a bag and rapidly shoves Timmy's clothes in it. His eyes are burning from the putrid stench, and he can't catch his breath. At the same time, Mosley is scared of getting jumped from behind while being bent over. He stands up quickly and rushes out of the bathroom with the clothes hanging out of the bag. On the way out, he flips the switch for the exhaust fan and leaves the door open.

Making a beeline for the exit, Mosley reaches the door just as Doc buzzes it open. Coughing and gagging from the bathroom smell, he hurries through the doorway and tosses the bag of clothes to Cottrell. Using his black marker, Cottrell labels the bag: **WILD ONE** and places it next to the others.

"What's that smell?" The Doc wrinkles his nose.

"Man! It's from the bathroom! That old boy must have swallowed a skunk! DAMN! In all my years of cleaning shit, I've never smelled anything that rotten before!"

The Doc looks back at the dayroom with the bathroom door wide open and the reactions of all the Bonds to the odor. George is looking around the room with a furrowed brow... Roger, in his tranquilized state, is rubbing his nose... even Sean, who supposedly has no sense of smell, is twitching his nose. Doc finds these behaviors very interesting. And over near the right corner of the room, Timmy is sitting nonchalantly with his hands behind his head in his own little world.

"That smell is pretty strong, huh?" the Doc asks.

"If I hadn't turned on that exhaust fan when I did, the shit smell would have peeled the paint!"

"Don't worry, it will dissipate. Go ahead and get the other bed. And I'll tell *Kilt Man* to take a shower."

"Better let that bathroom air out for a while or somebody will have to go in there and revive him!"

"Yeah, sure."

Mosley leaves the observation room to get the second bed, and the Doc turns his attention to Sean. He notices Sean's nose twitching.

I wonder if his sense of smell is returning? This could be the first indication that he's coming out of R.R.D. It's well documented that scent is the strongest sense linked to memory. Perhaps the stink is so strong as to awaken a sleeping olfactory. It could be acting like smelling salts! Quite possibly, he is familiar with that odor and is recalling a specific past incident!

The Doc notices that Roger has stopped rubbing his arm across his nose and Sean's nose has stopped twitching. George's undivided attention is again centered on the *Evangeline* musical.

Doc concludes that the stench has subsided and it's now safe for George to go into the bathroom. Doc electronically turns off the TV from the observation room and gets George's attention. He motions for George to come over to the window, and when he does, the Doc instructs him to take a shower.

George is glad to get a bath. He knows that the two previous *baths* he had in the river, with no soap and cold water, didn't really get him clean. He walks in the bathroom and can smell the remains of the stink.

Timmy must have eaten some bad caviar. That's why I always insist upon Beluga.

George is showering while Mosley is trying to wheel the second bed down to the dayroom. He's having trouble trying to get it to roll. The brake is on, and one wheel seems to be jammed. Already on edge from having to deal with four new patients, one of which is a violent, unpredictable maniac, and angry at having to work late, Mosley doesn't need the aggravation of a stuck brake!

Struggling with the bed, Mosley kicks at the lever, trying to release the brake. That failing, he tries to push the bed across the floor and makes a large, black skid mark across the white tile floor! He curses and kicks at the brake lever one more time, then picks up the corner of the bed and slams it on the floor, hoping to force the brake to unlock. But it just won't roll! He decides to get a hammer in the maintenance room and takes off in a huff.

Meanwhile, George is taking a shower and summarizing the day's events. But as much as he's enjoying the warm water and the luxury of soaping up, he tries not to take too long since he wants to finish watching the musical. With the shower over, he dries off and takes a gown from the closet.

"Well, at least it's clean!" he mutters.

George looks in the mirror as he puts on the gown and ties it in the back. Over in Room 18, Mosley kneels down to tap the brake lever with the hammer. He notices a black button on the side of the wheel and remembers that it's the lock release for the brake lever! He grits his teeth.

"DAMN! All this time I've been trying to unlock the brake, and a simple push of the button is all it takes!" Really pissed off now, he slides the hammer across the floor, stands up, rolls the bed into the hallway, then down to the dayroom, cursing all the while.

"I can't wait to get the hell out of here and go home! I'm setting up this bed, and that's it!"

Mosley pushes the bed into the observation room and patiently waits for the Doc to finish writing something before he's given instructions about the bed.

"I'll be with you in just a minute, Mosley!" the Doc says.

Glancing into the dayroom, Mosley's mood goes from pissed off to petrified! Timmy is pacing in a circular pattern on the right side of the room near the TV, Sean is still leaning against the windowsill and looking angrier than ever, and Roger is rolling his head from side to side and mumbling *"hey, baby"* again and again. George emerges from the bathroom in a relaxed attitude and strolls over to his TV chair. Just then, the Doc looks up, and George signals him to turn on the musical. The Doc gives George a thumbs-up and flicks on the TV from the observation room.

Already beginning to sweat, Mosley formulates his final trip into the dayroom. *I'm going to beeline it in, place the bed, and beeline it out!*

"OK, Mosley, sorry about the wait." The Doc closes his notebook.

"Ah... just go ahead and put that bed to the right of the gurney."

The Doc unlocks the door, and Mosley starts through the doorway, confident that he has every move calculated.

"And Mosley, get Kilt Man's clothes out of the bathroom before you leave."

SHIT! More stinking clothes! That wasn't part of my plan!

With no time to formulate a Plan B, Mosley forges ahead into the dayroom with the bed, which he places next to Roger and the gurney. He sets the brake and hurries over to the bathroom to retrieve the last bag of clothes. Just as before, he fears an attack from behind while stuffing the clothes into the bag. He rushes out of the bathroom and runs over to the door with the clothes trailing out of the bag! The Doc sees him coming and quickly buzzes open the door.

Mosley sprints into the observation room like a runner at the finish line. He is winded and shaking. He'd felt as if all the Bonds were on his heels! He hands the final bag of clothes to Cottrell, who doesn't bother to look up from the card game. As Mosley tries to catch his breath, the chief, with a jail cot under his arm, walks into the observation room.

"Here you go," he says, handing the cot to Mosley.

Before he realizes what he's doing, he takes the cot from the chief and stands there stunned. *What the hell did I just do? How did I end up with this?*

"Go ahead and set that up, Mosley, then you can get going. Put it in the far right corner, behind the TV."

Mosley can't believe it! It all happened so fast! In one clean sweep, he was roped into going back in there! He cringes at the thought! He turns slowly, defeat splashed across his face, and takes a few slow steps toward the door to the dayroom. He feels as if he's about to walk down death row! As Doc buzzes the door open, the electronic lock seems to clang louder than usual. Although Mosley's heard that sound a thousand times before, this time the cold, institutional echo chills his bones! His feet are like lead weights as he trudges into the dayroom.

Is this all real? he asks himself. Just as he passes through the door, the chief's radio goes off, and the sound throws Timmy into his Bond mode.

Mosley looks over at him and is suddenly frozen in fear. Timmy's Bond-like gaze bores right through him! Looking to his left, Mosley can see Sean, Roger, and George. To his right, he sees the chief talking to Doc while Wax and Cottrell are at the card table. Cottrell is busy marking the last bag of clothing: **KILT MAN.** Nobody is paying attention to the dayroom! Mosley feels deserted in this *den of insanity!*

I can do this! I can do this! he nervously reassures himself.

Mosley, determined to get this done, musters up enough courage to take a few steps, and at the same time, Timmy senses that Mosley wants to come over to the corner. Mosley walks forward and to the right. Timmy steps to the left, which is Mosley's right. Mosley moves left, and Timmy slides right, which is Mosley's left. They sidestep in front of each other in a type of directional awkwardness, but Mosley perceives it as a threatening standoff.

"Are we going to dance or what?" Timmy asks.

Sean is watching the whole scene from his windowsill. *Timmy's going to try and take him!* he says to himself excitedly.

Finally, Timmy shuffles left, and Mosley does the same. They switch positions by going around each other. Mosley, now with his back to the wall, can scan the whole room and get a fix on everyone's position.

They're unchanged except for Timmy, who, looking wild and shifty-eyed in his Bond mode, has resumed his circular pacing in front of the observation room door. Mosley can feel trouble brewing as he sets up the cot.

He's either going to try and block the door and hold me hostage, or he's going to try and escape! Mosley thinks as he watches Timmy.

Hot and sweaty and more than a little jumpy, Mosley is having trouble setting up the cot. It's a heavy canvas military-type cot with scissor-like legs and sturdy springs. But the springs are slightly rusted; it's becoming quite difficult to get the legs apart! Mosley keeps an eye on the Bonds while struggling with the cot. Still, nobody in the observation room is even glancing his way!

Mosley begins to feel a very real danger. Timmy's looks are becoming more menacing, and his pace is increasing.

I'm not too worried about the guy preoccupied with the TV. I think the one on the gurney is still out of it... or is he? The next time he freaks out, it could be deadly! That sumbitch could jump up and really come unglued. And Mr. Straitjacket is still able to kick and stomp! He keeps staring at the maniac pacing, and the maniac is staring right back at him, and I don't like the looks either one of them is giving me!

Mosley continues to fumble with the cot. Bink... bang... clank! Clunk... bang... bang. *This damn cot!* Bang... bang.

Mosley's hassle with the cot has become a full-fledged fight! And he, Sean, and Timmy all continue to exchange glances. Mosley feels like they're all predators about to pounce any second, and he's convinced it will happen soon!

Timmy's going to try and take him! Sean thinks as he watches Timmy's pacing become more and more agitated. *Yeah, that's it, Timmy.*

You can take him! I know if anybody can get us out of this shit, it's you! Roger's had it... George has never had it... I have it, but my hands are tied! So it's all up to you, Timmy! Come on, Timmy!

Finally, what seems like a never-ending battle with the cot suddenly comes to an abrupt end! Right before Mosley was about to smash it to smithereens, the cot springs open and locks into position! Mosley's frantic struggle ends in an instant, and for a brief moment, he feels relieved. He snaps out of that sensation, swallows hard, and stands up. He has bigger fish to fry with the likes of Sean and Timmy. Luckily,

Timmy's pace has taken him a slight distance from the door, and Mosley thinks his timing couldn't be better. He starts walking toward the observation room door.

Come on, Timmy! Sean silently cheers him on.

Mosley walks slowly, standing tall and trying to project an air of confidence while caving inside. Timmy's eyes are darting from Sean to Mosley to the door and back again from the door to Sean to Mosley and over to the door! Out of the corner of his eye, Mosley is keeping tabs on Sean while watching Timmy come straight toward him. Mosley's goal is the door, but the attack feels imminent!

HELP ME, SOMEBODY! Mosley screams inwardly.

Come on, Timmy! Sean encourages.

Mosley panics. He can see into the nurse's station and notices a young intern named Brenda entering the room.

Come on, Timmy! Come on, Timmy! Come on, Timmy! Come on, Timmy! Sean is pumped up by his inner dialogue.

Mosley reaches the door with Timmy right in his face. Mosley makes a grab for the doorknob.

Just then, Brenda drops her book on the desk, accidentally keying the mic. The sound snaps Timmy out of his Bond mode.

He leans into Mosley's face. "If you hear anything, let me know," Timmy says in a soft, secretive whisper.

"Uh... yeah, right!" Mosley says with an eye-popping expression.

What's Timmy doing? Sean is angry and disappointed. *DAMN! He could have taken him! DAMN!*

Timmy backs away from Orderly Mosley and nods his head along with a thumbs-up gesture that says, *"We got a deal."* Timmy saunters away with a lost look on his face and wanders over to his cot.

Mosley, now "safe" in the observation room, wearily sits down and pulls out his sweat-filled handkerchief to mop up more sweat.

"Mosley, are you all right? You're wringing wet!"

"Yeah, I'm OK. It's just *really hot* in there!"

"I noticed the wild one had something to say to you."

"Yeah. Get this—he said if I hear anything to let him know!"

"What'd I tell you, Chief? Classic *Schizophrenia!*" The Doc turns to the Chief with a look of confidence.

"Yeah, and what'd I tell you? *Classic Criminal!* And why is this guy uncuffed in the first place?" The Chief asks Officer Wax.

"We had to uncuff him so he could shower and dress."

"Oh... I don't like this! I don't like it at all!" The Chief shakes his head.

"Ah, Mosley, we need to get the *Wild One* a pillow and some linens," the Doc says.

"Oh no, not me!" Mosley stands up in a panic. "I've got to go right now! I've got to feed my dogs! Sorry, but I'm outta here!"

"I guess it is a little late. Sorry about that. See you in the morning, then."

With a disgusted look, the Chief stares through the glass at Timmy. "We've got just the *linens* a criminal like him deserves over at the jail. Standard jailhouse issue! A hard sponge pillow and a thin, burlap-textured blanket! That'll make him feel right at home! Wax—run next door and get our boy here some real linens!"

"Sure thing, Chief!"

"Well, I've got to go." The Chief sounds reluctant. "I'm gonna check on the dredging operation and the search of the boat. We've got spotlights set up so the guys can work through the night."

"Let me ask you something, Chief. If these guys are getting off on diplomatic immunity, then it won't make any difference whether you find something or not... right?"

"Not necessarily, Doc. Diplomatic immunity is not exactly *the free walk* it used to be now that we have the Patriot Act! If I find enough to stack the deck against these guys, they're not going anywhere! I don't give a damn what their lawyer says!"

Just then, the phone rings and the Doc answers. "Bellefontaine Clinic."

"Hello, Doc. Warren Perrin here. How's everything going?"

"Speaking of their lawyer... it's Perrin." The Doc covers the receiver with his hand. "Hello, Perrin. Well, we've got your clients all cleaned up and fed and ready for bed."

"Sounds good, Doc! Do you think you can have them ready to go around mid-morning? Tony Blair and his bunch will be here about noon."

"Sure, I can have them ready."

"You don't anticipate any problems, do you?"

"No, we always use a mild sedative when we transport patients if need be. They are in good hands and will be ready in the morning."

"Great! Then I'll be in touch with you in the morning. Good night."

"Good night, Mr. Perrin."

"What did Perrin say?" the Chief asks.

"He said that Tony Blair and his bunch will be here tomorrow morning."

"Tomorrow morning?" the Chief asks, sounding discouraged.

"Actually, about mid-morning."

"Damn!"

"You know, looking at those guys, you wouldn't think they have such powerful political connections! If you're going to stack the deck against them, you'd better find some *cards* real quick!"

Just then, Wax walks into the observation room carrying a lumpy pillow and a blanket.

"OK, Chief... I've got the linens!" Wax says with a smart-assed grin.

"Yeah, look. I've got to get going. Call that maniac over to the door, recuff him, and hand him his pillow and blanket. If he tries anything..."

"Don't worry, Chief!" Cottrell interrupts. "If he tries anything, Mr. *Coldcocker* will make minced meat out of him!"

"You know, with that kind of talk, I'm surprised you and your buddy there have never been brought up on brutality charges! That blackjack looks like it's on steroids!"

Cottrell strokes the blackjack like a proud papa. "I whittled this baby out of a 28 Louisville Slugger! Brutality charges? Hey, can we help it if prisoners sometimes *fall down* when they're getting arrested?"

Cottrell chuckles softly, but Doc is not amused. The Chief has left the clinic. Brenda, the young intern, is reading her book, and Doc resumes his note-taking. He has noticed that Roger's bulge under the sheet has returned. Officer Wax walks over to the Doc.

"Doc, when you get done there, can you unlock the door and call that guy over to get his linens? I need to recuff him."

"OK, Wax. Are you ready?"

The Doc unlocks the door and calls Timmy over. "Excuse me, would the patient near the cot..."

Timmy points to himself in a *who, me?* manner.

"Yes, you. Please come over to the door," the Doc says.

The director probably wants to go over some script changes. Timmy heads for the door.

"Doc, when that maniac gets close, I want you to step out of the way."

"OK, Wax. But no rough stuff!"

Timmy steps up to the opened door. "I need to recuff you," Wax says. "And here's your bedding."

Timmy submissively raises his wrists to Officer Wax and gets recuffed. Wax places the pillow and blanket in Timmy's arms and then steps back inside the observation room. Timmy can see the Doc at the window gesturing for him to return to his cot. He stands there for a moment and says to himself, *Well, so much for script changes!*

Timmy returns to his cot with the pillow and blanket. Sean has been watching the whole cuffing scenario and is disgusted with Timmy for giving in so easily. Still leaning against the windowsill, Sean sums up the situation.

Poor Roger! The boys in the Psych Department really did a number on him! And along with the drugs, shock treatments, and whatever else, he doesn't stand a chance! STEALTH EXAMINATION, my ass! STEALTH SCREWING is more like it! Maybe he'll be better by morning. Judging by that bulge in the covers, we really need to get him to New Orleans!

And that damn George... the way he pigged out on that chow, he's got so much truth serum in his system, he would confess to his first wet dream if they asked him! He's taken Stockholm syndrome to a whole new level! He's hypnotized by that TV and absolutely useless when it comes to the completion of this mission! By morning he may be a hair better than dead weight!

Sean looks over at Timmy. *And talk about a chameleon! The way Timmy sublimates that Shakespeare, it's like he's a few centuries removed from the here and now. He's impossible to communicate with, even by Double O standards! And his hearing problem is not helping either. With a good night's sleep, maybe he'll wake up in the here and now! Primeaux's gang will be changing shifts in the morning, and they'll be getting off to a groggy start. Maybe there'll be some miscommunication or commotion that will provide an opportunity for escape! Then we could make our way over to the control facility, get the Aspic data, and get the hell out of Melville! Well, I guess I'd better get some sleep myself.*

Doc watches as Sean lies down on the bed. *Thank God, for that old boy's sake, it's about time he relaxes a little. Hell, it's time they all relax and get some shut-eye!*

(SCRRRRR)... The Doc keys the mic and Timmy jumps to his feet, immediately in Bond mode. "It's time you boys get some sleep," he announces. "I'm going to turn off the TV and lights now. We'll have a nice breakfast for you all in the morning. Goodnight!"

(SCRRRRR)... He switches both the mic and Timmy off.

"Hey, Doc, you've got to leave on at least one of those lights so we can see in there," Wax says.

"Oh sure, I'll leave the one on near the bathroom." He turns off the TV and all the lights except one. "Is that OK?"

Wax looks into the dayroom and is satisfied that he can see across the room all the way to Timmy's cot in the corner. "That's just fine, Doc," he says.

Sean notices that the light is brightest on his side of the room. *They're leaving that light on to inflict sleep deprivation before they turn up the torture!*

CHAPTER V

Anna, the Doc's daughter, comes in to talk to her dad before going home.

"How's it going, Pop? I see you've got them all settled in for the night," she says cheerily.

"Yeah, I guess so," the Doc replies with a tight-lipped expression.

"What's wrong? Earlier, you were so upbeat."

"Well, that was a *'glory days of ER'* rush I was having," he says sadly. "I used to thrive on emergencies! When I did my internship at Tulane, there were hours and hours of nonstop action."

"Well, nothing lasts forever," she says kindly. "How are they doing?"

"Physically, for the most part, they're stable."

"How about mentally? You know, it just so happens I'm studying initial assessment in my Psychology class."

"Oh yeah?"

"Do they exhibit any mental deficits? Have you made any diagnosis in that area?"

"I did begin to piece together some assessments... similar symptoms, common denominators, plausible logic..."

"Oh, you mean like that name thing? What is it... Bond James Bond?" she asks.

"Yes, that's one aspect of common denominators. It was enough to start me thinking. Can you imagine having a first name and last name the same? I wonder what kind of parents would name their kids like that?"

"Yes, that is strange. But I began to look at the bigger picture and see what was really going on with those guys. Although they share the same name, they're seemingly from different walks of life based on their dress and demeanor. The puzzling thing is how they all ended up in the same place at the same time. The Chief thinks they're all criminals and this common name thing is an alias used in a bombardment fashion to throw off law enforcement. But I don't agree with him."

"From what I understand, they did wreak havoc on the whole community."

"Yes, but was it *harmonious* havoc? Was it a joint effort?"

"I see what you mean."

"Even though there is no real camaraderie amongst them and they appear to be disconnected from one another, I still sense something more is going on with them than what we can see or hear."

"Are you saying that they're strangers?"

"Well, there's been no real communication between any of them except for one brief incident in the lobby, and that can be construed as a simple social encounter. After all, they were in a lobby where it's not uncommon for strangers to chit-chat."

"Well, yes, but..."

"It was the nature of that brief conversation that led me to factor in another common denominator."

"Which is?"

"Schizophrenia."

"*SCHIZOPHRENIA? In all* of them!"

"Yes, all of them!"

"But that's not possible! That's not even plausible! What are the chances of encountering *four* schizophrenic patients at the *same* time or even the four of them ever connecting to one another?"

"I know! The odds are probably a million to one!"

"Unless they escaped from another mental facility in the area."

"I considered that possibility. Surely, we would have been notified if that had occurred, and the Chief would have been aware of it, also."

"But four at the same time!"

"I know! That's what I said to myself. But I can't deny my own observations. As a scientist, I'm trained to deal with the facts and to keep an open mind, as well as an open eye out for the unexpected. You know, Anna, just as I do, that many of the major breakthroughs and discoveries in the world have happened simply by chance."

"Yes, I know that."

"For instance, think about how Alcoholics Anonymous began. Two old drunks stumbled upon each other in the same facility and formulated a very successful program to overcome the addiction of alcohol. And now their accidental meeting has helped millions of people in all areas of addiction! It's my understanding that many other twelve-step programs began the same way—by chance meetings!"

"That all makes sense, Dad, but schizophrenic chance meetings?"

"Well, you know I've always been fascinated with the audio aspects of schizophrenia."

"Yes, I know you've written and submitted plenty of peer-reviewed articles on the subject."

The Doc looks through the window into the dayroom. "Take, for instance, that patient in the corner sitting on the cot. We've nicknamed him *Wild One*. I can confirm without any doubt that he is schizophrenic. If I key the mic on this PA system, he will completely change his behavior, even his voice. I can turn him on and off like a light switch with this mic."

"I guess in his case, schizophrenia is pretty obvious."

"And the one in the bed next to him..."

"Wasn't he the one in the kilt?" she asks.

"That's right. We call him *Kilt Man.* Anyway, I talked with him at length and really *tuned* into him, no pun intended. He's got *songs* going off in his head!"

"There's nothing unusual with that. Just this morning, I was humming a tune in my head."

"No, you don't understand, not *a* song but songs. Meaning more than one! And they're playing simultaneously!"

"Now that is unusual!"

"And not only that, but one of the songs has been playing for thirty *years!*"

"For thirty *years?!*"

"Yes. And the other song is brand new to his brain. He has no concept of time or the here and now."

"Could it be that he's an oldies fan and something new struck his fancy?"

"Hey, I like oldies just as much as the next guy, but I never had one playing for thirty years in my head!"

"Yes, that is quite extreme!"

"And that's not all. He readily admits to having trouble figuring out what's real and what's not!"

"Well, then he's a pretty clear-cut case of..."

"And he also claims to be wrestling with a status issue and seems to be caught between the rungs of the ladder."

"Ah... you mean like the corporate ladder? Do you think he's climbing or falling?"

"I wish it was a simple matter of social or economic status. But the ladder I'm referring to is that of the schizophrenic, and the rungs represent worlds... I mean *literally!*"

"Of course! What was I thinking? We had a lecture about that analogy in Dr. Nina Pearl's class last semester."

"Like most schizophrenic patients, he must have suffered a traumatic experience that propelled him into the illness. Whatever happened thirty years ago, he was never able or willing to deal with it."

"It's like sweeping something under a rug. It leaves a lump," Anna muses.

"It damn sure doesn't just disappear!"

"Speaking about a lump... what's with the guy on the gurney? It looks like there's something under the covers."

"A... er... this is a little awkward, you being my daughter and all."

"Oh Pop, we're both professionals!"

"Yes, you're right. Well, my guess is that *Gurney Guy* there is a Viagra user. He could be addicted to it or, at the very least, a *heavy* user! I'm waiting for his blood work to confirm that diagnosis."

"I saw him when they first brought him in, and he looked really out of it. How were you able to draw a schizophrenic diagnosis with him in that condition?"

"Audio indicators, as well as visual indicators. He was shot with a tranquilizer dart and is supposed to be totally immobilized."

"Supposed to be?"

"From time to time, he has these startling outbursts. The triggering mechanism could be audio in origin. But the outbursts also occur while he's in contact with people close to him. He may be seeing something real or imagined that frightens him."

"Yes, but if he is totally immobilized by the tranquilizer, wouldn't all of his senses be dulled to the point of no response?"

"Non-responsive for the average man, but not for the schizophrenic! Don't forget, the schizophrenic patient has heightened hearing and sensitized sight, and sometimes his senses are connected to finely-tuned frequencies."

"That makes a lot of sense, Pop!"

Over in the corner, Officers Wax and Cottrell are still playing cards, and Cottrell sneaks a peek at Anna.

"Man, look at the ass on that Anna!" Cottrell says in a hushed voice.

"You keep looking at *that* ass and Detective Coco is going to have *your* ass!" Wax warns.

"So you've told me about three of them. What about the fourth?" Anna asks.

"Ah—*Mr. Straitjacket*. Now, his case is more complex than any of the other three. He's afflicted with a secondary condition called Rage Reflex Disease, commonly referred to as R.R.D."

"Rage Reflex Disease? I've never heard of that."

"It's a relatively new description of the 'Swallowed Scream' Theory proposed by Dr. Fred Arven in the 1950s. It's a complicated condition caused by extreme rage, sometimes coupled with violence, that becomes internalized."

"Is it kin to the acid reflux that we're all familiar with?"

"The names reflux and reflex sound similar, but they are worlds apart! Reflux is a flowing outward, whereas reflex is a bending back. One is a release, and the other is a restriction. Totally opposite of one another."

"But rage is always a component of this disease?"

"Absolutely! We know that some schizophrenic patients are capable of violent behavior. Correct?"

"That's right."

"Well, it appears that *Mr. Straitjacket* was in the process of going into a raging, maniacal fit of potentially extreme violent behavior that was fueled by exceptionally high levels of adrenaline when he was suddenly arrested. Both literally and figuratively! The entire outburst was halted, then redirected inward, and internalized!"

"Yes, but I don't..."

"That much adrenaline, riding on the outburst, flooded his central nervous system in a constricting manner and temporarily turned off most of his senses and motor skills. In layman's terms—he got so pissed off, he paralyzed himself! We can't underestimate the effects that even one negative thought may have on the body and brain, and especially on the spirit!"

"I don't know, Pop. That all seems a little far-fetched!"

"Far-fetched? Not in the least. We know an asthma attack can be brought on by an emotional upset as well as dust, pollen, chemical vapors, and odors that constrict and paralyze the bronchial tubes."

"Yes, I know. But you're still not making the case for schizophrenia and *Mr. Straitjacket*. Which one of the four basic types of schizophrenia would you say he falls under?"

"Oh, he definitely matches three out of four types of schizophrenia and maybe even all four! Catatonically speaking, he exhibits the usual rigid posture, lack of movement, and/or attempts at frenzied movements, negativism, and silence."

"OK. Go on. I'm gonna play the devil's advocate here," Anna says playfully.

"That's fine. You do that," Doc replies with a smile. "Now, regarding *Disorganized Schizophrenia*, our patient here evidences a restricted range of emotions. In other words, he's got *one* gear... pissed off!"

"Isn't that due to his Rage Reflex?"

"Restricted range of emotions is partly responsible for the reflex reaction. But at this point, the Rage Reflex Disease is a secondary condition overlapping his underlying schizophrenia."

"How have you come to that conclusion?"

"First of all, I considered the amount of drugs I had to give him to counteract the results of the rage reflex... 20 cc's of Perzonia and 30 cc's of Quintellizine!"

"Wow, that's a lot!"

"But that's how much it took to stop the contorting. I was afraid he was going to break something. It took every cc to stabilize him! That's why I'm convinced this is not just Rage Reflex Disease. He was in a psychological vise!"

"Do you think he has Obsessive-Compulsive Disorder as well?"

"That's very possible. We know that obsessive-compulsive disorders and addictions are prevalent in the schizophrenic community. But that's putting it mildly for the intensity he displays!"

"Maybe he's *religiously* intoxicated. Now that's intensity! Rampant religious intoxication around the world is the worst addiction affecting planet Earth today! In my opinion, it's more destructive than an atom bomb and more deadly than an incurable disease!" Anna is adamant.

"Well said! Religious intoxication could explain some of the unbending, unyielding rigidity that *Mr. Straitjacket* displays. No doubt, he has a strong belief system, depending on what world he's in and who he's worshipping. But I don't think it's religious intoxication in his case. It's more than that."

"But if he comes from a repressed religiosity, the anger he expresses could be his spirit crying out for an unshackling or a breaking free. His spirit could be suffocating! It's almost as if he's in a *psychological* straitjacket to match the real one he's got on."

"I think it's more than that. Besides, most people his age have struck a balance between religious repression and unrestrained behavior, and they mellow out. No, it's something else with that guy!"

"What about the *paranoid* perspective?" Anna suggests.

"You're talking about delusions of grandeur or persecution. As far as a persecution complex goes, there's not an ounce of victim mentality in this guy! But yet, on the other hand, he carries himself in a grand manner. He acts as if he were a big shot!"

"Oh yeah? How's that?"

"Well, he's a *Mr. Tee-Dah*, all right! Underneath all that cow shit and diesel was an expensive suit and handmade Italian shoes!"

"Oh really?"

"Yes, he actually exudes an air of authority and sophistication. If there's a pecking order among the four of them, my guess is *he's the leader!*"

"Well, Pop, dressing like a *Mr. Tee-Dah* and being sure of himself doesn't make him delusional."

"No, but if you had only seen the look on his face. It was a look that could kill! He really looked as if he would kill anyone who got in his way! And when you factor that in with all the other indicators, it adds up to only one conclusion—*schizophrenia!*"

"Was he hallucinatory?"

"Damned near! It was enough to scare the hell out of Debra and Mosley, although they wouldn't admit it!"

"Yes, Pop, I understand all that, but you're still not making a solid case for a diagnosis of schizophrenia."

"Schizophrenia is a psychotic mental illness that is characterized by a twisted view of the world. It's a disorder that makes it impossible to differentiate between what's real and what's not; hence, *split mind*. The onset of the disorder is often related to a stressful life event."

"I agree completely."

"The Chief told me that *Mr. Straitjacket* drove a railroad truck off the trestle, straight into the river, and had to swim for his life!"

"Wow—that changes everything! When they first brought him into the clinic and I saw him in the lobby, he appeared to be in shock or having a seizure."

"He was seizing all right... bursting at the damn seams is what he was doing! His blood pressure was off the charts! I don't know how he avoided a massive stroke, or at the very least a Grand Mal seizure. That old fart must be made out of steel!"

"So how did he..."

"My guess is that he had two conditions taking place simultaneously. He had the rage reflex response, whereby he internalized the maniacal outburst at the precise moment he was schizophrenically shifting worlds."

"At the precise moment?"

"Yes, at the *precise* moment!"

"What are you saying? The *outburst* was absorbed into the split?"

"Exactly!"

"That doesn't even sound humanly survivable, especially when you consider the blood pressure, shock, and seizure!"

"I know! That's why I said that guy must be made out of steel!"

"So how did he survive?"

"Well, the Rage Reflex Disease is a condition that is constrictive in nature, while the schizophrenia is more of a *reflux* or expandable condition."

"It's hard to keep it straight! *Reflex... reflux!*"

"He was able to survive because of expanding and contracting at the same time, and with equal intensity, the opposing forces combined and became concentrated. The drugs created a calming catalyst. This chemical action prevented a deadly implosion. The components of R.R.D. and schizophrenia are now connected in a dormant state."

"Talk about being put through the wringer!"

"That term doesn't do him any justice. Not for what that poor sombitch has been through! The grinder is more like it!"

"Yes, well that leaves only one other type of schizophrenia, and that's *Undifferentiated.*"

"Yes... the type that is a mixture of *all* types of schizophrenia. He fits this category to some extent, but there's something else that I can't quite put my finger on!"

"What about *acceptable addiction?* You know, a socially acceptable use of a substance or product considered safe, and in reality, it's extremely harmful and difficult to discontinue. Things like perfume, scented laundry products, and air fresheners. Maybe he's a *Fume-a-holic!* We know that fume, from whatever source, is debilitating to the brain and body and accounts for erratic symptoms and behaviors."

"That's absolutely correct! And like other addictive substances, Fumeaholism is a real vice! The fume goes up your nose, down your throat, on your skin, and through it. Once a level of saturation is reached, a lack of tolerance sets in and spills over into a whole array of mental and physical symptoms. The intricate workings and reactions of the brain are *infinite!*"

"Do you think *Mr. Straitjacket* is a Fumeaholic?"

"It's hard to tell. He was caked in cow shit and drenched in diesel, but I didn't notice any overbearing scent on the others. That could indicate a level of *scentual* awareness among them."

"And then there's Brain Lock Syndrome."

"He's definitely a candidate for Brain Lock Syndrome! Whatever his goals or intentions are, he's hell-bent on achieving them at any and all costs! He's extremely focused and consistent. These are admirable qualities in moderation, but when they are pursued in excess and with an attitude of aggression, they imprison a person. Like the scripture, II Peter 2:19... whatever overcomes a man, to that he is enslaved."

"So Pop, in summation, would you say *Mr. Straitjacket* is a catatonically grandiose schizophrenic who is compulsively driven to attain a delusional destiny which may be fueled by religious intoxication or acceptable addictions? Or, on the other hand, is he merely a collection of *tendencies?*"

"*BRILLIANT* summation, Anna! But the possibility of *mere tendencies...* absolutely not! The many worlds of the schizophrenic are deeply embedded in their everyday existence, and he is no exception. In fact, all four of them seem firmly planted in the soil of schizophrenia. And like plants in the same soil, there are variations in appearance and adaptability. Like I said before, they seem to come from different walks of life and may have just met. Or perhaps, they were brought together."

"How so?"

"We know that most schizophrenic patients are tapped into another audio link... a higher frequency. They *hear* and sometimes *see* things that so-called *normal* people don't."

"That's true."

"Well, suppose that Darwin's Theory of Natural Selection is at play here."

"WHAT?"

"Why not? We have always believed the schizophrenic patient lived in his own world or worlds with his own audio link or links. What if these worlds meshed via the audio link? Maybe their vibrational megahertz collided and merged into a single transmission frequency that they heard at the same time, and that brought them together."

"That's kind of a stretch, Pop! It sounds like an old scary movie... *Invasion of the Schizo's!*" Anna laughs.

"This is no laughing matter! I'm serious."

"Yeah, I know. Sorry, but I just couldn't resist!"

"It's well known that athletes and risk-takers are necessary for the survival of our species... the whole *fittest* thing!"

"OK, I can see that."

"Could it be that these four split-minded individuals were following the combined frequency in search of single-mindedness?"

"*Audio athletes* on a trek? We're not talking *fittest*, we're talking *freakiest!*"

"Actually, it is the *fittest of the freakiest*. Society labels the schizophrenics as freaks, and maybe that's the wrong way to look at them. Maybe they're not sick at all... just exceptionally adept at hearing and seeing beyond the *normal* range! Maybe this is one of the ways our species will evolve."

"That's an awful lot of *maybes*."

"Science has confirmed that we only use about 10 percent of our brains. The schizophrenic could be using or attempting to use 20 percent, 30 percent, maybe 40 percent or more! This reminds me of the chemically sensitive community and their highly sensitized olfactory. Those who have been injured with various chemicals and are deemed *sick* by the medical establishment may actually be *gifted* with their incredible sense of smell and brain/body reactions!"

"Yes, that's possible."

"With regard to heightened hearing, some scientists claim to have found evidence of sound waves associated with the crop circles in England and around the world. If we placed schizophrenic patients in those crop circles, imagine what they could tell us! We've spent millions on audio equipment trying to communicate with extraterrestrials without any success. Why not *signal outer space* with *the schizophrenics?* They could be like the canaries in the coal mines... birds sent into the coal mines, and if they keeled over, that would indicate the presence of toxic gases. But instead of being sacrificed, the schizophrenics would be supported and encouraged by the scientific, medical, political, and religious communities."

"That audio equipment is highly sensitive... maybe more so than the schizophrenic patient!"

"Maybe, maybe not. What if it's only capable of picking up the frequency of other equipment, whereas the schizophrenics could pick up the frequency of other life?"

"You might have something there, Pop! It would be worth a try. But back to Darwin's Theory... you said there was no camaraderie amongst them."

"Not on the surface. But it's possible that on a deeper level, they were poised to unite, and more than likely, *Mr. Straitjacket* was the appointed leader."

"That sounds plausible. You said he carries himself with great authority."

"Yes, he is the more dominant force, but he's no more or less important to the total equation than the other three."

"What equation?"

"The *frequency equation!* Suppose all of them tapped into this same frequency. Let's call it the *Phrenia Frequency*... and they were about to converge when the whole process was halted because *Mr. Straitjacket* suffered the Rage Reflex episode, and at the same time, they were arrested both literally and figuratively. I believe this convergence was intended to create a higher order of development and adaptation, with each of them bringing his unique megalomania aspects of schizophrenia to mesh and erupt into a single consciousness from which they could fully function. When that convergence was canceled, they were forced to tap into a corresponding frequency. I believe that frequency was emitting from the patients in this *very* clinic. I think they found their way here by following that frequency."

"But they didn't *follow* anything! The police brought them over here!"

"*Seemingly so...* when in reality, survival of the fittest is achieved by any means possible. Seeds carried on the wind, wildlife washed away to other lands, and schizophrenics shackled and deposited at their eventual destination! It's all about gravitating to that circle of life where you belong."

"Well, they certainly do seem to belong here!"

"With all of our intelligence and medical arrogance, we may have overcomplicated and undervalued schizophrenia and overlooked what might be a very simple explanation for this whole illness. Maybe schizophrenia is an evolution for man's mind, brain, and thinking. It could be a gift rather than a source of grief. Our current treatments suppress this gift and the future advancement of the species!"

"Drug therapy is necessary for severely disturbed patients."

"Well, of course! But many patients complain of drugs stifling and suppressing their spirits and robbing their souls. In some cases, drugs are a form of bondage. That's an example of *acceptable addiction* that is pharmaceutically justified. If these patients were free from drugs, they'd be free to soar!"

"Come on, Pop! Some of these patients would soar right on out of here!"

"Sure, some of them would, but there are many more who could greatly improve with better nutrition and supplements instead of only drugs. With the psychiatric community stifling them and society stigmatizing them, schizophrenics don't stand a chance. Instead of forcing them to conform, we should learn to respect their view of reality and strive to uncover the mysteries of their brains. This disorder could be the gateway to our next order."

"That's quite a theory, Pop!"

"God works in mysterious ways, and I've come to believe he has a hell of a sense of humor! The schizophrenic patient needs to be seen as a great adventure and worthy of discovery. We need more curiosity like the early explorers Lewis and Clark and a spirit of wonder like the team at NASA. We need to think outside the box or, in this case... the ward!"

"You're outside the ward, Pop! Way outside!"

"Is it crazy to be sensitive to others? We cannot underestimate the *power of sensitivity*. A decade or so ago, people who were diagnosed with chemical sensitivity/environmental illness were thought to be 'off their rocker' because of a heightened sense of smell and intolerances to everyday odors, both good and bad. Unscented products were nearly impossible to find, except in specialty stores. Construction rarely gave air quality a second thought. Some in the medical community even suggested the problem with such people was psychological and they needed odor counseling!"

"WHAT?!"

"ODOR COUNSELING!"

"Odor counseling! I thought I'd heard it all, but that takes the cake!"

"Today, we're seeing extreme allergies and heightened sensitivity running rampant throughout the world! Everything from scented products to peanut butter to sunlight is an allergen or sensitizer! And for almost every toxic product, there is a non-toxic counterpart, as well as unscented products readily available at stores nationwide! Indoor air quality has become a billion-dollar industry. The Food and Drug Administration is engaged in a massive relabeling program of all products containing peanuts, and schools throughout the country have implemented safeguards for children allergic to peanuts because of the *very real danger of death*! This slow but steady evolution of chemical and dietary awareness has validated the many sensitive people in our society. These are prime examples of how all truth passes through three stages—first it's *ridiculed, then violently opposed*, and finally, it becomes *self-evident!*"

"And the point is?"

"The point is that through allergy or sensitivity, we become aware and begin to avoid. The very things we avoid are what enlighten us and send us seeking alternatives, ultimately culminating in a greater awareness and healthier lifestyle for all."

"So avoidance breeds awareness?"

"Yes, but it has to be *balanced*. Otherwise, you could avoid yourself right into a damn hole!"

"It's like that saying—*a person's greatest strength can also be his greatest weakness!*"

"Exactly!"

"We need to look at these maladies as abilities. We need to embrace sensitivity as a strength and a weakness and to see what it teaches us and, more importantly, where it takes us. A lack of tolerance, physical weakness, and mental instability are not shameful conditions. They are badges of courage earned on the battlefield of life."

"In relation to sensitivity, how does schizophrenia fit in?"

"I know schizophrenia is a frightening, debilitating illness, but it can teach us about cerebral allergy, electromagnetic fields, audio frequencies, insight, foresight, and the ability to be exquisitely sensitive. From that sensitivity will come enlightenment and improvement in our society."

"You make it all sound so hopeful!"

"And it is hopeful!"

"Well, Pop, that sure was a lot of food for thought, and some of it very palatable."

"It all came to me like a great feast! At the very least, I'm sure I can write a few interesting articles about all this."

"What made you throw in the towel?"

"It was that lawyer. He came in here claiming that those guys worked for the English government."

"I guess that really blew your theories out of the *ward*, so to speak!"

"To some extent. But I still stand by my initial diagnosis of schizophrenia. In fact, the information about their employment only reinforces my assessment of them as schizophrenics! How else could four guys that sick get hired on with the English government?"

"That makes sense, Pop."

"Actually, it's Chief Basile that I'm worried about. He's got the biggest bust of his career, and he's not even getting a conviction."

"Why not?"

"Those guys are eligible for diplomatic immunity. They'll be out of here tomorrow morning and on their way back to England. It's my understanding that Prime Minister Tony Blair is coming here on the Queen's yacht to pick them up!"

"Wow! That's exciting!"

"And that's not all. There's going to be a ceremony on the yacht's deck where that lawyer, Warren Perrin, and Governor Blanco will be accepting the apology for our expulsion in 1755!"

"Is that THE Warren Perrin... the *Apology Perrin?*"

"Yep. One and the same!"

"I didn't recognize him when he came in earlier. Boy, you sure have to admire that guy's tenacity! He's been working on that apology for years!"

"Yeah, he's been at it for around fifteen years or so!"

"Ooooh... the Queen of England will be here!"

"Oh, I don't think she'll be here. It's my understanding Tony Blair will be presenting the apology on her behalf."

"Nevertheless, this is all very exciting! A real *right-the-wrong* scenario being played out right here in tiny Melville and on the deck of the Queen's yacht! It reminds me of..."

"The WWII surrender and treaty signing, right?" the Doc interrupts.

"I thought the same thing."

"Yes! The symbolism is striking."

"It sure is. But more importantly are the redeeming consequences."

"Redeeming consequences?"

"Whenever a wrong is made right, even after 250 years and especially a wrong of this magnitude, the effects on a community are *profound!*

"Yeah, Pop, I see what you mean. And from a sociological perspective, the self-esteem factor could be far-reaching. An apology, no matter how long it is in coming, has the power to transform people."

"I agree, Anna. An apology can create a sense of being restored or made whole. It's a form of justice, and one of the founding principles of this country is—*justice for all!*"

"That's right."

"Unfortunately, there are folks in our community who could not see the significance of an apology. Years ago, I remember when Warren Perrin started petitioning the Queen of England for an apology, and many people criticized his efforts. They thought it was ridiculous to ask for an apology for an incident that happened so long ago. And some people actually thought he was crazy!"

"Well, I never felt like that! And now that Mr. Perrin is about to reap the rewards of his labor, not just for himself but also for Cajuns everywhere, we need to express our gratefulness to him. After all, this is a historical event! It's cause for a large celebration... a parade... a festival!"

"I agree! This is a wonderful opportunity to infuse our community with dignity and pride."

"A real *shot* in the arm."

"I like that analogy! It could also be the *antidote* for feelings of shame and inferiority. The attempt to eradicate French from our schools in the 1920s caused a sense of shame and feelings of being *less than!* Without a clear understanding of who we are and what we have been through, those negative attitudes were passed on generationally. And the result of those attitudes created levels of dysfunction still seen today in many Cajuns. The apology may be the beginning of a renewed spirit in the Cajun community."

"Well, I think we need to get the word out about this incredible event!"

"Oh, the word is out or it will be. I'm sure the media will be present. Oh, you know what else is going on tomorrow? I've volunteered to help escort a class from the Baton Rouge Episcopalian Church to the Mardi Gras Children's Parade in the morning. Wouldn't it be a great field trip for the kids if they could also witness the apology ceremony?"

"That would be a memory they could cherish forever and tell their children and grandchildren about! I'm sure Mr. Perrin will be here first thing in the morning. I'll ask him about it. The class probably won't be able to go on the yacht, but they can watch the ceremony from the riverbanks."

"That sounds like a good idea! This is all so *wonderful!* I'm so excited! I don't think I'll get any sleep tonight!" Anna says enthusiastically.

"Well, you'd better try!"

"What about you? Aren't you going home?"

"I don't think so. The night nurses, Meredith and Christy, will be here at 11:00 p.m., and I might as well sleep in my office. I want to be nearby in case of any problems with these patients."

"Well, Pop, I'm gonna get going. Now make sure you get some sleep!" She kisses Doc on his cheek.

"OK, I'll see you tomorrow."

"Goodnight, Pop." As she walks out of the observation room, she turns to Wax and Cottrell. "Goodnight, boys!" She waves cheerily.

Officers Wax and Cottrell smile and say goodnight to Anna, then resume playing Bourré, a favorite Cajun card game.

Meanwhile, back on the boat, a full-scale search is still underway. The officers and volunteers are well organized and methodical as they tear apart and look through every crate on deck and into every nook and cranny of the boat, right down to the engine room. The bloodhounds are sniffing and snorting, with their tails wagging endlessly like antennas in the wind.

Sean's car is also searched, and surprisingly, none of the gadgetry is set off during the search. The railroad watchman is questioned extensively, and the tracks and trestle are expertly examined, along with the pipeline. Dozens of photos are being taken of everything involved in the crime spree. The river is being dragged near the boat, railroad trestle, and along the banks. Huge spotlights illuminate the whole area. They have been searching for hours and have found nothing. Some of the cops and volunteers are getting tired and restless and are beginning to complain that it's all a waste of time. The chief is convinced that they're close to uncovering something *big* and encourages them to keep up their spirits and to press on. He admits that it'll be a *long* night but reminds them of the overtime benefits.

Back at the police station, a K-9 officer is checking out both the rented Lincoln Navigator and the stolen Lincoln from Krotz Springs. Detective Coco is on the computer for any news that might come up, and Dispatcher Lynette is filing her nails, watching the clock, and waiting for the night dispatcher, Jenny, to arrive. It's almost 11:00

p.m. Over at the clinic, Officers Wax and Cottrell in the observation room and Officer Wane, who's been sitting outside near the windows, are all waiting for their replacements: Officers Galantie, Mathews, and Adkins. Every available officer and volunteer has been working around the clock. The shift changes go off without a hitch for the police department. As for the clinic staff, the shift change has brought Nurse Meredith and Nurse Christy to the observation room, where they check in with the Doc and learn of his plans to spend the night in his office.

On the other side of the Atlantic, Pierce has arrived at MI-6 headquarters.

"Good morning, 'N'! So what's going on with the mission?" Pierce inquires jauntily.

"We're calling it a success." 'N' shuffles papers on his desk.

"So was it accomplished?" Pierce asks, more curious now.

"We're calling it a success, and we'll leave it at that, Double O."

Hmmm... I wonder what the hell went on over there? I know Sean would never negotiate with the terrorists!

"I've got other news for you," 'N' says.

"Oh yeah?"

"Some good and some bad—which do you want to hear first?"

"Give me the bad."

"You're being put on inactive duty."

"Man, that's a body blow!" Pierce is taken aback.

"I know."

"But why?"

"They're bringing in a new guy."

"*A new* guy?! But I'm..."

"I'm waiting for him now," 'N' interrupts.

"But I... so, what's the *good* news?"

"You can apply for a transfer and maybe get on AMALGA."

"That would be great! You know I always wanted to work with Sean!"

"Well, it's a *maybe*. You can request it, but there's no guarantee you'll get it."

"Yes, of course. I realize that."

"You'll go through the normal declassification just like any other Double O."

"OK."

"The AMALGA missions are classified as Semi-classified, Unclassified, Classified."

"You know, the acronym for those words spells out SU..."

"Yes, I'm well aware what it spells out! And that acronym is no reflection on the nature of these missions. They were designed to be a public relations success. They will have a limited budget at first but will be no less exotic than past missions. These SUC missions will exemplify the maturity and dignity of the Crown."

"Does this transfer carry with it a Double O status?"

"Of course! During your declassification process and subsequent transition period, you'll be able to keep your car and some basic gadgetry such as your gun, briefcase, watch, etc. Depending on how well you handle the transition, you could be back in the saddle in no time! On the other hand, you could end up on *permanent* inactive duty. It's all up to you."

"I really want to work with Sean! I'll do *whatever* it takes!"

"Well, you can start by finishing the physical that you walked out on after the imprisonment in North Korea. Then you can report to the boys in the Psych Department."

"The boys in the Psych Department?"

"For a complete evaluation."

"*Complete evaluation?* But whatever for?" Pierce asks in confusion.

"It's a new standard procedure for all transfer requests. We've got to make sure you're fit for AMALGA."

"All right, is that it?" Pierce heads for the door.

"Well, there is one other matter. You might want to explore your *grudge* problem while you're down at Psych."

"What?! What *grudge* problem?" At the door, he turns to stare at 'N'. "Looking over your file, I noticed you've cooked up, harbored, and personalized quite a few grudges in the past and even more recently!"

"Let me tell you something!" Pierce erupts. "Anybody messes with Sean and they're going to deal with me!"

'N' looks over the top of his glasses at Pierce and makes a notation for Pierce's file. "Precisely my point! Ms. Munynickle has your paperwork ready. Good luck, Double O!"

Pierce angrily walks out of 'N's office and into Ms. Munynickle's office. "I understand you have some paperwork for me?"

"Yes!" She hands Pierce a large envelope marked AMALGA.

"How did you know I wanted to go to AMALGA?"

"I figured you wanted to work with Sean," she said sarcastically.

"They all want to work with Sean! *Everybody* wants to work with the *great* Sean!

"You know, Munynickle, I..."

"Don't even start! I'm waiting for Roger and that's that!"

"ROGER?! He's not even..."

"He's not what?" she asks in a huff.

"Oh, nothing."

"When Roger gets back, we're getting together!" she says confidently.

Pierce turns and leaves. *Oh, yeah! I'm sure he'll have a ring in his pocket!* Once outside the building, Pierce bursts out laughing.

A few minutes later, Danny, the new Double O, walks into Munynickle's office. She's busy filing and doesn't look up right away.

"Excuse me. I'm the new O reporting for duty! I was told to report here." He holds his hat at waist level in front of himself.

Out of the corner of her eye, she can see his hat in his hand. "You can put your hat on the rack over there," she says without looking up.

Danny walks over and places his hat on the rack. "You must be Ms. Munynickle?" he says.

Ms. Munynickle raises her eyes to look at the new O. "Your hair—it's *blond!* Are you sure you're in the right place? This is a large complex. Maybe you're lost!"

"Yes, I'm sure. I'm here to see 'N'. I'm ready for an assignment. I haven't been assigned a car yet, but I'm ready! I was hoping I could team up with Sean. Do you know Sean?"

"Unfortunately, yes!" she says in disgust as she rings 'N'. *Here we go again!* she thinks. "The new O is here!" she announces.

"Send him in, please."

"Go ahead," she says with an insincere smile as she waves him in.

"Thank you, Ms. Munynickle!" Danny heads for the padded door.

Hmmm... with buns like that, maybe I could get used to the hair! she thinks, watching him walk away.

Meanwhile, back in Melville, it's 6:00 a.m. and the normal hustle and bustle of Monday morning is taken up a notch with the activity around the Bonds. Doc has been up since 5:00 a.m. and looked in on the Bonds, who were still asleep. Nurse Meredith and Nurse Christy informed him that it had been a quiet, uneventful night and that Mr. Perrin had called late last night to inquire about the patients in the dayroom. Doc is sitting in the observation room studying the charts of other patients in the clinic while keeping an eye on the Bonds in the dayroom. With little time left, he's anxious to observe their waking moments. Although most of his theories didn't pan out, his curiosity as a good doctor/scientist urges him on to study and obtain all the data he can. He's ever vigilant and trained to expect the unexpected. In the town of Erath, Louisiana, Warren Perrin is drinking his morning coffee and talking with his wife, Mary.

"Mary, pinch me so I know I'm not dreaming! I can't believe that after fifteen years, today is the day that the apology will become a reality!" Just then, the phone rings, and Perrin answers.

"Hello," he says.

"Mr. Tony Blair calling for Mr. Perrin," a very British, female voice informs.

"Speaking."

"Hold, please."

Perrin covers the receiver with one hand and whispers to Mary, "It's him, Tony Blair!" he says with child-like glee.

"Well, no need to pinch you now!" Mary says with a smile.

"Hello, Mr. Perrin! How are you this morning?"

"Just fine... and you?" Perrin wonders if something has gone awry.

"Just great!" Blair replies.

"Then we're still on for today?"

"Absolutely! All systems are to go on this end! All the necessary documents have been prepared and are ready to present. How about on your end?"

"Likewise here. I've had the documents for the apology drawn up for some time now."

"That's good. The Queen sends her deepest regret that this apology took so long in coming, and she's apologetic for not being able to present it herself."

"We appreciate that sentiment. With respect to the documents for releasing your *boys*, the Chief of Police has assured me that he will have all the paperwork completed. Hopefully, everything will be in order from the chief and your embassy representative. Also, I've drafted something that will help the transition go smoothly and help process the mountain of political documents. The promissory notes, for all the injured parties to be paid in full, are ready for your signature. As we agreed, full restitution will be expected within thirty days."

"In other words, we'll be paying through the teeth!" Blair chuckles.

"More like your ass! Those 'boys' did an incredible amount of damage!"

"I won't argue that. Speaking of my boys, how are they doing?"

"When I left the clinic last night, everybody appeared calm and comfortable. And I called late last night, and they were all sleeping peacefully."

"That's wonderful news. Well, our yacht is just now entering the mouth of the Atchafalaya River. The captain informs me that our ETA to Melville will be about 11:00 a.m. That puts us an hour ahead of schedule!"

"You sure are making good time!"

"It's that hefty tailwind I mentioned yesterday. The captain thinks it might be part of a storm that's brewing. It's very overcast, and the sky is getting pretty dark. What's your weather like there?"

"I hear thunder rumbling to the south. I'm listening to a local weather report right now; they're calling for a 100 percent chance of showers and thunderstorms."

"We won't let that deter us, will we?"

"After waiting 250 years, we're certainly not letting some rain stop us! I have to say, though, that this system is coming out of nowhere! It's similar to the popcorn showers we have in early spring, only magnified. Even the weather people were taken by surprise! I don't mean to sound superstitious, but it's almost like you're bringing this weather with you!"

"It must look like that!"

"I'm just joking! This storm could even be out of here by the time you arrive. At any rate, it won't make a difference."

"If need be, we can conduct the ceremony inside the yacht."

"That would be fine."

"Have you notified your local dignitaries?"

"Yes. Governor Blanco is quite busy, but she said she wouldn't miss this for the world!"

"And your media?"

"I haven't notified them yet. There's always been a bit of a rivalry between our two local stations as to which one is the first to cover an event. I wanted to wait until I had a more definite time to give them and avoid a frenzy."

"I can understand that."

"As soon as I get to my office this morning, my secretary and I will simultaneously place calls to the two stations. That way, each of them will have a fair shot at getting the story first."

"That sounds very fair and also quite humorous."

"It's a lot funnier than you think! The funniest thing about this rivalry is that almost everyone who once worked for one station now works for the other!"

"Sounds like a bit of fence-jumping going on there!"

"You got that right!"

"Well, I'll see you around eleven o'clock."

"See you then."

By now it's 7:00 a.m., and Perrin hangs up the phone. He looks over at Mary. "It's all systems go!" he says enthusiastically. "How about meeting me down at the office about nine o'clock? Or you could ride to Melville with Darylin later on."

"I think I'll ride with Darylin... OK?"

"Sounds good, honey. I'll see you soon." Perrin kisses Mary goodbye and heads out the door.

Meanwhile, the shift changes at the clinic have taken place. Nurses Hebert, Debra, and Ashley have replaced Nurses Meredith and Christy. Orderly Mosley is walking down the hallway to the observation room. Anna is in the lobby along with Officers Wax and Cottrell. Officer Wane is outside standing guard near the windows of the dayroom. He hasn't seen any action there, but he's not complaining. The hot topic of the morning is the weather and how it wasn't even predicted! Outside the observation room, a kitchen worker arrives with breakfast for the Bonds. She rolls the cart into the nurse's station/observation room, and Mosley walks in behind her. The Bonds are beginning to wake up. Doc looks at the food cart and says...

"Hmmm... Let's see now. We don't want this to be a major production," the doc says, rubbing his chin. "We'll try to respect their space and avoid a commotion. I'll send in one nurse with the food and see what happens. If *Mr. Straitjacket* wants to eat, Mosley, you'll go in and feed him."

"*DAMN! Here we go again!*" Mosley mutters under his breath.

"If the *Gurney Guy* has trouble getting up or eating, Debra, you'll assist him."

"Nurse Hebert, I'd like you to go in with the food and add some *lively bedside manner*. It might make them feel more at home."

"Have you ever known me to not be lively?"

"Come to think of it, no! Go ahead and do your thing... be yourself!"

Officers Wax and Cottrell have come into the observation room on the tail end of Doc's comment to Nurse Hebert.

"Don't worry, Nurse Hebert, we'll be right here," Wax says.

"I'm not worried about anything!"

"I got my eye on that *Wild One* in the corner. Any inkling of violence out of him and me and my partner here will be all over him!" He taps the blackjack at his side.

"Oh, those guys are just a bunch of teddy bears! I'm sure their barks are much worse than their bites!" Nurse Hebert says. "Doc, would you open the door, please?" She rolls the food cart into the dayroom. "OK, boys... RISE AND SHINE! It's CHOW TIME!" she exclaims cheerfully.

Sean slides out of the bed quickly and stands near the windowsill. He's braced in a cautionary stance with a furrowed brow, scanning the room in Bond-like fashion.

The doc takes out his hand-held tape recorder and begins his observations. *Mr. Straitjacket is getting around quite well this morning. He won't be needing the wheelchair anymore.*

George sits up in bed and cranes his neck to check out the food. He licks his lips in anticipation of another feast. Timmy rolls over and just lies there looking up at the ceiling while Roger is lazily stretching his legs and arms and waking up.

Patient Wild One is slow to respond this morning. However, patient Kilt Man looks ready to devour the entire cart! Gurney Guy is responding better than expected. Movements appear normal... only slower, the doc notes.

"Come on, you boys! Up and at 'em! We've got eggs, hash browns, Paul Primeaux's famous Taso, New Orleans-style French toast, and delicious Community Coffee to top it off! Get it while it's hot!" the nurse encourages.

"Are we in New Orleans?" Roger slurs, partially rising from the gurney.

A breakthrough! The Gurney Guy is beginning to speak and appears to have heard Nurse Hebert offering food, the doc notes excitedly.

Roger suddenly has an agonizing look of pain on his face and grabs his privates. He then notices Nurse Hebert and sits straight up on the gurney, blinking and rubbing his eyes as if trying to focus.

The Gurney Guy must be feeling the effects of the catheterization by the expression on his face and the way he's holding himself. Those effects will probably linger for another day or two. He seems to be regaining his eyesight. The tranquilizer serum seems to have dissipated more quickly than I anticipated.

George is not shy. He jumps out of bed and hurries over to the table and digs in! Sean shakes his head in disgust as he watches him hungrily attack his food. *That's it, George... just keep shoveling more truth serum into your mouth! In no time at all, you'll be puking up confessions!*

"How about some of this nice hot coffee?" Nurse Hebert asks George.

George tries to answer her, but his mouth is so full that all he can do is nod his head. Nurse Hebert pours him a cup of coffee. Roger is sure he hears a woman, and as his vision clears, he can almost see her. He tries to swing his legs over the side of the gurney but is halted by the pain in his private area.

Although Gurney Guy continues to orient himself to his surroundings, he seems to be plagued by penile pain. He may need to be re-examined, the doc voices his concern.

The doc observes as Timmy slowly gets up and sits on the side of his cot facing the wall. *Patient Wild One is malingering. He continues to stare at the wall and perhaps is looking for a point of reference from his many worlds in order to start his day. He clearly demonstrates anti-social behavior.*

"You can sure say that again!" Cottrell says as he eavesdrops on the doc's comments.

"Do you mind? I am taking private notes for my professional diagnosis!" the doc exclaims.

"Uh... sorry, Doc!" Cottrell walks over to the card table and busies himself with putting loose cards back into their packs.

"Hot coffee over here... come and get it!" Nurse Hebert cheerfully hollers over to Timmy.

Timmy doesn't respond, but Roger does. He carefully turns and dangles his legs off the side of the gurney. Sitting there, he sways from side to side and taps a foot around, trying to touch the floor. In the observation area, Nurse Debra notices Roger's dilemma and reaches for the PA mic to alert Nurse Hebert, but the doc stops her. He knocks on the window to get Nurse Hebert's attention and motions for her to give Roger a hand. She quickly puts down the coffee pot and rushes over to help.

"We don't want to jump-start *Wild One* this morning. Mosley, we need to shut off the breaker to the PA system until further notice," the doc announces.

"Sure thing, Doc!" Mosley replies and heads down the hall.

The doc returns to his memo taking. *Without artificially stimulating the Wild One, we may be able to establish a personality baseline and determine a prominent identity.*

Nurse Hebert puts her arm around Roger to help him off the gurney. "Do you think you can stand? Do you think you can walk?" she asks.

Her voice, her touch, and her smell seem to revive him. More importantly, his touching her really begins to orient him. Her softness and femininity breathe new life into him. As she lifts Roger off the gurney in a bear hug embrace, he is comforted and excited by her caring and tender touch. But he continues to be confused by the stabbing pain in his penis.

Sean watches Roger and Nurse Hebert. *That's all he needed... a WOMAN! I tried to tell 'N' that, but he psychoanalyzed it all! Now that my right-hand man is on the mend, maybe we can make a break for it!* Nurse Hebert places one arm around Roger's waist and then expertly guides his arm across her shoulders. His hand brushes over her breast, and as a reflex, Roger gently cups it. Nurse Hebert is surprised at first and then chuckles as she moves his hand aside. It's not the first time she's handled a horny old man!

As Nurse Hebert helps the Gurney Guy, he appears to be unusually responsive to human contact, as if he is extremely relaxed while at the same time quite alert, the doc notes.

Nurse Hebert and Roger shuffle over toward the table. Roger walks stiffly, like he's got a broomstick up his bottom.

Sean watches the slow progression. *Oh, no, the food! Roger can handle the truth serum... he's not like George... but it's the ONE WORLD TASTE I'm worried about, not to mention the magic seasoning! No telling what effect all of it may have on him!*

The doc is also watching. *Concerning Mr. Straitjacket... his posture and range of motion have dramatically improved, but he continues to display rigidity in his stance—classic schizophrenia symptom! He has no visible signs of convulsive or combative behavior, and this leads me to believe that his central nervous system dysfunction is reversing itself. He is closely watching the activity in the dayroom, and this is an indication that his eyesight is functional. However, he may have a slight blurring, which is evidenced by the way he squints his eyes while scanning the room. His movements are deliberate and controlled. My guess is that his remaining senses are still impaired. The mute condition is symptomatic of R.R.D. and schizophrenia.*

Nurse Hebert and Roger have reached the table, and he sits down and begins to eat. Beside him, George is literally feasting!

Sean worries as Roger slowly begins to eat. Poor Roger. *He's still half out of it! I know he's hungry, but hopefully he won't eat too much, unlike that buffoon, George! That guy swills his food down without coming up for air!*

It's so good to see Gurney Guy eating, even though he's taking small bites and eating slowly. The Wild One is still staring at the wall and sitting on his cot. Very disturbing behavior! the doc observes.

The chief walks in the observation room.

"You don't look too well! Did you get any sleep?" the doc asks.

"I had an investigation to conduct!" The chief replies curtly.

"Did we come up with anything, chief?" Wax asks.

"Nothing but *JUNK!* We searched *every bit of that cargo!* If they had anything of value, they already made the drop or threw it overboard. Probably damned near to the Gulf, by now! How are things going here?

That Cagney character give you any trouble?"

"Nah . . . not yet." Cottrell answers.

"You know, Doc, those guys look damn good for being as bad off as you said! They should have slept in the jail!" The chief says.

"Yeah, looking at them now, hindsight is *20/20!* But yesterday, they needed . . ."

"Yeah, I know . . . *MONITORING!*"

"You don't have to get all bent out of shape! I know you're tired, but you don't have to take it out on me!"

"We're about to get some coffee, Chief. Do you care for a cup?" Wax and Cottrell stand up.

"Yeah, thanks . . . cream and sugar."

"How about you, Doc?" Wax asks.

"Yes, black, please."

The officers leave to fetch the coffee.

"Frankly, Chief, I don't know why you knocked yourself out like that when you knew they were getting off with Diplomatic Immunity!" The doc shakes his head.

"You should talk—look at you with your tape recorder in hand! You're *never* going to get to treat those guys! You'll *never* see them again after today!"

"I've got a report to make!"

"I've got a report to make, too!"

"Yeah, I guess you're right." Doc relents.

"Damn, I sure hate to see them walk when they're guilty as sin! They did a helluva lot of damage out there! It's like a bomb went off, it all looks so *terroristic* in nature! If I could have found a weapon of mass destruction, like a dirty bomb or some type of explosive, we'd have nailed them! The Patriot Act would have easily trumped Diplomatic Immunity!"

Both men sink into their own private reverie, silently grieving, what would have been, their *finest hour*. Doc continues to observe the Bonds in the dayroom and the chief takes a seat at the card table. He is completely exhausted and disgusted. Just then, Officers Wax and Cottrell return with the coffee and they all sit down for a moment to enjoy it.

CHAPTER VI

*M*eanwhile, over in Erath, Louisiana, Warren Perrin arrives at his office at the same time as Darylin. They exchange "good mornings" and go into the building. He tells of his plan to simultaneously contact the two news networks, and she starts laughing.

"Given their long-standing rivalres, that's a fair and reasonable plan to contact them." She shakes her head and laughs again. "Laughter is such a wonderful way to start the day!"

Darylin starts the coffee pot, and Perrin calls Governor Blanco to coordinate the time and place of the ceremony. They agree to meet in Melville at 10:30 a.m. to discuss any last-minute details and await Tony Blair's arrival. Before calling the clinic, Darylin walks into his office with the coffee.

"Mary would like to ride with you to Melville. Is that OK?"

"That'll be just fine. I'd like the company."

Darylin sets the coffee on his desk and returns to her office. Perrin dials the number to the clinic.

"Hello. This is Warren Perrin calling for Dr. Bellefontaine."

"Speaking."

"How are y'all doing over there this morning? I trust all is well."

"Very well. In fact, better than expected. Your clients are doing much better except for one who's getting off to a slow start, but I'm sure he'll be OK."

"Good. Does the chief happen to be over at the clinic?"

"As a matter of fact, he's sitting here right now."

"I need to speak to him, please."

"All right." The doc hands the phone over to the chief.

"Hello?"

"Chief Basile, how are you this morning?"

"OK... considering."

"Have you found any more damage that my clients may allegedly be responsible for?"

Damn, there he goes with that word again! The chief represses a grin. "No, not anything else yet."

"Good. Tony Blair will be here about 11:00 a.m. to pick up his boys. Will you have those release papers ready?"

"Don't worry... they'll be ready. The embassy guy from Dallas just dropped off their documents."

"I'm glad to hear that. Well, I should be in Melville around 9:30 or ten o'clock."

"OK."

"I'll see you all then. Good-bye!"

The chief heads over to the station to finish the paperwork and get cleaned up. In Erath, Perrin asks Darylin to come into his office.

"Well, everything's set with the Governor and the clinic. Are you ready to call the TV stations? Remember they both get the information as simultaneously as possible. I'll use my cell and call TV-10 while you call TV-3 on the office phone. Ready, set, GO!"

Both local stations have just wrapped up their morning programs when they receive the info about the news event. Immediately, a frenzy of activity ensues. At TV-10, the CBS affiliate, Bob and Laurie volunteer to cover the story, but Gary says he wants a piece of the action, too. The bickering between Bob and Gary quickly escalates, with Laurie in the middle. Just then, the station manager, Dee, walks into the newsroom, and Laurie tells him what's going on.

"I should be the one to cover this story! After all, I speak French!" Bob, the morning news anchor, says.

"The ceremony will probably be in English! The timing will put the story in my time slot!" Gary, the noon anchor, says.

"Yes, but I live in Erath and I know Warren Perrin personally! We're damn near neighbors!" Bob retorts.

"That doesn't cut any ice! I've got *seniority* here!" Gary exclaims loudly.

"This is *unbelievable!*" Dee says soberly. "This is *BIG*... really BIG! We'd better put both our six and ten anchors on this story!"

"We need to be on the scene by 10:00 in the morning. We'll get Chuck out of bed and have Lon, in the news van, pick him up at the Northgate Mall. That'll save some time. We've got to be *FIRST* on the scene! After all, we are *Acadiana's News Leader!* We'll have Blue, here at the station, go live with the exclusive. We'll break in on the morning game shows as things progress, then do a follow-up on our noon program with a full recap at 5:00, 6:00, and 10:00."

"But—that noon program has been my..." Gary protests.

"Where are we shooting today?" Dee interrupts.

"Brown's Furniture, they're having a big *Going Out of Business Sale*," Gary says.

"Good," Dee says. "Let's maintain that schedule. We'll start out with you, Gary, at the furniture store. You'll segue into *Breaking News* with the furniture store in the background—man, they'll love that— and then you'll hand it off to Blue at the station, then she'll go live to Chuck on the scene. We'll do the weather and then we'll go back to Gary at Brown's Furniture. Then back to Blue and over to Chuck for a live wrap-up."

"I can't believe you're going to stick with that furniture spot on a news day like this! They're on a rotation plan, and it's not the first time they've gone out of business," Gary whines.

"They'll be glad to pay, and we need the revenue!"

"What about me?" Bob complains.

"You'll do a sound bite translation in French from the studio," Dee says. "And when Chuck gets back from Melville and works it up, maybe you can do another one for the 5:00, 6:00, and 10:00."

"What about me?" Laurie asks.

"Sorry, Laurie—but you're gonna have to sit this one out." Dee leaves the office, yelling out, *"OK, PEOPLE, LET'S GET MOVING!"*
"I should have been a furniture salesman," Gary mutters out loud.

"If I didn't speak French, I wouldn't even have a job!" Bob commiserates.

Over at TV-3, the ABC affiliate, things aren't so complicated. They don't have a noon program to worry about, and being a smaller station, there's less back-biting. They know exactly how they're going to cover this story. News anchor Tom is going out on a live feed van with his driver/photographer, Lance, while the evening news co-anchor, Debra, will break the news from the studio, then cut live to Tom on location. The newsroom is busy poring over road maps to find a shortcut to Melville before TV-10 gets there. With a shortcut route in hand, Tom rushes out the door with Lance.

"I'll be damned if TV-10 beats us to this story!" Tom says as they run for the news van and quickly climb in.

"Yeah! This baby is ready to roll, and boy does it *roll!*" Lance exclaims.

Over at the clinic, Roger is almost finished eating, and Nurse Hebert has been helping feed him and wiping his mouth because he's still a bit groggy and uncoordinated.

"I need to go to the john," Roger manages to mumble.

Nurse Hebert helps him over to the bathroom and waits outside while Roger goes in and begins to urinate. *Damn! Did I have sex with that woman? She sure must like it rough! Or maybe I was just dreaming! But I've never had such a painful piss before!*

Out in the dayroom, George has finished eating, and he signals to Doc, at the window, to turn on the Evangeline musical. Doc turns on the TV and VCR, and George lies down on his bed to watch the continuing saga. Sean is still leaning against the windowsill, and Timmy is still staring at the wall. Roger comes out of the bathroom and wants to lie down as well, so Nurse Hebert helps him up onto his gurney.

No use making a move on her now with this terrible pain! Roger thinks.

Meanwhile, the evening news anchor, Chuck, has arrived at the Northgate Mall to meet up with Lon.

"This is *BIG!* This is really *BIG!* The Queen's yacht with Tony Blair in Melville, Louisiana! This will be our top story for a while! Man—this is gonna look great on my job tape, what a resume! Let's go, Lon, you know our motto: 'Acadiana's First! So—Punch It, *Lon*—PUNCH IT!'"

"You got it! But—hey, what's with this weather? Look at those clouds."

"I don't know. Our weather service didn't forecast this."

"It looks pretty bad! Hope we can put the dish all the way up. Turn this whole setup into one big lightning rod if we're not careful."

"Damn! Forgot about that! Blue's at the station getting ready for a live feed!"

"Well, we can always go to tape and run it back!" Lon chuckles nervously.

"Still, we might get lucky. Remember the time our old weatherman, Rob, forecasted a flood? People were lined up for a mile to get sandbags and supplies, even the drag races were canceled, and not a damn drop of rain hit the ground! He really blew it on that one!"

"Well, today it looks like it's fixin' to come down in buckets. Hey, we've got company coming! Channel 3 remote van at two o'clock!" Lon points over his shoulder.

"Where?" Chuck spins around.

"Coming down the I-10 ramp!"

In the Channel 3 van, photographer Lance spies the competition.

"TV-10 coming up on I-49!" he calls out to Tom.

"Don't let them get ahead of us!" Tom shouts.

Chuck, in the TV-10 van, strains to see the other rig. "Damn! That looks like Tom Vaunchee riding shotgun!"

"Looks like Chuck in there! They're pulling out the big guns for this one!" Tom exclaims as he and Lance fly down the ramp.

Just then, Lon, driving the TV-10 van, has to change lanes to avoid the merge ramp. "*What* are you doing?" Chuck yells frantically.

"You're letting them on!"

"I had to move over for the incoming ramp! Sorry..." Lon says glumly.

The TV-3 van merges onto Interstate 49, and for a moment, both live news vans are side by side. With a big grin, Lance, in the Channel 3 van, gives a little wave, then hits the accelerator and pulls away from the competition. The TV-10 van looks like it's standing still!

"DAMN!" Lon exclaims.

"PUNCH IT!" Chuck yells.

"It's punched!" Lon shouts back.

"Man! Did you see the look on Chuck's face when we pulled away?" Tom laughs out loud.

"Yeah! He had that *Mr. Whipple* look. Like someone had squeezed his Charmin a little too hard!" Lance guffaws.

"Damn!" Chuck halfheartedly punches the dash. "We're *Acadiana's News Leader!* We're supposed to be first! Why did you let them get ahead?"

"Just instinct. When you're driving and you see ramp traffic trying to merge, you move over."

"FLOOR IT! We still have a chance!" Chuck demands

"It's floored! We're doing 80!"

"But they're pulling away!"

"They must have a Hemi in that thing!"

"Damn! Maybe the traffic will slow them up some. We've got to be *FIRST* on this story!" Chuck grits his teeth nervously.

The two news crews are speeding down I-49 and approaching the town of Opelousas. Lucky for Lon and Chuck in the TV-10 van, the traffic has slowed, and now Lance and Tom, the TV-3 team, are only a quarter of a mile or so ahead.

Tom quickly scans the road map. "Looks like a shortcut here. We can take the Creswell Extension over to Port Barre, pick up 190 to Krotz Springs, then Hwy 105 to Melville."

"Yeah, in miles maybe, but not in minutes!" Lance replies. "I know that road; I used to work at an alligator farm down there and had to drive it every day. It's got a lot of curves, and believe me, it's no shortcut! We're better off taking 190 from Opelousas. It's a straight shot through Port Barre all the way to Krotz Springs."

"Man—look at those clouds!" Tom cranes his neck, looking out the window. "Pretty dark to the south there. I hope we can get to Melville before they open up. Can you still see them back there?"

"Yep, they're back there all right, and they're gaining on us! Damn traffic!"

In the TV-10 news van, Chuck wonders aloud. "I wonder if they're stupid enough to take that Creswell Extension or if they'll go straight on to 190?"

"I'll tell you what we ought to do—take exit 24. It's real close to Palmetto where my in-laws live," Lon says. "My wife and I take it all the time. From there, it's a straight shot to Melville."

"I don't know about that; looks like some heavy weather up that way. Look—they just passed up Creswell; that means they're taking 190. Yep, there's his turn signal!"

"Let them. They'll have to slow up in Port Barre; that's a well-known speed trap. If Lance keeps his foot in that Hemi, the way it has been, the cops will stop him for sure. OK—so which is it?" Lon looks over to Chuck.

"Palmetto it is! It's our only hope of being *first* on the scene!"

Meanwhile, over at the clinic, Warren Perrin has just arrived, and he walks immediately to the observation room where he finds Doc, Nurse Debra, and Officers Wax and Cottrell, who are still playing their Cajun card game.

Sean watches Perrin walk into the observation room. *There's Primeaux's diversionary expert. If I can just read his lips, maybe I can get a handle on what they've got up their sleeves.*

"Good morning, Doctor Bellefontaine!" Perrin says enthusiastically. "Good morning, Nurse Debra, officers! How's everything this morning?"

"Good morning," the doc says.

"Looks like some bad weather headed this way. Have you seen those clouds?"

"No. I haven't been outside yet. But everybody who's come in to work has been commenting on it. I guess it's looking real bad."

"Looks like some pretty rough weather coming up from the south. I've never seen anything like it, not this time of the year, anyway. I hope it doesn't interfere with our plans." Perrin turns his attention to the Bonds in the dayroom. "Are the boys ready to go?"

Plans... huh? Ready to go? They must be taking us to another location to turn up the torture! Perhaps a concentration camp! Sean reads Perrin's lips.

"Yeah, they're ready to go," the doc says. "But I'm a little worried about that one in the corner over there." The doc gestures toward Timmy.

"Is he the one getting off to a slow start? Does he need any medication or something?"

"Maybe, maybe not. I'd rather wait until he becomes active on his own. That way I can establish a reference point from which to gauge the depth of his delusion. A patient like him lives in many worlds. Understanding his level of delusion will enable me to assess his need for medication and then determine what to give him, the dosage, frequency of dosing, etc."

Out on the road, the news crews are getting closer to Melville. Tom and Lance in the TV-3 van are just leaving Krotz Springs on Hwy 105. They have about twelve miles of curved road to go. The TV-10 van with Chuck and Lon is leaving Palmetto on Hwy 10 and has about fifteen miles of straight road to go before reaching Melville.

"We're making good time on this straight highway!" Chuck smiles over at Lon.

"Yeah! And Lance is on that curvy-ass road! If he tries to stand on his Hemi there, he'll *roll* it!"

In the TV-3 van, Tom looks worried; he glances over at Lance. "Do you think they'll beat us?" he asks.

"I hope not! But I don't believe these curves! They may be on a straight road, but that was a helluva jog to the north! We're probably ahead of them."

Also on the road to Melville is Governor Blanco, with her driver, John, and secretary, Arlyne. They're being followed by two vehicles carrying security agents and personal assistants. As they cross over the bridge on Hwy 190 and look north up the river, they can see the Queen's yacht headed for Melville.

"The Queen's yacht sure is something, isn't it?" the Governor smiles broadly.

"Yep! That's taking *tee-dah-ness* to a whole new level!" John responds.

"Yeah, you're right about that!" Arlyne says. "But yet, they still put their pants on one leg at a time just like the rest of us!"

"Sure looks like we might be in for some bad weather. Look at those clouds, Governor." John points out the window. Both women look out at the threatening clouds off to the south. Back at the clinic, Perrin takes a call from Tony Blair on his cell phone.

"Good morning, Mr. Perrin!" Blair says. "Looks as if we're running ahead of schedule a little. We've just passed the 190 Bridge at Krotz Springs and should be there shortly."

"That's great! We're just about wrapped up on this end, and by the time you arrive and dock, we'll have your boys ready to go."

"Speaking of docking, the captain has asked about the docking facilities. He said a U-turn in a vessel of this size and in a strong current is going to be a tricky maneuver. He would prefer to make that turn upon approach rather than departure. It has something to do with momentum."

"Well, there is no dock, but there is a ferry ramp on both sides of the river. The ferry normally docks on the West ramp, and right now there's a crew boat anchored north of the East ramp. Better have him anchor near the East ramp, and we'll take the ferry over to you."

"OK. I'll relay that information to the captain, and we should see you soon."

"OK." Perrin pockets his cell phone and turns to the doc. "That was Blair. They're running a little early; the Queen's yacht is almost here."

Sean, reading Perrin's lips, suddenly feels a glimmer of hope. *Blair! The Queen's yacht! This changes everything!*

Just then, the chief returns to the observation room with the release papers. He's showered, shaved, and in a clean uniform, but his expression is still tired and discouraged.

"Good morning, Chief! Do you have those release papers?" Perrin asks.

Release? Sean's heart races at the thought.

"Yeah, I've got them. I just can't believe that those guys have the political connections to get diplomatic immunity and then to have Tony Blair escort them out of here!" The chief shakes his head.

Diplomatic immunity! We're getting the hell out of here!

"They definitely have friends in high places," Perrin says.

"Friends in *high places*... huh? That's the problem with our society," the chief says angrily. "The big shots don't pay for their crimes anymore! Well, they're still guilty as sin in my book!"

"Don't worry, they're paying, monetarily," Perrin says.

"That's not *paying* for your crime! Especially if you're loaded or someone else is picking up the tab! That's not even a slap on the hand!"

"Well, Chief, who knows... maybe when they get back to England, they'll have hell to pay."

"I doubt it. This is no different than some young punk tearing shit up and his rich daddy bailing him out! I've seen it a thousand times! Rarely do the rich *pay* for their crimes! They just pay. I tell you, it's sad... very sad." The chief shakes his head.

"Well, we don't make the laws; we just follow and enforce them," Perrin offers.

"In our justice system, it used to be that a man was innocent until proven guilty. Anymore, he's innocent until proven *broke!*"

"I'll go along with that!" the doc adds. "And with money comes power to twist and shape reality to your own liking!"

"I'm ashamed to say it, but justice is not always *fair!* But I have to believe that nothing happens by mistake. Everything happens for a reason, and that reason isn't always clear at the time, but it works itself out." Perrin gestures broadly. "Look at today... after 250 years, we're getting an apology for that terrible exile!"

Apology. I can't believe it! Why couldn't those Cajuns just forget about that exile thing? It was 250 years ago! What's the big deal anyway? Maybe they deserved what they got! Sean thinks, watching the discussion.

"Apology? Whatever happened to an eye for an eye and a tooth for a tooth? Now, that's real justice! " the chief demands.

"We're human. We do the best we can. The important thing is to learn from our mistakes and move on. Speaking of which—I'm sure Blair is just around the bend. What about transportation to the ferry?" Perrin asks.

"We'll run them down there in a couple of squad cars."

"I think the clinic van would be better," the doc offers.

"Yes, maybe the van would be better... more subtle," Perrin says. "Oh yeah! Criminals of their stature, God forbid, they should show up in a cop car! That would be *embarrassing!* " The chief rolls his eyes.

"It's not just that, but we have to consider the space on the ferry. There'll be the Governor's limo, security vehicles, the media trucks, and my car. And to be honest, a cop car generates a *hostile energy.* With the dark, gloomy sky out there, we need to keep things more positive. After all, this is truly a day of celebration."

"Yeah, I guess you're right."

"Oh, I just remembered," the doc speaks up. "My daughter, Anna, who's our receptionist, wanted to ask you about some students attending the ceremony. She's bringing them to town for the parade."

"Sure, if we can fit them on the ferry. In fact, it would be wonderful for them to witness this historic event!" Perrin smiles.

Well, so much for the mission... the Aspic... the Queen's gold! I can't believe HQ is pulling us out of here. We could have turned this mission around! Sean feels a deep sense of regret.

"Doc, we can't wait all day for the guy in the corner. We need to start moving them out of here," Perrin says.

Officer Cottrell comes to his feet. "You want to move that Wild One in the corner? I'll put Mr. Coldcocker here on his ass and he'll move!"

"We don't have to get that forceful! But we do need to get going. Tony Blair is only about thirty minutes away!"

"We need to check those cuffs and leg irons!" the chief says.

"Really now, don't you think leg irons are kind of extreme?" Perrin asks.

"Not for riding in a hospital van! I don't want that maniac getting loose between here and the river! He could kill someone, take a hostage, or God knows what he's capable of! Oh no! I've been agreeable long enough. He's leaving here in those irons and cuffs! I've got a responsibility to protect this community, and I intend to do my job!" The chief is adamant.

"OK—OK. Go ahead, check him, then get the others ready and let's go!"

Suddenly, Timmy jumps up from his cot and begins to shout. *"TO EAT OR NOT TO EAT? TO EAT OR NOT TO EAT? TO EAT OR NOT TO EAT? THAT IS THE QUESTION!"*

"Shakespeare! I knew he was an actor!" the doc exclaims excitedly.

"It's all just an act, Doc." The chief shakes his head in disgust.

"Do you think you need to medicate him, Doc?" Perrin asks.

"No. In that frame of mind, he's more likely to go with the flow."

"What about the one in the straitjacket?"

"Better leave it on, for his own protection. He could still seize and hurt himself. We've gotten this far without grounds for a lawsuit; no point in chancing it now."

"Good enough. Let's go!"

"OK, Debra, you and Mosley go in the dayroom with the officers and help move the patients," the doc instructs.

Damn! Mosley mutters under his breath and cringes. He'd been hoping he wouldn't have to deal with the Bonds again.

"Don't worry, Mosley, we got you covered!" Cottrell pats his side.

"Should we wheelchair any of them?" Nurse Debra asks.

"No. I think they can walk on their own, with some assistance. You help Mr. Straitjacket, and Mosley can help Gurney Guy."

Officer Wax stands up. "I'll help Cottrell with the other two."

The doc turns off the TV and unlocks the door to the dayroom. The musical George is watching has ended, and George gets off the bed and looks toward the dayroom. Timmy wanders over to the table where Nurse Hebert is stacking the breakfast dishes and food back onto the food cart. Cottrell is the first in the dayroom and heads straight toward Timmy to check his leg irons and cuffs.

"OK, you—let's go," Cottrell says.

"Go where?" Timmy asks.

"Sit down!" Cottrell yells.

"Which is it?"

"...and shut up!"

"To sit or not to sit? To sit or not to sit? That is the question. To speak or not to speak? To speak or not to speak? That is the question." Timmy speaks eloquently, staring Shakespearian-like off into space.

Cottrell grabs Timmy's shoulders and shoves him down to sit. "You see the notches on this blackjack handle?" he says angrily. "They ain't just for grip! And there's room for one more! You've been asking for it ever since you got here! Try something—anything... I'm begging you!" Cottrell's face reddens.

Meanwhile, Officer Wax has cuffed George and calls out to the chief.

"Do you want me to cuff the Gurney Guy?"

"HELL YES! I want them all cuffed!"

Nurse Debra and Mosley are attending to Roger and Sean, so Officer Wax decides to see if Cottrell needs a hand with Timmy. He walks over to the table.

"Here, let me give you a hand with him." Wax unlocks Timmy's cuffs. "I'll just recuff him behind his back."

"Hell, yes... behind his back! A good idea; a maniac like this will try to strangle someone with his cuffs in front! I'm tightening these leg irons."

Wax finishes recuffing Timmy and begins to walk away. In the observation room, Doc and Perrin are watching all the dayroom activity. "I should check their vitals." The doc reaches for his stethoscope.

"There's no time for that! I'm sure the Queen's yacht has a physician and complete medical facility on board," Perrin says.

"Well, I'll bring my bag along in case something happens between here and the ramp. Sometimes waiting for the ferry can take a while."

The chief is satisfied that everything in the dayroom is secured and under control. As he's walking into the observation room, his radio goes off. At the same time, Cottrell is bent over and has almost finished securing Timmy's leg irons.

(SCRRRRR)... Timmy reacts to the sound by quickly pulling his feet away from Cottrell and standing up! Cottrell is startled by Timmy's sudden movement and falls backwards. Humiliated and pissed off, Cottrell regains his balance, stands up, and in a rage, lunges and grabs Timmy by the throat and pins him down on the table! Cottrell rips his blackjack from his belt loop and raises it high above his head in one swift move. Officer Wax runs over to the table, grabbing Cottrell's arm on the downswing and pushes him away from Timmy. Wax is trying to restrain Cottrell, and he's trying to break free.

"What the hell is going on?" the chief yells out.

"EASY, MAN! EASY!" Wax tries to calm Cottrell down.

Officer Cottrell, furious with Timmy, frantically tries to free himself from Officer Wax's restraint. His face is blazing red, and his whole body is trembling. "We'll kill that sombitch!" he screams.

"COTTRELL, CALM DOWN! EASY, MAN! EASY!" Officer Wax yells above Cottrell's screaming.

"Your radio going off is what started it—you might want to turn it off," the doc says to the chief.

"Yeah, right! I'm gonna turn off my radio to accommodate a criminal! There'll be snowballs in hell when that happens!"

"I can't believe what I just saw! Do you think he ought to be a cop?" Perrin asks the chief.

"Actually, he's one of my best men! He's just a little worked up."

"I knew it! I saw it coming! That Officer Cottrell could definitely use some anger management classes!" the doc retorts.

"My agent's going to hear about this shit! I'm through with these low-budget productions and untrained nobodys!" Timmy rubs his throat.

"HEY! Let's just *all* calm down now!" the chief shouts. "OK, Doc—now where is that van of yours?"

"It's parked around back. We don't use it much, but I had Mosley air up the tires a few days ago."

Just then, Anna knocks on the large dayroom window facing the hallway, and Doc leaves the observation room to speak with her.

"Well—is it OK for the children to attend the ceremony? What did Mr. Perrin say?" she asks excitedly.

"He said yes. He thinks it's a wonderful idea! We're getting everyone ready to leave for the river right now."

"That's terrific! The kids are all on the bus out back—we'll follow you down there."

"Now what were you saying?" The doc returns to the chief.

"OK. Here's the plan... we'll form a single procession to walk out of the clinic and get into the van. Mosley will drive, and Cottrell will ride shotgun."

"I should be riding in the van with the patients," the doc complains.

"PRISONERS! They're leaving the clinic! Now, they're *PRISONERS!"*

"Well, technically..."

"Don't get technical with me, Doc! I've had enough of this SHIT!"

Perrin taps Doc on the shoulder and gives him a signal to cool it. "OK, chief. You're calling the shots," he says, hoping to end the argument.

The chief pulls himself up proudly. "Like I said before, Mosley is the driver and Cottrell rides shotgun. I'll take the lead in an unmarked unit, followed by the van, and Wax and Wane will take up the rear in a squad car. And—I don't want to hear jack-shit from anybody!" he adds with authority.

"That's fine, Chief. Doc can ride with me," Perrin says.

It's a tight squeeze as everyone files out the door and down the hallway. The chief in the lead, followed by Mosley holding onto Sean, Nurse Debra with her arm around Roger, Cottrell nudging Timmy with his blackjack, and George next to Officer Wax.

As George approaches Doc, he thanks him for his words of wisdom and encouragement and asks how he could get a copy of the musical, *Evangeline.* Without hesitation, Doc produces a new DVD from his bag.

"Here, this is for you. And I'm glad if I was able to help you." He places the DVD between George's cuffed hands.

"Thanks, Doc. Yes, you helped a lot!"

They continue down the hall, through the kitchen, and out the back door to the van. It's locked, so Mosley leans Sean against the side of the van and runs inside to get the keys. They stand there silently waiting for Mosley and the keys.

Meanwhile, both the news crews, having arrived simultaneously, are barreling through Melville, despite some minor road construction. Lance and Tom from TV-3 approach an intersection littered with bright orange caution cones that extend along the right side of the road till the pavement ends.

"DAMN!" Lance, driving the TV-3 van, looks to his left and hollers out. "Here they come!"

"GO FOR IT!" Tom shouts to Lance.

Lance doesn't come to a complete stop and quickly pulls out from the intersection, making a wide right turn because of the caution cones. "DAMN! There's Channel 3!" Lon yells loudly.

"Damn! Go around them!" Chuck hollers back.

The Channel 10 van slows down some and tries to go around the TV-3 vehicle, but because of Lance's wide turn, there's no room. Lon swerves and spins on the gravel to the left of the road, temporarily losing control, then over-correcting and sideswiping the TV-3 van! A distinct, blunt, crunching, metallic thud of a crash echoes throughout the small town and reverberates between the levees. The group waiting outside the clinic hears the sound.

"That sounded like a car wreck!" the chief exclaims.

"That crazy sombitch!" Lance fights to regain control of his steering.

"GO FOR IT, LANCE!" Tom shouts.

In the other van, Chuck yells at his driver. *"PUNCH IT, LON!"* White-knuckling the steering wheel, Lon hollers back, "We're half on the shoulder and half on the road! Look at him hogging the whole damn road!"

The trucks swerve and scrape and bash against one another. The sound is heard all over town.

"Sounds like they hit again!" Officer Wax exclaims.

Another loud crunching sound follows. "And again! Damn!" Cottrell says.

The two news vans hit each other so many times that it sounds like a multi-car accident! The bowl shape of Melville bounces the loud, grating sounds, one on top of another, and produces one hell of a racket! The chief radios the station.

(SCRRRRR) . . . "Ah, Lynette—get a hold of the officers on road patrol and have them check out a possible auto crash somewhere near Main and Hwy 10. It might be a pileup!"

"I'm on it now, chief!" Lynette responds.

"Sounds like they're still moving, chief," Wax says.

"Sounds like some crazy hit-and-run shit headed for the river!" Cottrell adds.

I hope that's not TV-3 and TV-10 jockeying for first coverage! Perrin worries.

The two vans reach the pavement's end where the road turns to gravel and rises up and over the levee in an "S" shape. They're neck and neck and, at times, stuck together!

"It sounds like all hell is breaking loose! We better get going. What's taking Mosley so long with those keys?" the chief asks.

The news vans have passed over the levee and are heading to the large gravel parking lot next to the ferry ramp. They separate and pick up speed heading for the ramp and sideswipe, once again, in a bone-jarring crash that sends their vehicles spinning in opposite directions. With gravel flying everywhere, they come to a screeching halt. The two vans, mangled from bumper to bumper, end up nose to nose. The crews scramble to get out. Chuck's door is jammed shut, whereas Lance's door swings open and almost falls off the hinges and then flops back to close with a clunk. Lance surveys the damage.

The front fender is bashed in, with the turn signal lens busted out, and the socket, wires, and shredded metal are hanging down over the fender. The hubcap is squashed against the tire, and the door has deep, ugly gouges scarring its surface. The door swings back open and just hangs by springs and wires. The side view mirror was sheared off at first attack, and its perch is now a gaping wound of twisted metal and scraped paint. The entire side panel is a collage of deep dents, long gashes, and wide holes. The back taillight looks like fresh road kill, with the colored strands of wire and connectors dripping onto the ground. The rear hubcap has vanished, and the once-beautiful chrome fender is now hammered metal folded in on itself. Lance stands there, numb and in disbelief.

"My baby! Look what they've done to my baby!" he blurts out in shock.

Tom comes around to the front of the TV-3 van and stands there, dumbfounded, staring at the damage. Chuck, still in the TV-10 van, is frantically kicking and pounding on his door that won't open. Held hostage by the jammed seatbelt, he screams at Tom through the broken window.

"ACADIANA'S NEWS LEADER! WE WERE HERE FIRST!"

Lon makes his way around to the back of his van, and the first thing he notices is the right back door is bent open. The right rear bumper is twisted, torn, and lying on the ground. There's a jagged deep slice along the entire right side of the truck. It's a grand canyon of gashes compared to the dozens of smaller gaping holes and chiseled grooves. The side view mirror is dangling by a frayed wire. The headlight assembly was shattered by the final impact, and broken pieces of glass and chrome are scattered everywhere. Both hubcaps are flattened but still clinging to the wheels, and the front bumper is creased and crunched into a 90-degree angle.

"Damn! Look at this shit!" Lon shakes his head in disbelief.

Chuck is still struggling to get loose from the seatbelt and keeps tugging and twisting and even biting at it to release him. He looks like he's fighting an anorexic anaconda. Finally, the struggle pays off, and the belt snaps open. He crawls over to the driver's door and out onto the gravel, then marches over to Tom. Their confrontation is the same as Lon and Lance's: loud voices, hand movements accompanying the spirited arguments, and heightened emotions. The crew from the ferry emerges from the galley onto the deck and can hear and see the impending fight near the ramp.

Back at the clinic, Mosley has returned with the keys, and the Bonds are loaded into the van onto the two bench seats. It's an old, white, rusted van with dirty windows, cheap hubcaps, brown plastic upholstery with white piping, shag carpeting, and a broken door handle on the sliding door. A screwdriver is wedged in the handle hole and can be wiggled around to open and close the door from inside. After debating who sits where, George hops in first and sits in the left rear seat. Next is Sean, who needs a hefty push to make it up the step. He is seated in front of George and behind the driver. In Bond-like fashion, Sean inspects the shabby van. He glances to the right at the broken door handle and just shakes his head in disgust. He has never sat in a vehicle this pathetic.

He worries that it could somehow taint his image but assures himself that he won't be in it for long. Looking up front, he catches a glimpse of himself in the rearview mirror. Nurse Debra helps Roger climb into the van, and she starts to sit him next to Sean when Officer Cottrell stops her.

"Put him in the back seat because I want the Wild One up front near me and Mr. Coldcocker!" Cottrell smirks.

Oh, great! I get to sit next to Shakespeare! If I'm lucky, maybe he'll do an encore! Sean looks over at Timmy, now sitting next to him.

Officer Cottrell glares at Timmy and warns him once more about trying something, and then Cottrell slams the rusted side door shut. The chief, Wax, Cottrell, Doc, Perrin, Mosley, and Nurse Debra are standing next to the van, and Debra keeps eyeballing Roger and smiling at him. He looks back at her with a quizzical expression.

Hmmm . . . was she the one that I . . . uh, did I . . . could I have . . . ? Roger shakes his head in disgust. Nah! He notices the sliding door and screwdriver. *Finally, a sliding door! But what's that sticking out of it?*

Officer Wane is still standing guard outside the windows of the dayroom when Wax radios him to be ready to go in a few minutes. Chief Basile orders Cottrell and Mosley to pull the van up to the front of the clinic, while he, Wax, Doc, and Perrin walk around to the front and get their cars.

Nurse Debra can't join in the festivities because she's needed at the clinic. She gazes lovingly at Roger and realizes she'll *never* see him again. She is suddenly saddened and filled with longing. Roger has seen that look from thousands of women, and he does the only decent thing he knows to do . . . he flashes his trademark smile and winks goodbye.

As everyone is dispersing to meet out front, Mosley squeezes past Nurse Debra, and the blending of their faces momentarily resembles a voodoo monster and freaks Roger out! Doc immediately notices Roger's reaction.

"Maybe I should ride with the patients. They might need me! I have my bag and medications right here."

"C'mon, doc! We have our plan. Let's stick to it! And I told you, they're *PRISONERS*, not patients!" the chief reminds sternly.

"It's a short ride. I'm sure they'll be all right," Perrin says reassuringly.

The van slowly pulls away, leaving Nurse Debra standing alone and heartbroken as she waves a final goodbye to Roger. Her depressed mood matches the darkened skies and overall gloominess of the impending storm. The wind gusts are getting stronger and the thunder louder.

The officers on road patrol are searching for the possible pileup and have found nothing except a crumpled hubcap, a few broken pieces of colored plastic, and a squashed side view mirror strewn along the road. When the patrol car crosses over the levee, Officers Poole and Vaughn immediately notice the TV news vans parked in the gravel lot and can see the extensive damage to the vehicles and can hear the loud arguments. Officer Poole turns on the flashing lights and siren to get their attention, and it quiets the yelling for a moment.

"The cops are here! They'll straighten this mess out!" Lance yells.

"*You* pulled out in front of me!" Lon yells back.

"*You* were doing a hundred miles an hour and tried to pass me in a no-passing zone!" Lance retorts.

"*You* were hogging the road!" Lon hollers.

"There was construction; I had to pull around the cones!" Lance screeches.

Just then, the Queen's yacht came into view. Everyone stood stock still, awestruck, unable to move.

"Quick!" Chuck yells, suddenly coming to life. "Let's get that dish up!"

"Are you *crazy?* I'm not putting that lightning rod up in this weather!" Lon replies.

"OK . . . what's going on here?" Officer Poole steps up.

"Excuse me, officer, I'm Chuck Hebemer from *TV-10 . . . Acadiana's News Leader.* As you can see . . . we've got a very important story that has to be covered!" Chuck points to the Queen's yacht coming up the river.

"I don't give a damn if you're *Chuck Yeager!* I want an explanation of why you left the scene of an accident!"

Officer Vaughn joins the group, clipboard in hand; he begins to take notes.

"It happened back there at the stop sign!" Lon blurts out. "They ran the sign and pulled right out in front of us!"

"I looked to see if anyone was coming—they were at least a block away!" Lance retorts loudly. "The next thing I knew, they were on top of us, and WHAM—they sideswiped the hell out of the van! They had to be doing a hundred!"

"OK—so you failed to stop at the sign," Officer Poole points at Lance. "And you were speeding in a construction zone." He nods toward Lon.

Officer Vaughn quickly notes: Violations—No. 923 . . . No. 647 . . . No. 859."Me—speeding!" Lon yells. "*They* failed to stop at a stop sign! They came around that corner on two wheels! Sideswiping us was the only thing that kept them from turning over!"

The heated accusations continue to fly between the two news teams, while back at the clinic, everyone is in their vehicles and the procession proceeds to the river. Chief Basile is in the lead, with the clinic van behind him. Officers Wax and Wane are following the van, with Doc and Perrin in Perrin's car wedged between the smoking squad car and the yellow school bus containing Anna, the other volunteers, and the kids.

Sean is anxious to be free of the whole nightmare. He looks up and once again sees his reflection in the rearview mirror, and the image is *Mr. Perfect* from his days as a young, suave, sophisticated 007 agent. He reassures himself that HQ is not going to blame any failures of this mission on him.

It was a combination of faulty intelligence along with those two buffoons, George and Timmy, and that new Quartermaster packing all that junk! Sean mutters to himself. No—HQ isn't putting this monkey on my back! I've got a reputation to protect!

Roger squirms uncomfortably in his seat, rubbing his privates. *I wonder where we're going? I still can't believe this pain in my crotch! I've had sex a million times, and I've never experienced anything like this! Maybe it's the voodoo! That must be it . . . voodoo!* He thinks of the possibilities.

While Sean and Roger are lost in their own private thoughts, George has been reading the *Evangeline* DVD jacket. *My girlfriend, Adena, is sure going to love this! It's the ultimate in love stories! I'd put it right up there with Romeo and Juliet!*

Timmy has decided they must be headed back to the studio. *That's fine with me! I've had enough of these cheesy, low-budget productions!* He stares at Cottrell with the blackjack in hand. *I'm through ad-libbing with untrained gorillas like him! He damned near killed me! My agent and I are going to have a long talk!*

(SCRRRRR) . . . "Unit One to Unit Two," the chief radios.

(SCRRRRR) . . . "Unit Two . . . go ahead," Wax answers.

(SCRRRRR) . . . "I can see the Governor's limo and what looks like her Secret Service agents and some other vehicles topping the levee now. When we reach the ramp, we'll semi-combine our forces with those of the Governor's Secret Service. Our main objective is to ferry the prisoners to the yacht, and their job is to protect the Governor. Since we'll all be on the same ferry, it won't be easy. We don't want to get into any territorial disputes over security with them, so try not to step on any toes."

(SCRRRRR) . . . "Roger that. But sometimes Secret Service can be pretty obnoxious!"

(SCRRRRR) . . . "You got that right! I'm approaching the levee now. Still no sign of that pileup!"

Governor Blanco's limo and Secret Service vehicles are now pulling up at the ferry. The news crews are immediately impressed and silenced. They are caught up in the royal splendor of the yacht and the pride of this Cajun procession. Darylin and Mrs. Perrin are pulling into the lot to park. And further up the levee, everyone's attention is on the parade of vehicles from the clinic.

"This is BIG! Really BIG!" Chuck says, adjusting his Channel 10 jacket importantly.

"Officer, can't we handle the accident thing when this ceremony is finished?" Tom asks Officer Poole as he looks over at the mangled news van.

"Looks like we're gonna have to," Poole replies.

(SCRRRRR) . . . "Wax, I'm topping the levee now," the chief informs.

(SCRRRRR) . . . "I see that. Wow—look at those TV vans! There's your pileup, chief!"

(SCRRRRR) . . . "Yeah! They must have hit each other a dozen times!"

Doc and Perrin cross over the top of the levee and see the Queen's yacht before them.

"Pinch me, Doc! I feel like I'm dreaming! After all these years, they're going to finally say . . . *WE ARE SORRY!* There's my wife and secretary and the Governor and the press! And Tony Blair is on that yacht!"

Everybody, except the Bonds, gets out of their vehicles to discuss a game plan. The Double Os remain in the clinic van, and the children are still on the bus. Just then, the wind surges and the thunder explodes. The air is cool and smells like rain. The Queen's yacht overshoots the ferry, sounds its horn, and begins the difficult U-turn without getting too close to the railroad trestle.

The noise and activity grab the attention of the crew boat captain, deckhand, and engineer. The deckhand leaves his TV show to walk out on the back deck and is amazed at the size and beauty of the Queen's yacht. He is also surprised to see the dark sky and to hear the rumbling thunder. The engineer, who was down below and could feel the powerful vibration of another boat's engine, knew it had to be a large vessel. He's come up to the back deck to take a look, and he can't believe the splendor of the magnificent ship! The weather steals his attention because it's so dark outside. He wonders if he has his days and nights mixed up!

"What time is it?" the engineer asks the deckhand.

"Almost eleven o'clock. Hey, what do you think about all that action on the West Bank? And what's the deal with the *giant yacht*? Maybe it's a new casino!"

"Man, I don't know. I could feel it rumbling in from down below.

It looks like some kind of celebration over there. Probably some Mardi Gras shit going on! Well, I gotta get back down there and get those engines fired up. I'd like to get out of here before that storm hits!"

The captain is sleeping when the yacht's horn blasts and wakes him. He gets out of his bunk, rubbing his eyes and yawning, and walks slowly into the wheelhouse to check out the noise. The yacht has accomplished the turn and is now blocking the captain's view of the west side of the river and all the commotion going on over there. His attention is drawn to the black clouds blocking out the sunlight, the sound of distant thunder, and the raging wind. Then he sees the British flag and the Queen's own banner flying proudly from the main mast of the royal yacht, and immediately he understands its purpose there.

The apology! Somehow, Warren Perrin has succeeded at last! The captain's face breaks into a wide grin and his heart swells with pride.

On the other side of the river, the chief, Perrin, and the Secret Service have decided how to conduct this operation. They agree that if the storm breaks out before reaching the yacht, the vehicles aboard the ferry will be used for shelter until the storm passes.

"My car will go on first with me, Doc, Wax, and Wane, followed by the clinic van, then one Secret Service Suburban with all their personnel, and the Governor's limo with her driver and secretary, Perrin, his wife, and secretary. Last but not least, we'll squeeze the school bus on with everyone still in it," the chief summarizes.

"What about our news trucks?" Chuck asks, Lon standing at his side.

"There's not enough room! Now, move those *junk heaps* out of the way so we can get loaded! You too!" the chief motions to Tom and Lance.

"But—but—but . . ." Chuck stammers.

"But nothing! If it starts raining, you boys can jump on the bus with the kids!" The chief looks across the river at the yacht. "It looks like the *Queen* is almost anchored. Let's get a move on!"

Lon and Lance back their mangled TV trucks out of the way and park on the far side of the gravel lot. While the ferry is being loaded, the two news photogs grab their gear. Glad not to be tethered to their truck's giant satellite dishes during a bad storm, they hurry to the ferry. Along with Tom and Chuck, they're the last to board.

"Ah—Lon, go ahead and get some establishing shots of the river and the ferry and pan the parking lot with all the vehicles. I'll get a sound bite going," Chuck directs.

"Yeah, Lance," Tom says. "Let's get some footage of the yacht and then a slow pan into a close-up of me at the front of the ferry."

"DAMN!" Lon yells suddenly.

"What's the matter?" Chuck asks with concern.

"The cam is busted!"

"*WHAT?*" Chuck yells.

Lance tries to hold back his reaction to TV-10's bad news, but he can't help it and starts laughing out loud. Tom, trying to maintain a professional courtesy toward Chuck and his dilemma, tries unsuccessfully to stifle a snicker.

"The whole damn case is *cracked!* It won't even turn on!" Lon moans.

"*DAMN! DAMN! DAMN!*" Chuck slaps his palm against his forehead. "It must have happened when they hit us!" Lon glares at Lance.

"*You* mean when *you* hit *us!*" Lance glares back as he flips his cam's 'ON' switch. "Looks like mine's working just fine." He steps back playfully and lines up a shot with Lon and Chuck in the frame.

"How about you guys giving me a big smile?"

"Hey, Tom, old buddy, old pal . . ." Chuck sidles up to Tom. "What are the chances of us getting a copy of the ceremony after you shoot it?"

"Well, let's see . . . as soon as we get back to the station, Debra will do a few 'breaking news' announcements, then segue into a full-blown promo at three—then she and Brashaw will do a partial story at 5:00 p.m., then our 6 & 10 anchors, Hoyt and Darla . . . *you remember* Hoyt *and Darla* . . . well, they'll do a full story at six and again at ten. Let's see—that's only four runs. It won't exactly be old news, but it won't be breaking news, either. Sure—I could get you a copy—probably a little after midnight. TV-10 could air a special *'news break'* for insomniacs—that's a good-sized audience!" Tom smiles broadly.

Unable to control themselves, both Tom and Lance burst out laughing. Chuck looks like he could cry, and Lon is ready to toss the broken camcorder into the river. The ferry pulls away from the ramp, and suddenly, the whirling winds spin themselves into a warming breeze. The heavy black clouds begin to move quickly in all directions, allowing glimpses of sunlight that are begging to shine through. Everyone on the ferry is oohing and aahing at the amazing shift in the weather. The sky is a kaleidoscope of changing colors hovering above the river. Governor Blanco and Perrin leave the limo to lean against the ferry's handrail.

"Well, the weather looks like it wants to cooperate with us, doesn't it?" the Governor offers.

"Yes, it does," Perrin replies.

"I've been wanting to speak to you privately," the Governor says sincerely. "To thank you personally and on behalf of all Cajuns, past and present, for your tenacity, devotion, and sacrifice to attain this apology."

"Thank you for your kind words, Governor, but I have to tell you, it's really those who suffered so indignantly who deserve the praise and appreciation. Their injustice inspired me to care enough to do something, no matter how small or great. My mission . . . my passion has been to rectify that injustice and to help spark in Cajun people today a sense of the greatness within us all. It is truly this *greatness of spirit* that has traveled so far and endured so many hardships and believed so strongly in *finding a place to call home that could never be taken away!* I am merely the messenger—it is the message of the Acadians that matters most!" Perrin says emphatically.

The Governor's eyes fill with tears as she imagines the ancestors of the Cajuns rejoicing in the heavens! All the thousands of Evangelines and Gabriels who carried their love for one another to their graves, all the thousands of families who never again touched, looked upon, or even spoke to one another after that hateful, hellish day, and all the hundreds of Acadians who perished in filthy, lonely ships that sank . . . were reunited and embracing with shouts of love and laughter!

"And that *message* is one of hope and renewal. It's the age-old message of love that survives and comes full circle. With each revolution, it only gets stronger." The Governor wipes her tears away and gazes out across the river.

"I know an apology is not enough to right a wrong of this magnitude," Perrin says. "But if it serves as a catalyst to propel people around the world to start righting the wrongs being inflicted on fellow human beings, then this apology will have been well worth the effort."

"I agree. A mere apology can never repay or erase the heinous acts that took so many lives and inflicted so much heartache. But like you said, if one apology can create a domino effect worldwide, then some measure of debt has been paid this day. I also want to tell you that I'm signing an official proclamation to commemorate today as the Day of *Acadiana Apology.* And I would like to create the *Warren Perrin Award* that will be presented yearly to a deserving person who rights a *wrong against all odds.*"

"The proclamation is a wonderful way to keep the memory and the honor of our ancestors alive. And the award is an ongoing tribute also, but you don't need to name it after me," Perrin says humbly.

"Mr. Perrin, you worked how many years on this apology?"

"About fifteen years."

"You, sir, deserve the *Nobel Prize!*" The Governor looks Perrin square in the eye. "I'm just sorry that all I can offer is an award named in your honor! Don't be so modest, Warren—and enjoy the fruits of your labor. God knows you've earned it!"

The weather has become unbelievably beautiful. A balmy breeze and spring-like temperatures are wafting over the river. The rain-filled clouds have departed, and in their place are ribbons of sunshine and the fragrance of flowers. The captain, at the helm of his old crew boat, is still smiling proudly as he stands at the wheel, surrounded by a shaft of sunlight streaming through the window. The deckhand is on the back deck watching the ferry and the Queen's yacht come about and marvels at the change in the weather. The captain on the Queen's yacht comments to Tony Blair that it's the damnedest weather he's ever seen in his fifty-two years at sea!

Perrin and the Governor stand at the ferry rail and look over at the yacht. "Well, we're almost there," Perrin says. "That looks like Tony Blair coming out on the back deck. I've arranged for the chief to take Blair's four guys from the van onto the boat first. They'll quickly move them to the infirmary. Then you and I, along with your staff, my wife and secretary, the Secret Service, the Melville personnel, the children, and the press—all in that order—will board the yacht."

The sky is clear and bright, and the air is fresh and alive. The ferry docks in between the crew boat and the Queen's yacht. The deckhand connects the catwalk and lowers it to the ferry's metal deck. The chief and Officer Wax are standing by the clinic van with Officer Cottrell when both news crews walk up from the right side of the ferry.

"Hey—where do y'all think you're going?" Officer Wax calls out.

"Up on the yacht," Tom answers with authority.

"No, you're not! Not yet!"

"But we've got press passes!" Chuck protests loudly.

"Back away now! Get back!" the chief orders gruffly. "This is official police business we're conducting! We'll let you know when you can go on the yacht! Move on back behind the limo."

"Come on, Lon," Chuck says. "We'll try to get a statement from the Governor." They move around the backside of the limo, and a Secret Service agent stops them.

"Hold on there, where do you two think you're going?" The agent reaches out and grabs Chuck's arm.

"To get a statement from the Governor." Chuck points importantly to the press badge pinned above the Channel 10 logo on his jacket.

The agent, unimpressed, glances at Chuck's badge. "You're not getting near the Governor until *after* the ceremony, and then it's her decision to grant an interview. I'll have to ask you to step back, please. Move on out of the way, back behind the school bus."

"But I have a *PRESS PASS*!" Chuck laments as he and Lon walk back around behind the bus. "And we're Acadiana's News Leader!"

"News Leader, my ass!" Tom snorts as he and Lance follow along behind.

Meanwhile, Officer Cottrell has been struggling with the clinic's van door, then yanks it open as the chief gives instructions.

"Go ahead and get the leg irons off him," the chief points to Timmy. "If he tries to run, he'll drown! We'll take their cuffs off when we officially hand them over."

Cottrell removes Timmy's leg irons, and along with Officer Wax and the chief, the Bonds are taken out of the van and led up the catwalk, followed by Doc, clutching his precious medical report to his chest. They reach the top of the walkway, and Sean, who still can't talk, looks at Tony Blair and nods his head as if to say, *Mission Accomplished.*

Their handcuffs are removed, and Doc proudly hands over his report to the yacht's physician.

With the Bonds now *officially* released and whisked away to the infirmary, the chief motions for everyone on the ferry to board the yacht. Leading the way are Governor Blanco and Warren Perrin. Prime Minister Tony Blair warmly welcomes them with handshakes and friendly greetings. Moving over to the tables set up on the back deck, they prepare to begin signing papers.

"Should we get the release papers for your boys signed and out of the way before we move on to the apology?" Perrin asks Blair.

"Yes, I think that would be best." Blair quickly scans the papers and adds his signature. "They all seem to be in order. The Queen really appreciates this. She assures me that as soon as all the damages have been tallied, payment will be wired immediately to all the injured parties!"

The children are now on deck with Anna and the chaperones, and they gather around the tables and the dignitaries. Anna positions the shortest children in front so they can easily see what's going on. The news crews are jockeying for the prime location from which to watch and report. The Secret Service have taken their places alongside the chief, Wax, and Wane. Doc stands beside Mrs. Perrin and Darylin. The papers for release and reimbursement are now signed and stamped, and the ceremony progresses to the main event. The warm sunshine and refreshing breeze accompany a spirit of excitement and expectation. Tony Blair addresses the crowd of onlookers.

"Thank you all for being here on this very important day. What we are about to do here today has been 250 years in the making. No words can sufficiently express the sorrow, shame, and regret that England feels for the despicable displacement of the thousands of Acadians from their homes in La Acadie. The British soldiers who planned and executed the expulsion are long since dead, but their blood flows through our veins, and their sins have become our own. We cannot change the past, but we can begin to right the wrong by this small gesture of apology today. The gentleman to my right, Mr. Warren Perrin, has fought the good fight and has finished the race by bringing a measure of justice to the Acadian people through this apology. He never stopped believing in the power of principle and the tenacity of truth. I am humbled by this man's mission and devotion to his people. And I am reminded of another great American who said these words about a group of honored heroes like your ancestral Acadians."

"The world will little note, nor long remember what we say here, but it can never forget what they did here."

Blair quotes the immortal words of Abraham Lincoln, then continues, "The Acadians forged a new nation for themselves and readapted to a life of change and struggle. Their ability to persevere under extreme humiliation and deprivation is the cornerstone of the Cajun community today. This kind of strength is not taught and cannot be bought . . . it is passed like a torch from one generation to the next. *That flame of hope and survival must never be extinguished!"* Blair looks out at his audience and pauses for emphasis.

"In 1755, my countrymen tried to eradicate the Acadians by scattering them to the wind, but their efforts were in vain. For the Acadians not only survived but have thrived. May the future generations of Cajuns never forget what the Acadians have done here. On behalf of the Queen and the people of England, I am sincerely sorry for what we did to the Acadian people in 1755."

The heartfelt sincerity in Tony's voice is unmistakable. The crowd erupts in a symphony of applause. An aide hands him the leather-bound parchment document that is the APOLOGY. It was delivered early that morning by a courier via the Royal Air Force from the Queen of England. She signed it and insisted it arrive in time for the ceremony. Tony takes a step forward and then turns and presents the document to both Governor Blanco and Warren Perrin.

"This apology is presented to the Cajun people of Louisiana and Acadians throughout the world from the Queen of England and the British people," Blair speaks loudly and clearly. "May this simple document symbolize profound remorse and be worthy of the Acadians' forgiveness."

At that exact moment, a spectacular surge of sunlight radiates warmth and brightness everywhere. On the crew boat, the captain is standing on the upper deck looking over at the yacht with an expression of wonder on his face. Infused with enthusiasm and validation, the crowd hurries to the catwalk and back onto the ferry, which will carry them to the celebration in Melville. Hundreds of Cajuns are streaming down to the river, and hundreds more are cheering and clapping on the riverbank as the ferry heads for the West ramp.

Suddenly, the engineer starts the crew boat's engines, and thick clouds of smoke billow into the air. When the Queen's yacht pulls anchor and begins to sail, George walks out on the back deck and sees the captain on the crew boat. The captain sees him, and they both look over to the ferry as Perrin turns their way. All together, they give a thumbs-up that seems to say, *"Well Done, Mission Accomplished!"* As the ferry chugs across the river, the railroad bridge is lowered, and moments later, the shiny silver Cajun Express shoots across the tracks!

Warren Perrin, standing on the ferry deck, looks up into the radiant sky. He can hear the jubilant music from *Evangeline,* and in the distance, above the trestle, he envisions a cloud of Cajuns rejoicing and dancing in the sky! *Ah . . . justice at last. Justice at last!*

WARREN PERRIN PETITIONED QUEEN ELIZABETH II OF ENGLAND IN 1990 TO ATTAIN AN APOLOGY FROM GREAT BRITAIN FOR THE ACADIAN DEPORTATION OF 1755. THE PETITION WAS FINALLY RESOLVED BY THE SIGNING OF THE QUEEN'S ROYAL PROCLAMATION ON DECEMBER 9, 2003. THE PROCLAMATION WILL RECOGNIZE JULY 28, STARTING IN 2005, AS THE ANNIVERSARY OF THE DEPORTATION ORDER.

BIBLIOGRAPHY

Carl A. Brasseaux, SCATTERED TO THE WIND, The Center for Louisiana Studies, University of Southwest Louisiana, 1991

Trent Angers, THE TRUTH ABOUT THE CAJUNS, Acadiana House Publishing, 1998

Jacob B. Berkson, A CANARY'S TALE, Baltimore, MD, Canary's Tale Publishing, 1996

Phyllis A. Balch, C.N.C. & James F. Balch, M.D., PRESCRIPTION FOR NUTRITIONAL HEALING, Penguin Putnam Publishing, 2000

ACADIE THE ODYSSEY OF A PEOPLE:

Historic Research:

Brenda Dunn James E. Candow

Graphic Design Cardinal Communications

Illustrations Claude Picard Lewis Parker Bernard Leblanc

Project Manager William H. Nethery A.R.O. Interpretation

Project Inspired by

Robert G. Leblanc's Research, revised edition, 1993

Formative Evaluation Acadian Consultative Committee Centre for Acadian Studies Stephen White R. Gilles Leblanc

FILM: AGAINST THE TIDE (the story of the Cajun People of Louisiana) Produced by Zachary Richard, Directed by Pat Mire, Written by C.E. Richard

FILM: <u>THE ACADIAN MEMORIAL</u> (a documentary) Produced by Acadian Memorial Foundation, Inc.

FILM: <u>EVANGELINE</u> (silent film/partial sound, circa 1920) Produced by United Artists, Directed by Edwin Carewe

MUSICAL: <u>EVANGELINE, THE MUSICAL IN CONCERT</u> (1999) Story, Music, and Lyrics by Paul Taranto and Jamie Wax

<u>WWW.EVANGELINETHEMUSICAL.COM</u>

ACADIANMUSEUM.COM

Missions abound!

Anthony J. Lomas

About the Author

*A*nthony J. Lomas, a proud Cajun and lover of all things James Bond, has managed, with Amalgamated Spy, to combine his two loves in a humorous, yet heartfelt tale of hope and hilarity. He also loves cooking Cajun food and divides his time between the Ozark Mountains of Arkansas and Lafayette, Louisiana. He enjoys hearing from readers, you may write him at *tony/amalgamatedspy@gmail.com*